THE GESTURAL COMMUNICATION OF APES AND MONKEYS

Josep Call
and
Michael Tomasello

 LAWRENCE ERLBAUM ASSOCIATES, PUBLISHERS
2007   Mahwah, New Jersey   London

Lawrence Erlbaum Associates, Inc., Publishers
10 Industrial Avenue
Mahwah, New Jersey 07430
www.erlbaum.com

Cover design by Tomai Maridou

Library of Congress Cataloging-in-Publication Data

The gestural communication of apes and monkeys / edited by Josep Call and Michael Tomasello.
    p. cm.
Includes bibliographical references and index.
ISBN 978-0-8058-6278-2 — 0-8058-6278-1 (cloth)
ISBN 978-0-8058-5365-0 — 0-8058-5365-0 (pbk.)
ISBN 978-1-4106-1636-4 — 1-4106-1636-3 (e book)
1. Apes—Behavior. 2. Monkeys—Behavior. 3. Animal communication. 4. Gesture. I. Call, Josep. II. Tomasello, Michael.
QL737.P96G47   2006
599.88—dc22   2006035560
                                                CIP

Books published by Lawrence Erlbaum Associates are printed on acid-free paper, and their bindings are chosen for strength and durability.

Printed in the United States of America
10 9 8 7 6 5 4 3 2 1

THE
GESTURAL COMMUNICATION
OF APES AND MONKEYS

An accompanying

DVD is enclosed

inside this book

Contents

Preface

This volume represents the culmination of over 20 years of observational research on great ape gestural communication by our research team. We began with one group of chimpanzees at the Yerkes Primate Center Field Station, and then made observations on a second, newly formed group of chimpanzees there as well. After we moved to the Max Planck Institute for Evolutionary Anthropology in Leipzig, and before the Wolfgang Köhler Primate Research Center was built, we decided to expand our research to the other great ape species, as well as to some other primate species, observing them in various kinds of zoo settings. We paid particular attention to the flexible use and development of gestures by observing youngsters of different ages. Whenever possible, we observed more than one group per species to be able to establish broader comparisons both within and between species. Our attempt in this volume is to bring together all of this work into a single place, looking for both similarities and differences among the different species, perhaps giving us some hints about the evolution of communication in our nearest primate relatives—and perhaps even about the evolution of human communication and language as well.

ACKNOWLEDGMENTS

The enterprise obviously involved many different people over 20 years. Students who participated in the early chimpanzee studies at Yerkes were Ann Kruger, Barbara George, Jeff Farrar, Andrea Evans, Thomas

Frost, Debbie Gust, Kathy Nagell, Kelly Olguin, Malinda Carpenter, and Jennifer Warren. We thank them all for their efforts, and we also thank the caretakers and scientists at Yerkes, especially Tom Gordon who supported us throughout—and for all of their help as well. The students and colleagues observing the nonchimpanzee species appear here as authors of their own papers: Simona Pika, Katja Liebal, Nana Hesler, and Julia Fisher. Anja Dube helped in some early stages of the new studies as well. We thank these collaborators, and we thank the following institutions that allowed us to observe their animals; Howletts Wild Animal Park and Chester Zoo (UK), Zürich Zoo (Switzerland), La Forêt des Singes (France), Wild Animal Park Planckendael (Belgium), Zoo Appenheul (the Netherlands), Krefeld Zoo and Leipzig Zoo (Germany).

Back on the home front in Leipzig, we thank Henriette Zeidler, Annette Witzmann, and Knut Finstermeier for their help in getting the volume into shape and Katja Liebal both for providing some gesture videoclips and for helping us find others that are included in the CD that accompanies this volume. Thanks also to Cathleen Petree of Lawrence Erlbaum Associates for her editorial guidance as well.

CHAPTER 1

Introduction: Intentional Communication in Nonhuman Primates

Michael Tomasello
Josep Call
Max Planck Institute for Evolutionary Anthropology

O rganisms seek information to help them make adaptive behavioral decisions. Some of that information comes from the behavior of conspecifics. For example, if a small youngster sees a large adult approaching food, she knows that there is no use contesting it. In this context, some organisms have evolved physical characteristics and/or behavior patterns that influence what others perceive and do in ways that accrue to their advantage. For example, many animals have developed ways of making themselves look bigger—puffing out parts of their bodies, raising their hair, and so forth—such that others are less likely to oppose them in contests of various kinds.

Physical characteristics and behavior patterns that have evolved to influence what other organisms perceive and do, especially conspecifics, are typically referred to by ethologists and behavioral ecologists as communicative signals. Since the arguments of Dawkins and Krebs (1978), the focus has been on the extent to which such signals are deceptive versus honest. Dawkins and Krebs argued that because only signals that favor the signaling individual could evolve, most signals provide others with misinformation (deceptive information) that gives the signaling individual an advantage it would not have had without the signal. On the other hand, often in the context of sexual selection, other theorists have argued that it is useful for an individual to advertise some advantage it has to potential mating partners or other potential interactants. Because 'cheap' signals are easy for individuals not possessing this advantage to fake, organisms have evolved a number of 'honest' signals that are so costly to produce that they cannot be faked; for example, only extremely strong and healthy male peacocks can afford to have huge tails because these represent a large handicap both energetically and in fleeing predators (Zahavi, 1997).

The kind of signals that are the topic of these debates are those that have been phylogentically ritualized under specific selection pressures (Tinbergen, 1951). But some social behaviors that would also seem to qualify as communicative signals have not arisen from evolutionary processes directly, but rather have been created and/or learned by individuals during their individual lifetimes. The most striking example is the many communicative signals and symbols that make up the 6,000+ different human languages of the world. Of course, although the ability to create these signals and symbols has evolved biologically, the signals themselves—for example, the greeting "Hello!" used by some but not all humans—would not seem to be subject to evolutionary pressures directly (even if greeting itself, as a general social function, somehow is). We may thus say that these signals have been ontogenetically ritualized, as individuals have in one way or another created or learned them during their own lifetimes—perhaps for more transitory functions. These signals quite often serve to regulate social interactions among individuals in ways that are mutually beneficial to both signaler and recipient alike.

The communicative signaling of the various species of nonhuman primates is a complex mix of phylogentically and ontogenetically ritualized signals used in many different social contexts. And indeed, many individual signals themselves arise from a confluence of different processes. For example, the alarm calls of some monkey species are made even by individuals raised in complete social isolation, suggesting that they have been crafted by evolution. However, knowing precisely when to use these signals, and how to respond to them when they are produced by others, appear to involve significant learning processes during ontogeny (Seyfarth & Cheney, 2003). There are also some signals in the gestural modality that seem to have been invented and used by only a single individual (Goodall, 1986). The important point in the current context is that communicative signals that involve a significant degree of learning require the signaler to make informed decisions about when and perhaps how to use them. That is, using communicative signals flexibly and appropriately requires learning and complex cognitive processes (Tomasello & Call, 1997).

In this book, we focus on the gestural communication of the four great ape species, along with that of one species of small ape and one species of *cercopithecine* monkey. The actual behavioral form of some of these gestural signals is at least partially phylogentically ritualized, whereas others would seem to be ontogenetically created and/or learned. In all cases, however, our focus is on gestural signals—no matter their source as behavioral forms—over which the signaler has significant behavioral control. In other words, the signals we are interested in are not signals that are invariably elicited by particular external or internal stimuli, but rather they are signals that the individual chooses to produce, or not to produce, in particular situations for particular social goals. Although the term sometimes creates confusion, we know of no better way to designate these strategically used signals than with the term intentional communication.

In this introductory chapter, we provide a brief review of what is known about primate vocal and gestural communication, with particular focus on those aspects that involve individual decision making and cognition. We also set the stage for our six case studies of primate gestural communication—involving chimpanzees, gorillas, orangutans, bonobos, siamangs, and Barbary macaques—by outlining the major theoretical and methodological issues involved.

PRIMATE VOCAL COMMUNICATION

By far the greatest amount of research has been done on primate vocal, as opposed to gestural, communication. Primates vocalize to one another in various contexts such as avoiding predators, defending against aggressors, traveling as a group, and discovering food. For the most part, all of the individuals of a given species use the same vocal signals, and no new vocal signals are invented individually. However, there is some flexibility in the precise manner in which a given call is produced. For example, rhesus monkey "coo" calls are acoustically more similar within than between *matrilines* (Hauser, 1992), and chimpanzees (and some other species) display population-specific "dialects" in some vocal signals (Mitani, Hasegawa, Gros-Louis, Marler, & Byrne, 1992). But experimental studies have suggested that such flexibility is severely limited (see Hammerschmidt & Fischer, in press). Thus, Owren, Dieter, Seyfarth, and Cheney (1992) found only minor modifications in the calls of two cross-fostered *macaque* species, and the modifications that were found mostly involved changes in the frequency of calls already in the animals' repertoires.

Unlike call morphology, call usage seems to have a bit more flexibility, although learning may still play a highly constrained role to particular emotionally-charged situations. Thus, in most cases, calls are used in adultlike contexts from early in ontogeny, but then there is a learning phase in which more adultlike usage is fine tuned (see Snowdon, in press). For example, infant *vervet* monkeys often make mistakes by giving an eagle alarm call to various moving things in the sky, and they produce intergroup calls whenever they are distressed. Only later do they confine these to adultlike contexts (Seyfarth & Cheney, 1997). Tamarins that heard (and observed) a conspecific alarm calling after tasting peppered tuna fish, which the listeners themselves had not tasted, subsequently reduced the consumption of that food item even after the pepper had been removed (Snowdon & Boe, 2003). An especially important type of flexibility concerns audience effects, in which an individual uses its vocal signals differently depending on the social communicative situation. For example, some *tamarins* produce food calls when discovering food, but rates depend on whether or not other group mates are present (Caine, Addington, & Windfelder, 1995); male chimpanzees pant hoot more frequently in traveling contexts when their alliance partners are nearby (Mitani & Nishida, 1993); and *vervet* monkey females adjust the rate of alarm calling depending on whether their own offspring are present, whereas males call more often when females are present (Cheney & Seyfarth, 1985). On the other hand, in an experimental study, *macaque* females who saw a predator approaching their offspring in another location did not attempt to alert ignorant offspring more often than knowledgeable ones (Cheney & Seyfarth, 1990). This suggests that audience effects in primate vocal communication may not involve callers assessing the knowledge of recipients but only noting their presence or absence in the situation.

Undoubtedly, primates display most flexibility in the way they perceive and understand vocal signals. The classic case for context-sensitive comprehension is *vervet* monkey alarm calls in which individuals respond to acoustically distinct calls with particular types of antipredator responses even in the absence of the predator (Seyfarth & Cheney, 1990; Seyfarth, Cheney, & Marler, 1980). Convincing evidence that recipients are indeed responding to the meaning (reference) of such calls, and not to such things as their emotional intensity or the like, come from experiments in which individuals habituated to some call show dishabituation only when the meaning (referent) of calling is changed (e.g., Cheney & Seyfarth, 1988; Zuberbühler, Cheney, & Seyfarth, 1999). Interestingly, there are no convincing observations of such 'referential vocal signals' in any ape species, the closest possibility being the way chimpanzees adjust calling rate for food grunts used in the context of sharable and unsharable foods (Crockford, Herbinger, Vigilant, & Boesch, 2004; Hauser, Teixidor, Field, & Flaherty, 1993). In general, it may be said that the learning skills used in call comprehension show almost unlimited flexibility because a number of primate species can learn to effectively use the calls of other species, including some nonprimate species (Hauser, 1988; Zuberbühler, 2000).

Overall, then, nonhuman primates seem to have only limited control over their vocalizations—very little in terms of call morphology and a bit more in the case of call usage, including some adjustments for audience presence or absence. Current evidence suggests that nonhuman primates possess most flexibility in call comprehension, with some species even comprehending the calls of other species, which almost certainly requires learning.

PRIMATE GESTURAL COMMUNICATION

Primates also routinely communicate using manual and body gestures (see definition later), mainly in close-range social contexts such as play, grooming, nursing, and during sexual and agonistic encounters. These are in general less evolutionarily urgent functions than those signaled by acts of vocal communication, but nevertheless many of them are fairly involuntary facial expressions, body autonomic responses (e.g., piloerection), and the like. But an important subset of these seem intentional, in the sense of individual control. That is, unlike the case of vocal signals, there is good evidence that individuals of some primate species—most of the research is with great apes—invent new gestural signals as needed. Goodall (1986), for example, reported much variability in the gestures used by individual chimpanzees, including even a number of idiosyncratic gestures used by single individuals only, that could not have been either genetically determined or socially learned. Common gestures used by one or another ape species include such things as "arm raise," "wrist offer," "head-bob," "chest beat," "touch side," "ground slap," and "poke at."

Apes most likely acquire many of their gestural signals via a process of ontogenetic ritualization (Tomasello, 1996). In ontogenetic ritualization, two organisms essentially shape one another's behavior in repeated instances of a social interaction. The general form of this type of learning is:

- Individual A performs behavior X (not a communicative signal);

- Individual B consistently reacts by doing Y;
- Subsequently B anticipates A's performance of X, on the basis of its initial step, by performing Y; and
- Subsequently, A anticipates B's anticipation and produces the initial step in a ritualized form (waiting for a response) in order *to* elicit Y.

The main point is that a behavior that was not at first a communicative signal becomes one by virtue of the anticipations of the interactants over time. There is no evidence that any primate species acquires most of its gestural signals by means of imitative learning (Tomasello & Call, 1997). Indeed, de Waal and Johanovitz (1993) looked at the reconciliation gestures of juvenile *rhesus* and *stumptail macaques* who were co-housed for a period of 5 months and found that the nature of the gestures and displays for reconciliation remained unchanged for both species (even though the frequency of occurrence of some other behaviors did change).

With regard to flexibility of use, Tomasello and colleagues (1994, 1997) found that many chimpanzee gestures were used in multiple contexts, sometimes across widely divergent behavioral domains. Also, sometimes different gestures were used in the same context interchangeably toward the same end—and individuals sometimes performed these in rapid succession in the same context (e.g., initiating play first with a poke at followed by an arm raise). The gestural signals of many monkey species have not been studied much; however, those that have been studied do not appear to have this same degree of flexibility, but rather they are tied to particular communicative situations more in the manner of their vocal signals (Maestripieri, 1999). For what it is worth, in some studies both monkeys and apes have been observed learning to use some gestures to outwit competitors (e.g., Mitchell & Anderson, 1997; Woodruff & Premack, 1979). Although it is still unclear what level of psychological processes support those cases of "tactical deception," they at least indicate that individuals can display a gesture outside its ordinary context of use (Whiten & Byrne, 1988).

In terms of audience effects, Tomasello and colleagues (1994, 1997) found that chimpanzee juveniles only give a visual signal to solicit play (e.g., arm raise) when the recipient is already oriented appropriately, but they use their most insistent attention getter, a physical poke at, most often when the recipient is socially engaged with others. Tanner and Byrne (1993) reported that a female gorilla repeatedly used her hands to hide her playface from a potential partner, indicating some flexible control of the otherwise involuntary grimace—as well as a possible understanding of the role of visual attention in the process of gestural communication (see also de Waal, 1986, for a similar observation for chimpanzees). In an experimental setting, Call and Tomasello (1994) found that at least some orangutans also were sensitive to the gaze direction of their communicative partner. Kummer (1968) reported that before they set off foraging, male *hamadryas* baboons engage in "notifying behavior" in which they approach another individual and look directly into their face, presumably to make sure that the other is looking before the trek begins.

Because the gestures of apes are produced so flexibly, flexible skills of gesture comprehension are required as well. Virtually no ape gestures are referential in the sense that they indicate an external entity (e.g., there is no pointing for conspecifics in the human fashion), but rather they mostly serve to regulate either dyadic interactions with others or triadic interactions over food or requests to groom specific body parts or grab specific objects. Interestingly for the process of comprehension, Tanner and Byrne (1996) have reported on a number of gorilla gestures that seem to be iconic. That is, an adult male gorilla often seemed to indicate to a female playmate iconically, using his arms or whole body, the direction in which he wanted her to move, location he wanted her to go to, or the action he wanted her to perform (see also Savage-Rumbaugh, Wilkerson, & Bakeman, 1977, for bonobos). However, these might simply be normal ritualized gestures with the iconicity being in the eyes of the human only; in fact, a role for iconicity in gorillas' and other apes' comprehension of gestures has not to this point been demonstrated (Tomasello & Call, 1997).

Overall, then, nonhuman primate gestural communication shows much more flexibility than vocal communication, perhaps because it concerns less evolutionarily urgent activities. Apes create new gestures and use most of their gestures quite flexibly, with audience effects and flexibility of comprehension being routine. More research is needed with monkeys.

DEFINITIONS AND THEORIES

The classic definition of communication, as opposed to social behavior more generally, is articulated by Smith (1977, p. 389) as follows:

> [Communicative] acts achieve their ends indirectly. That is, the actor does not act physically to alter things to suit his needs, pushing or dragging other individuals about, beating them into submission, or the like. Instead, the actor's behavior provides other individuals

with information, and the actions that *they* take on the basis of this information lead to any functions that are obtained.

And so, for example, one individual might force another to leave its territory by actually attacking and driving it away—a social strategy—or else it might simply bare its teeth and growl—providing a signal to the intruder of what will happen if it does not leave. Baring teeth and growling, rather than actually biting, are communicative signals in terms of form because they are ritualized; that is, they are not the actual behavior itself but only some physically ineffectual portion of the real behavior. Gestural signals in particular concern all types of bodily, nonvocal communicative acts—especially hand motions, body postures, and facial expressions. Gestures can use as a perceptual channel either the visual (e.g., arm raise), the tactile (e.g., poke at), or the auditory (e.g., ground slap) modality—or some combination of these.

As outlined earlier, gestural signals may be under the voluntary control of the signaler to a greater or lesser degree, depending on the extent to which the ritualization process occurred during phylogeny or ontogeny. To the extent that communicative signals are produced automatically whenever an individual is in a certain mood state or perceives a certain stimulus—without flexibility, strategic choice, or voluntary control—they are not cognitive phenomena for the signaler and therefore not of direct concern to us here. Rather, we are concerned with gestural signals produced flexibly in pursuit of communicative goals. The basic criterion for goal-directed behavior is that the organism pursues the goal persistently around obstacles, and using different means in the face of failure, until the goal is attained—at which point the relevant activities cease (Bruner, 1981). To determine whether an organism has a communicative goal, we must determine if it is directing the act to another individual and expecting that individual to respond appropriately. Operationally, this means that as it produces the signal, the signaler orients to the recipient, at the very least, and that, even better, it waits for a response from the recipient. So, altogether, this means that the target of our investigation is primate behaviors that are:

- Goal directed or intentional in the sense that the organism uses them flexibly and strategically to pursue a goal;
- Communicative in the sense that an organism directs them at other individuals with the expectation that they will respond appropriately and so help them achieve their goal;
- Ritualized in the sense that these behaviors are only signals and so are not intended to effect a goal physically (i.e., they are mo-

torically ineffective), as would the real version of the behavior, but only communicatively; and
• Gestural in the sense that they involve bodily motions and/or postures rather than vocalizations.

Providing a full explanation of the gestural communication of a particular species involves a full description of its ecology and social structure. For example, it has been proposed that vocal communication predominates in arboreal species, when visual access to conspecifics is poor, whereas gestural communication predominates in more terrestrial species (Marler, 1976). Further, it has been proposed that species with a more despotic social structure in which the outcome of most social interactions is, in a sense, predetermined should have a smaller repertoire of gestural signals, whereas species with a more egalitarian social structure involving more complex and negotiated social interactions should have a larger repertoire of gestural signals (Maestripieri, 1999). We return to these issues in the final two chapters, after we have reviewed the current data. For the moment, we are most concerned with providing an accurate and useful description of the gestural signals of our six species, with particular concern for the cognitive and learning processes involved.

Toward that end, each of our six case studies focus on three major issues. The first is the goal-directed nature of particular gestures, operationalized as flexibility of use. We thus want to know such things as the variability in the gestural repertoires of different individuals, as an indication of the degree to which there is a fixed set in the species. Also important in this regard are differences in the gestures used by individuals of different ages and genders. Perhaps of most direct relevance to issues of flexibility, we want to identify gestures that are used by the same individual in multiple behavioral contexts, and also to identify contexts in which the same individual uses multiple gestures. Of special importance here are gesture sequences, or combinations, in which the signaler pursues a social goal persistently using different means in the face of failure.

The second issue is how particular gestures are learned. In the absence of experimental interventions, we are again interested in individual differences as an indication of whether gestures are learned or not learned—or perhaps even invented, as signals used by only one individual would seem to indicate individual invention. But most directly, we are concerned with whether particular gestures are ontogenetically ritualized in something like the manner outlined earlier, or whether, alternatively, they are socially learned from others using one or another form of social learning (e.g., imitation). In general, signals used by all or most members of one group, but not by the members of any other group of the same species, would seem to indicate some of type of social learning or imitation. Conversely, if the variability in individual gestural repertoires within a group is just as large as that between groups of the same species, then it is very unlikely that social learning or imitation is the major learning process—and much more likely that ontogenetic ritualization is what has occurred.

The third issue is adjustments for audience. As previously noted, it is fairly common for primate species to produce particular vocal or gestural signals only when certain types of individuals are present—and indeed such audience effects are also characteristic of the vocal signaling of some nonprimate species as well (e.g., domestic chickens; Evans, Evans, & Marler, 1993). But our more specific concern is with the question of whether an individual chooses a particular type of gesture depending on the attentional state of a particular recipient. For example, we are interested in whether individuals use visual gestures only when the potential recipient is visually oriented to them, and whether they use tactile signals preferentially when the potential recipient is not visually oriented to them. Such adjustments would seem to indicate that the signaler knows something about how its signal is being perceived, and perhaps understood, by the recipient.

Related to all of these issues is the distinction between two types of gestures; intention movement and attention getters. Intention movements are typically abbreviations of some full-fledged social behavior; for example, arm raise is a ritualization of play hitting. As such, intention movements are mostly used within a restricted set of social contexts, namely, those in which the real behavior typically occurs, and so their 'meaningfulness' is basically insured from these contexts. Attention getters, on the other hand, are such things as slapping the ground, throwing things at others, or poking others in the back. Because they are not ritualizations of preexisting social behaviors, these signals are more context free and occur quite widely across contexts. At the same time, this means that attention getters do not carry with them their meaning in the same way as intention movements. Most typically, an attention getter is used when the signaler is already displaying its mood in some other, often involuntary, way (i.e., facial expression, piloerection). For example, a youngster might have a play face and posture and slap the ground so that a nonattending potential playmate will notice this face and posture and so start to play. Or a sexually aroused adult male with an erection might make noise with a dead leaf (so-called leaf clipping) in order to attract the visual attention of a female to his erection—and so initiate sex. The upshot is that the meaning of an attention getter most often derives not from the signal itself or from the surrounding context but rather from some accompanying behavior. The ontogenetic ritualization of attention getters may also be somewhat different, as the initial behavior (e.g., slapping the ground) is not abbreviated/ritualized during learning in the same way as intention movements.

GENERAL METHODS

The methods of observation and analysis used in our six case studies derive ultimately from the series of studies on chimpanzee gestural communication conducted by Tomasello and colleagues over a 12-year period (Tomasello et al., 1985, 1989, 1994, 1997). We also conducted a follow-up study focused on the issue of gesture combinations (Liebal, Call, & Tomasello, 2004). The precise methods used evolved during this time period, and so the methods used in the current studies are based most directly on the two studies from the 1990s and the follow-up study. Of special importance, only the follow-up study used focal animal sampling—observers watch a particular individual for a specific length of time no matter what it is doing—and so only it can be used to estimate absolute frequencies (the earlier studies used all occurrences and *ad libitum* sampling in which observers simply look for occurrences of target behaviors from anyone in the group). All of the studies of other ape and monkey species reported here used either focal animal sampling, or some combination of focal animal and *ad libitum* sampling. To count in our observations, we had to observe an individual produce the same gesture on more than one occasion.

All of the studies reported here also used the same basic coding scheme for characterizing acts of gestural communication. For each act of gestural communication observed that is, for each observed behavior that met the four-part definition outlined earlier (goal-directed, communicative, ritualized, gestural)—the following was recorded:

- the initiating individual
- the gesture (later classified into type: visual, auditory, tactile)
- the context (such things as play, nursing, grooming, etc.)
- the recipient individual
- the state of recipient (visually attending or not)
- the behavioral response (attend, play, groom, gesture, etc.)

However, when observing different species, one cannot adhere to a single set of definitions and criteria too rigidly, and so some adjustments were made for particular species; these will be described, as appropriate, in the individual studies by their individual investigators. In some cases, the focus was mainly or even exclusively on juveniles of the species, as we were interested in the development of gestures. Additionally, youngsters seemed to engage in gestural communication most frequently.

This coding scheme allowed us to focus on our three main questions. The identification of individuals and their gestures in context enabled us to look at issues of flexibility of use and at gesture combinations. And it is perhaps worth noting that data on individuals are rarely used in studies of primate communication, of whatever type, and so it is impossible in these other studies to determine flexibility of use for specific individuals. Coding the state of the recipient before the initiator produced the gesture (and also its response) enabled us to discern adjustments for the recipient. To look at possible social learning, for five of the six species we observed more than one social group. This enabled us to look for group-specific gestures and also to compare individual variability within groups to the variability that occurred across different groups.

We now present the six case studies. The description of the chimpanzees is a composite of all of our previous work. The other five descriptions are based on recently conducted studies with the other species. Following these empirical reports, we attempt to make some cross-species comparisons with regard to our three main issues; flexibility of use, learning, and adjustments for audience. In a penultimate chapter, we try to explain at least some of the cross-species patterns in terms of the ecology, cognition, and social structure of the different species. In a final chapter, we try to relate our observations of ape gestural communication to the emergence of gestural communication in human ontogeny, and also to the emergence of linguistic communication in human evolution. In this final chapter, we also present what we think have been three basic steps in the evolution of human language; the flexible production of communicative signals in the manual modality detached from urgent functions, increased sensitivity to the attentional states of others due to the demands of the visual (as opposed to the auditory) modality, and the development of an intrinsic interest in understanding and sharing and intentional states with others.

REFERENCES

Bruner, J. (1981). Intention in the structure of action and interaction. In L. Lipsett (Ed.), *Advances in infancy research* (pp. 41–56). Norwood, NJ: Ablex.

Caine, R., Addington, R. L., & Windfelder, T. L. (1995). Factors affecting the rates of food calls given by red-bellied tamarins. *Animal Behaviour, 32*, 470–477.

Call, J., & Tomasello, M. (1994). Production and comprehension of referential pointing by orangutans (*Pongo pygmaeus*). *Journal of Comparative Psychology, 108*, 307–317.

Cheney, D. L., & Seyfarth, R. M. (1985). Vervet monkey alarm calls: Manipulation through shared information? *Behaviour, 93*, 150–166.

Cheney, D. L., & Seyfarth, R. M. (1988). Assessment of meaning and the detection of unreliable signals by vervet monkeys. *Animal Behaviour, 36*, 477–486.

Cheney, D. L., & Seyfarth, R. M. (1990.) Attending to behaviour versus attending to knowledge: Examining monkey's attribution of mental states. *Animal Behaviour, 40*, 742–753.

Crockford, C., Herbinger, I., Vigilant, L., & Boesch, C. (2004). Wild chimpanzees produce group-specific calls: A case for vocal learning? *Ethology, 110*, 221–243.

Dawkins, R., & Krebs, J. (1978). Animal signals: Information or manipulation. In J. Krebs & N. Davies (Eds.), *Behavioral ecology: An evolutionary approach* (pp. 282–309). Oxford, England: Blackwell.

de Waal, F. B. M. (1986). Deception in the natural communication of chimpanzees. In R. Mitchell & N. Thompson (Eds.), *Deception: Perspectives on human and nonhuman deceit* (pp. 221–244). Albany, NY: SUNY.

de Waal, F. B. M., & Johanowicz, D. L. (1993). Modification of reconciliation behavior through social experience: An experiment with two macaque species. *Child Development, 64*, 897–908.

Evans, C. S., Evans, L., & Marler, P. (1993). On the meaning of alarm calls: Functional reference in an avian vocal system. *Animal Behaviour, 46*, 23–38.

Goodall, J. (1986). *The chimpanzees of Gombe: Patterns of behavior.* Cambridge, MA: Harvard University Press.

Hammerschmidt, K., & Fischer, J. (in press). Constraints in primate vocal production. In U. Griebel & K. Oller (Eds.), *The evolution of communicative creativity: From fixed signals to contextual flexibility.* Cambridge, MA: MIT Press.

Hauser, M. (1992) Articulatory and social factors influence the acoustic structure of rhesus monkey vocalizations: A learned mode of production? *Journal of Acoustical Society of America* (4, Pt. 1), 2175–2179.

Hauser, M. D. (1988). How infant vervet monkeys learn to recognize starling alarm calls: The role of experience. *Behaviour, 105*, 187–201.

Hauser, M. D., Teixidor, P., Field, L., & Flaherty, R. (1993). Food-elicited calls in chimpanzees: effects of food quantity & divisibility. *Animal Behaviour, 45*, 817–819.

Kummer, H. (1968). *Social organization of hamadryas baboons.* Chicago, IL: University of Chicago Press.

Liebal, K., Call, J., & Tomasello, M. (2004). The use of gesture sequences in chimpanzees. *American Journal of Primatology, 64*, 377–396.

Maestripieri, D. (1999). Primate social organization, vocabulary size, and communication dynamics: A comparative study of macaques. In B. King (Ed.), *The origins of language: What nonhuman primates can tell us* (pp. 55–77). Santa Fe, NM: School of American Research.

Marler, P. (1976). Social organization, communication and graded signals: The chimpanzee and the gorilla. In P. P. G. Bateson & R. A. Hinde (Eds.), *Growing points in ethology* (pp. 239–280). Cambridge, MA: Cambridge University Press.

Mitani, J. C., & Nishida, T. (1993). Contexts and social correlates of long-distance calling by male chimpanzees. *Animal Behaviour, 45*, 735–746.

Mitani, J. C., Hasegawa, T., Gros-Louis, J., Marler, P., & Byrne, R. (1992). Dialects in chimpanzees? *American Journal of Primatology, 27*, 233–243.

Mitchell, R. W., & Anderson, J. R. (1997). Pointing, withholding information, and deception in capuchin monkeys (*Cebus apella*). *Journal of Comparative Psychology, 111*(4), 351–361.

Owren, M. J., Dieter, J. A., Seyfarth, R. M., & Cheney, D. L. (1992). Evidence of limited modification in the vocalizations of cross-fostered rhesus (*Macaca mulatta*) and Japanese (*M. fuscata*) macaques. In T. Nishida, W. C. McGrew, P. Marler, M. Pickford, & F. B. M. de Waal (Eds.), *Topics in primatology: Human origins* (pp. 257–270). Tokyo: University of Tokyo Press.

Savage-Rumbaugh, E. S., Wilkerson, B. J., & Bakeman, R. (1977). Spontaneous gestural communication among conspecifics in the pygmy chimpanzee (*Pan paniscus*). In G. H. Bourne (Ed.), *Progress in ape research* (pp. 97–116). New York: Academic Press.

Seyfarth, R. M., & Cheney, D. L. (1990). The assessment by vervet monkeys of their own and another species' alarm calls. *Animal Behaviour, 40*, 754–764.

Seyfarth, R. M., & Cheney, D. L. (1997). Behavioral mechanisms underlying vocal communication in nonhuman primates. *Asnimal Learning and Behavior, 25*, 249–267.

Seyfarth, R. M., & Cheney, D. L. (2003). Signalers and receivers in animal communication. *Annual Review of Psychology, 54*, 145–173.

Seyfarth, R. M., Cheney, D. L., & Marler, P. (1980). Monkey responses to three different alarm calls: Evidence of predator classification and semantic communication. *Science, 210*, 801–803.

Smith, W. J. (1977). *The behavior of communicating: An ethological approach.* Cambridge, MA: Harvard University Press.

Snowdon, C. T. (in press). Contextually flexible communication in nonhuman primates. In U. Griebel & K. Oller (Eds.), *The evolution of communicative creativity: From fixed signals to contextual flexibility.* Cambridge, MA: MIT Press.

Snowdon, C. T., & Boe, C. Y. (2003). Social communication about unpalatable foods in tamarins (*Saguinus oedipus*). *Journal of Comparative Psychology, 117*, 142–148.

Tanner, J. E., & Byrne, R. W. (1993). Concealing facial evidence of mood: Perspective-taking in a captive gorilla? *Primates, 34*, 451–457.

Tanner, J. E., & Byrne, R. W. (1996). Representation of action through iconic gesture in a captive lowland gorilla. *Current Anthropology, 37*, 162–173.

Tinbergen, N. (1951). *The study of instinct.* New York: Oxford University Press.

Tomasello, M. (1996). Do apes ape? In J. Galef & C. Heyes (Eds.), *Social learning in animals: The roots of culture* (pp. 319–346). Academic Press.

Tomasello, M., & Call, J. (1997). *Primate cognition.* Oxford, England: Oxford University Press.

Tomasello, M., Call, J., Nagell, K., Olguin, R., & Carpenter, M. (1994). The learning and use of gestural signals by young chimpanzees: A trans-generational study. *Primates, 37*, 137–54.

Tomasello, M., Call, J., Warren, J., Frost, T., Carpenter, M., & Nagell, K. (1997). The ontogeny of chimpanzee gestural signals: A comparison across groups and generations. *Evolution of Communication, 1*, 223–253.

Tomasello, M., George, B., Kruger, A., Farrar, J., & Evans, A. (1985). The development of gestural communication in young chimpanzees. *Journal of Human Evolution, 14,* 175–186.

Tomasello, M., Gust, D., & Frost, T. (1989). A longitudinal investigation of gestural communication in young chimpanzees. *Primates, 30,* 35–50.

Whiten, A., & Byrne, R. W. (1988). Tactical deception in primates. *Behavioral and Brain Sciences, 11,* 233–244.

Woodruff, G., & Premack, D. (1979). Intentional communication in the chimpanzee: The development of deception. *Cognition, 7,* 333–362.

Zahavi, A. (1997). *The handicap principle: A missing piece of Darwin's puzzle.* New York: Oxford University Press

Zuberbühler, K. (2000). Interspecific semantic communication in two forest monkeys. *Proceedings of the Royal Society of London B, 267*(1444), 713–718.

Zuberbühler, K., Cheney, D. L., & Seyfarth, R. M. (1999). Conceptual semantics in a nonhuman primate. *Journal of Comparative Psychology, 113,* 33–42.

CHAPTER 2

The Gestural Repertoire of Chimpanzees (Pan troglodytes)

Josep Call
Michael Tomasello
Max Planck Institute for Evolutionary Anthropology

Figure 2.1. Chimpanzee.

1. INTRODUCTION TO THE SPECIES

1.1. Taxonomy

Chimpanzees belong to the great ape clade together with orangutans, humans, bonobos, and gorillas. Bonobos and chimpanzees are humans' closest living relatives. Current estimates suggest that humans shared a common ancestor with chimpanzees and bonobos around 5–7 million years ago (Bailey et al.,1992). Likewise, chimpanzees shared a common ancestor with bonobos between 1.2 and 2.7 million years (Bradley & Vigilant, 2002; Kaessmann & Pääbo, 2002). Currently, there are four recognized chimpanzee subspecies; *Pan troglodytes verus, Pan troglodyres vellerosus, Pan troglodytes troglodytes, and Pan troglodytes schweinfurthii* (Bradley & Vigilant, 2002).

1.2. Morphology

Chimpanzees are covered by black hair although some individuals turn gray with age in some areas of their body (e.g., legs). Infants have light faces that get darker as they mature and a white tuft of hair in their anal region that disappears at around 3–5 years of age. Chimpanzees are mainly a terrestrial species although they spend a considerable part of their day in the trees where they forage and rest. In addition, every night, chimpanzees make a nest in trees where they sleep. Knuckle walking is the chimpanzee adaptation to terrestrial locomotion and consists of using the second phalange in their fingers as the contact point with the ground during quadruped locomotion. Chimpanzees show a slight sexual dimorphism with males being slightly larger than females. Adult males and females weigh around 40–60 kg. and 32–47 kg., respectively (Rowe, 1996).

1.3. Distribution and Ecology

Chimpanzees inhabit a wide variety of habitats in sub-Saharan Africa ranging from dry woodland savannah, and grassland to secondary and primary rain forest. Current population estimates place the number of west African chimpanzees between 96,000 and 180,000 and that of eastern African chimpanzees between 173,000 and 300,000 (Butynski, 2003).

Chimpanzees are omnivorous. They feed on a variety of fruits, leaves, bark, seeds, insects, and meat from small mammals such as antelopes or monkeys. Chimpanzees use tools regularly in the feeding context.

Among other things, they use stones and logs to crack open nuts, sticks to extract insects, or leaves to absorb liquids from difficult to reach places. Some of these practices vary across populations and represent social traditions that persist across generations. Some of these techniques are hard to master and youngsters require several years of practice to become proficient tool users. For instance, individuals require several years to become capable of nut cracking, which incidentally only occurs in some west African populations. Another aspect of the feeding behavior of chimpanzees is hunting. Chimpanzees hunt small terrestrial mammals such as antelopes or more commonly, arboreal monkeys. In some populations, hunting is done cooperatively by groups of males whereas in other populations hunting is an individual activity. In cooperative hunting, males pursue their prey and different hunters appear to play different roles to catch the prey. Thus, some individuals seem to flush the prey out whereas others cut its escape routes.

1.4. Social Structure and Behavior

Chimpanzees form communities of males and females that vary in size between a dozen to more than 100 individuals depending on the site. Although individuals in a community occupy the same territory, all members of the community are virtually never together at the same place. Instead, chimpanzees form a so-called fission-fusion society in which they temporarily split into small parties that reunite at a later time. Thus, this is a fluid society in which party membership (but not community membership, especially for males) may change from day to day depending on factors such as food availability or the presence of estrous females, among other factors.

Chimpanzees are patrilocal. This means that on reaching sexual maturity, females leave their natal group and migrate to neighboring communities. In contrast, males remain in their natal group and become integrated in an adult male dominance hierarchy. Males actively defend their territory against males from neighboring communities by patrolling the border of their own territories. Occasionally, intergroup encounters occur that can lead to serious injury or even death of individuals.

Males within a community form a dominance hierarchy that is often based on the establishment of long-term alliances between community members. Thus male–male bonds are stronger than male–female or female–female bonds although there is some variation across populations in this regard. Mother–offspring bonds are the strongest and infants are very dependent on their mother even after the birth of a younger sibling. The interbirth interval ranges between 4 and 6 years and offspring become more or less independent between 6 to 8 years of age. Nevertheless, even after independence, offspring still maintain strong bonds with their mother.

1.5. Cognition

1.5.1. Physical Cognition

Chimpanzees are the most intensively studied of the great apes (see Call & Tomasello, 2005; Tomasello & Call, 1997 for reviews). Call (in press) surveyed the literature on ape cognition between 1988 and 1997 and found that chimpanzees alone accounted for 70% of all studies published in leading journals on animal behavior, anthropology, and psychology. Among other things, these studies show that chimpanzees can remember spatial locations and the type of food present in each location. Likewise, they are capable of traveling efficiently by using detours and shortcuts and they track the displacement of hidden objects and infer their new locations after various spatial transformations. Chimpanzees are proficient tool users and tool makers. There is even some evidence suggesting that they have some understanding of the properties that make a tool a suitable one. For instance, they know that pulling a cloth to get a reward closer only works if the reward is on top of the cloth, not beside it or over it. They also have some understanding about what constitutes relevant and irrelevant functional features of a tool, and they can represent the appropriate dimensions of an effective tool in a particular task. Nevertheless, other studies have also shown certain limitations, particularly in tool-using tasks (e.g., Povinelli, 2000).

At a more abstract level, chimpanzees are capable of perceiving relations of similarity and difference between objects. Moreover, chimpanzees can solve analogies regarding the similarity or difference between pairs of objects. Recently, chimpanzees have been shown to also solve spatial analogies involving the use of scale models to locate food in particular locations of the real world. Chimpanzees can also make inferences in transitivity and conjunctive negation problems of various types and they can solve quantitative problems that require combining or dissociating quantities and they can also develop the notion of ordinality and the use of Arabic numerals in various tasks.

1.5.2. Social Cognition

An area that has received much research attention in recent years is social cognition (see Byrne & Whiten, 1988; Tomasello & Call, 1997). These studies of what may be called a social problem solving thus demonstrate that chimpanzees have some knowledge about what others can and cannot see in the present, or in the immediate past. Thus, chimpanzees follow the gaze of conspecifics and humans, follow it past distracters and behind barriers, "check back" with humans when gaze following does not yield interesting sights, stop following the gaze of a looker who keeps looking at nothing, use gestures appropriately depending on the visual access of their recipient, know when they themselves have seen something, and select different pieces of food depending on whether their competitor has visual access to them—understanding transparent barriers and split barriers in the process (see Tomasello & Call, in press, for a recent review). There is also some indication that they may understand something about the intentions of others. Thus, chimpanzees can distinguish a human who is willing but unable to give them food from one that is simply unwilling. There is also some evidence that they can distinguish between the intentional and accidental actions of others (see Call, 2005; Tomasello & Call, in press, for recent reviews).

Although there is clear evidence of social learning among chimpanzees, the question of the precise mechanism involved in the transmission of behavior remains controversial (Tomasello, 1996). Whereas some authors have suggested that imitation is one of the main ways in which chimpanzees learn from each other, other authors have suggested that much of the social learning in chimpanzees can be explained as a case of emulation. This is not to say that chimpanzees are incapable of copying the actions of others. On the contrary, chimpanzees can be trained to imitate actions on command (Custance, Whiten, & Bard, 1995; Hayes & Hayes, 1952). Yet it is unclear how often they use this source of information when they are solving problems. An alternative to action copying that has gained support in recent years is the reproduction of results, not the actions that produce the results. In effect, chimpanzees are very attuned to the changes that others produce in the environment, and less concerned with the exact actions that bring about those changes (see Call & Carpenter, 2003; Whiten, Horner, Litchfield, & Marshall-Pescini, 2004, for reviews).

1.6. Communication: State of the Art

The communicative repertoire of chimpanzees is composed of vocalizations, facial expressions, and gestures. They use different vocalizations in various situations such feeding, alarm calling, and during social interactions. For instance, subordinate animals use grunts directed to dominant animals as a sign of appeasement and submission. Besides the vocalizations that they use to communicate with individuals that are in close proximity, chimpanzees also have long distance vocalizations that serve to communicate with other community members (or even outsiders) that are not currently present. These vocalizations are often combined with pounding on trees. Chimpanzees have about 10 distinct facial expressions indicative of a variety of emotions including fear, pleasure, aggressiveness, distress, or excitement. They are used in a variety of contexts including play and aggression and there is some evidence that subjects can recognize facial expressions across individuals (Parr, Hopkins, & De Waal, 1998).

Chimpanzees have a gestural repertoire of about 30 to 40 gestures that includes limb movements and body postures. Most studies of the gestural repertoire have taken an ethological approach and have described in detail the repertoire of communicative and noncommunicative behaviors. Thus, van Lawick-Goodall (1968) and van Hooff (1973) published the first chimpanzee behavioral repertoires (so-called ethograms). These ethograms contain many of the communicative gestures that have been observed in latter studies in the wild and the laboratory. Nishida, Kano, Goodall, McGrew, and Nakamura (1999) have produced the latest and most complete chimpanzee ethogram to date, which included a comparison with previous ethograms, particularly those developed by Goodall (e.g., Goodall, 1986; van Lawick-Goodall, 1986).

Plooij (1984) also investigated the behavioral repertoire of chimpanzees, but mostly focusing on infant behavior. One main difference between Plooij's and previous studies is that it took an approach closest to our own, inspired on the study of gestural communication in children. Berdecio and Nash (1981) is another example of this approach. Finally, de Waal (1988) conducted a comparative analysis of the communicative repertoires of bonobos and chimpanzees. De Waal (1988) devoted an entire section to gestures and like many of its predecessors, this analysis had its roots on the ethological tradition of cataloguing the different units of behavior into comprehensive repertoires.

The aim of this chapter is to offer an overview of the gestural repertoire of chimpanzees in relation to its contexts of use, variability, and flexibility in gestural production. In addition to descriptive information, this chapter includes comparisons between and within groups, development of gestures, combinations of gestures, adjustment to audience effects and the relation between gestures and contexts.

2. METHODS

2.1. Individuals

The data presented here are based on five studies that took place between 1983 and 1999 at the field station of the Yerkes Primate Research

Center in Lawrenceville, GA (Liebal, Call & Tomasello, 2004; Tomasello, Call, Nagell, Olguin, & Carpenter, 1994; Tomasello et al., 1985, 1997; Tomasello, Gust, & Frost, 1989). Due to the ontogenetic focus of this research program, the bulk of the observations was concentrated on chimpanzee youngsters. Taken together, these studies included a total of 28 individuals (14 males, 14 females) ranging in age from 1 to 10 years. The longitudinal nature of these studies meant that 21 individuals were observed in two consecutive observational periods. This means that there were 49 individual × period data points.

The first three studies focused on one group in three different observation periods separated by 4 years. The fourth study focused on two different groups of chimpanzees, the original group and a second group. The last study focused exclusively on the second group 4 years after our initial observations on this group. Although the bulk of the observations focused on how youngsters used gestures, we also focused on adults in this last study period.

2.2. Data Collection

We observed the chimpanzees in five different periods between 1983 and 1999 at regular intervals of 4 years. Each period covered around 3 months of observation that represented a total observation time ranging between 75 h and 240 h depending on the observation period. All studies combined represented approximately 815 h of observation. We used *ad libitum* and focal sampling. Additional details on the observational procedures for each study period can be found in the corresponding papers.

2.3. Description of the Gestural Repertoire

As stated in the introductory chapter, we considered as gestures those intentional movements of the limbs, head, and body as well as body postures used to communicate with conspecifics. We excluded facial expressions from our analyses. Later we present the ethogram resulting from combining the gestures observed in all five study periods. In some cases we have collapsed some of the original specific gestures into more general categories. For instance, belly offer and back offer have been collapsed into the category offer. We have indicated the correspondence of the current gestures with those from previous studies (both our own and others). The ethogram is organized as a function of the gestures' main sensory modalities; auditory, tactile and visual. Visual gestures rely solely on visual information, auditory gestures rely mainly on sound production (although they also have an important visual component), and tactile gestures depend mainly on establishing physical contact with the recipient. We observed the following gestures (see Table 2.1 for a comparison with the categories observed in previous studies).

2.3.1. Visual Gestures

The following are visual gestures.

- *Arm raise*—Lift stretched arm in the air more or less perpendicular to the ground.
- *Ball offer*—Present ball to the recipient and take it back when recipient approaches.
- *Bipedal jump*—Jump up and down while standing bipedally.
- *Crouch*—Press the front of the body against the ground so that body size is virtually minimized.
- *Finger curl*—Reach out to the recipient with an outstretched arm and curl the fingers.
- *Genito-anal offer*—Present the backside to the recipient.
- *Hand beg*—Place hand under the recipient's mouth.
- *Head bob*—Move the head rhythmically up and down.
- *Head shake*—Move the head horizontal and repeatedly.
- *Look back*—Look over the shoulder at the recipient while moving away from her.
- *Offer*—Present a body part such as the back, leg, or belly to the recipient [i.e., back offer, belly offer, leg offer].
- *Penis offer*—Present the penis to the recipient by leaning back and frontally orienting the body to the recipient.
- *Point*—Touch its own side (sometimes with a finger) and look at the recipient's face.
- *Raise object*—Lift and hold an object over the head.
- *Reach*—Extend the outstretched arm in the direction of the recipient.
- *Shake object*—Push an object rapidly back and forth in front of the body.
- *Swagger*—Move the body rhythmically from side to side.
- *Wave object*—Swing an object over the head.
- *Wrist offer*—Present the back of a flexed hand so that the wrist is pointed at the recipient.

2.3.2. Tactile Gestures

We observed the following tactile gestures.

- *Arm on*—Approach recipient with an outstretched arm and place it on the recipient's back.

TABLE 2.1

Comparison Between the Gestures Observed in the Current Study and Those Reported by Other Authors

Current study	van Hooff, 1973	Plooij, 1984	de Waal, 1988	van Lawick-Goodall, 1968	Nishida et al. 1999
arm raise			arm waving, arm up	bipedal arm waving,	raise arm*, dance bipedal
ball offer					
bipedal jump		jumping			leap bipedal on spot
crouch	crouch	crouching, bowing		crouching, bowing	crouch, bow
finger curl			finger flexing		
genito-anal offer	mount present, crouch present	present	rump present	present, sitting- hunch	present with limbs*
hand beg		begging with hand		beg with hand	beg with hand
head bob	squat bob, vertical head nod	bobbing		bobbing	bob
head shake	horizontal head shake				
look back				look back	look back, wait
offer	groom present	arm high, hands around head	ventral present	stretching out, present*	solicit grooming, lean forward, lie with back to another, lower,* raise leg,* turn face downward
penis offer	vacuum trust		concave back	male invite	thrust,* open thighs
point					
raise object					lift rock

(continued)

TABLE 2.1 (continued)

Current study	van Hooff, 1973	Plooij, 1984	de Waal, 1988	van Lawick-Goodall, 1968	Nishida et al. 1999
reach	hold out hand, finger stretched, stretch over	lie down on back, arm raise, extend hand*	begging gesture, stretch over, leg out	reach hand, beckoning, holding hand towards another	extend hand,* offer arm, extend leg
rub chin					
shake object		branch swaying, branching, shake detached branch		branch shaking, branching	flail, rinse, shake branch
swagger	sway walk, arm sway	bipedal swagger	bipedal swagger	bipedal swagger	swagger bipedal
wave object		branch swaying		branch swaying	flail, sway vegetation
wrist offer	wrist bent		bended wrist	wrist bending	
belly slap					drum belly
foot stomp	stamp trot		stamp trot	stamping, heel kicking	stamp,* heel kicking, slap-stamp
ground slap		banging, drumming, flapping		flap, drum, kick, slap ground	club ground, drum, flap, kick backward, rap, slap
hand clap			clapping	flapping	
arm on	cling, embrace	embrace half	lateral embrace	arm round	embrace half
direct hand	touch	hand leading		pull towards	
embrace	embrace	embracing full	ventral embrace	embracing	embrace full
face grab					pull face to face

	gnaw	open mouth kiss, bite-kissing, mouthing/gnawing	mouth kiss	open mouth kiss, submissive kissing	open mouth kiss, mouth
formal bite					
gentle touch	touch	pat	patting	pat, light touch, touch	pat, stroke, touch
lead	touch	hand in neck			
lip lock					
poke at	hit, poke	dabbing		tickling + poking, slapping, dabbing, hit	slap, club another, dab, hit, poke
pull	pull & shake limbs, tug	hair pulling			pull
push body				kick	push, kick
push object					
spit at					
throw stuff	aimed throwing	aimed throwing		aimed throwing	drop branch, lift & drop, push backward, throw at
			wrist shaking	hitting away	
			chest beating	rump turning	
	flinch/shrink	bending away	bending away		bend away
					bend shrub
					clip leaf
				branch dragging	drag branch

(continued)

TABLE 2.1 (continued)

Current study	van Hooff, 1973	Plooij, 1984	de Waal, 1988	van Lawick-Goodall, 1968	Nishida et al. 1999
				hold genitals, hold hand	hold genitals, hold hand
		mount		mounting embrace	mount
					pull through stem
		finger in mouth		finger in mouth	push finger into mouth
		arm raise		arm threat, arm raising	raise arm quickly
				scrub	rake/scratch dead leaves
				head tipping	tip head
		beg with mouth, put face close			beg with mouth, peer
		hand in neck			
		leg bending			
		lowering back		flexed knees	

- *Direct hand*—Place the recipient's hand on the subject's body.
- *Embrace*—Put one arm or both around the body of the recipient (includes arm-neck).
- *Face grab*—Grabbing the face of the recipient from behind to obtain the recipient's attention.
- *Formal bite*—Place the open mouth on any body part (back, neck, wrist) of the recipient, simulating biting.
- *Gentle touch*—Put the hand gently on any body part of the recipient [i.e., touch side].
- *Lead*—Place the arm around the neck/body of the recipient and pull it in a certain direction [i.e., grab head, grab face, pull head].
- *Lip lock*—Hold with the mouth while sucking the recipient's lower lip and then back away.
- *Poke at*—Hit or stab the recipient with hands, feet or with an object [i.e., back push, wrist hit].
- *Pull*—Pull quickly and rapidly on a body part (arm, leg) of the other.
- *Push body*—Apply pressure against the recipient's body with a rapid movement of the hands, feet, or head.
- *Push object*—Displace an object in the recipient's direction.
- *Rub chin*—Stroke the chin of the recipient while staring at her face.
- *Spit at*—Project water or saliva from the mouth toward the recipient.
- *Throw stuff*—Throw some detached object or material (e.g., stone, paper, toy, stick, dirt) at the recipient.

2.3.3. Auditory Gestures

The following are auditory gestures we observed.

- *Belly slap*—Hit the belly with one or two open hands.
- *Foot stomp*—Step forcefully on the ground with one or both feet either in a bipedal or quadrupedal stance.
- *Ground* slap—Hit the ground, wall, or an object with one or two open hands (or more rarely feet).
- *Hand clap*—Strike an open hand against the other.

3. GESTURAL REPERTOIRE

3.1. Overview

The gestural repertoire of chimpanzees varied between 25 and 30 gestures depending on the study period. Thus, Tomasello, Call, Nagell,

Olguin, and Carpenter (1994) described 30 gestures (18 visual, 3 auditory, 9 tactile) whereas Liebal et al. (2004) reported 27 gestures (12 visual, 3 auditory, 12 tactile). Combining all gestures from all studies produced an ethogram of 38 gestures (20 visual, 4 auditory, 14 tactile). More detailed information about the use of gestures by particular age–sex classes of individuals can be found in Tomasello et al. (1994, 1997).

3.2. Context of Use

Chimpanzees used gestures in a variety of contexts including affiliation, agonistic, feeding and nursing, sexual, grooming, travel, and play. For instance, they extend their arm to beg for food, slap the ground to call attention to themselves, and put their arm around their mother's back to request travel to a different location. Several studies showed that play was the most important context accounting for between 47% and 70% of the gestures depending on the studies (Tomasello et al., 1994, 1997). It is conceivable that group composition, and especially the age of the subjects, explains this variability. Tomasello et al. (1989) noted that the gestural repertoire changed with age and some gestures disappeared and were replaced by adult forms. For instance, gestures used in the nursing context decreased from 5% to 0% as individuals were weaned whereas gestures used in agonistic or sexual contexts increased its relative importance from 3% to 12% (Tomasello et al., 1997). Figure 2.2 presents the total number of gestures per context.

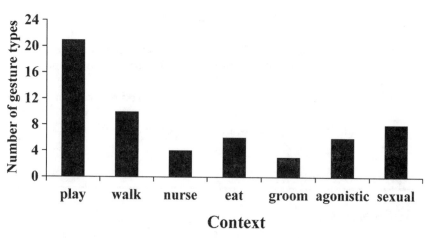

Figure 2.2. Number of gesture types as a function of context.

3.3. Variability

3.3.1. Individual Differences

Tomasello et al. (1994) compiled data from the first three studies and reported that 14% of the gestures were idiosyncratic, that is, unique to particular individuals. Moreover, 40% of the gestures (13 out of 30) were idiosyncratic at a given time point. That is, only one individual used them during that particular observation period. An inspection of the ethograms of previous studies also revealed idiosyncratic gestures (Table 2.1). Without exception, all previous studies have reported gestures that were apparently only observed in those studies. Although differences in sampling methods (including total observation time) may explain those differences among studies, this is unlikely to explain the differences observed in our series of studies in which we used comparable methods and observation periods.

Fifty percent of the gestures in the repertoire were used by four individuals or less (out of 22 individuals possible). We also calculated the amount of similarity that subjects shared with other members of their group by using Cohen's kappa. Tomasello et al. (1994) found that the intragroup reliability in gesture use was low for play gestures (mean Cohen's kappa across three groups = 0.48) and even lower for nonplay gestures (mean kappa = 0.20). Similarly, Tomasello et al. (1997) included four study periods and also found a low overall intragroup concordance regardless of the type of gesture (kappa = 0.42). This means that there was great interindividual variability in the types of gestures used by individuals. In fact, only six gestures (out of 29) were used by 50% or more of the individuals. The most commonly used gesture was ground slap (100%, i.e., all individuals used this gesture) followed by arm raise (86%), throw stuff, poke at, and head bob (59%), and hand clap (50%). Nevertheless, it needs to be pointed out that these represented the vast majority of gestures produced by individuals.

Tomasello et al. (1994, 1997) also documented the within-gesture variability for the three gestures that subjects used in the third and fourth study periods; ground slap, throw stuff, and poke at. Each of these gestures varied considerably depending on the object toward which it was directed or the style of the performed actions. For instance, ground slaps varied on nine objects to which they were applied and four different styles (Tomasello et al., 1997). Likewise, throw stuff varied depending on the material thrown (6 types) and the way it was thrown (i.e., overhead, sideways, underhand, or backward).

3.3.2. Age Differences

Gesture use increased with age. This does not simply reflect that older subjects were more active but it also shows that they had a greater variety of gestures. Figure 2.3 presents the number of gesture types as a function of age. The number of different gestures peaked between 5 and 6 years of age and deceased slightly afterwards (Tomasello et al., 1985, 1997).

The overall repertoire for one year olds was composed of 12 different gestures and it reached a peak at 3 years of age with 19 gestures (Tomasello et al., 1997). From this point on, the repertoire did not increase any further but some gestures were replaced by others. For instance, nursing gestures virtually disappeared whereas those related to agonistic and sexual behavior became more prominent. This means that no individual or age class ever displayed the full repertoire of about 30 gestures.

The number of contexts in which gestures were used also increased with age (Tomasello et al., 1997). Another important developmental aspect is that infant gestures were often replaced by adult gestures when new contexts became more important with age. Thus, nursing disappeared after 3 or 4 years of age and other contexts such as sexual or agonistic increased their importance (see Fig. 2.3).

Two other age-related changes occurred in the use of multi-context gestures (i.e., those gestures that were used in more than one context) and the length of gesture combinations. Whereas multi-context gestures

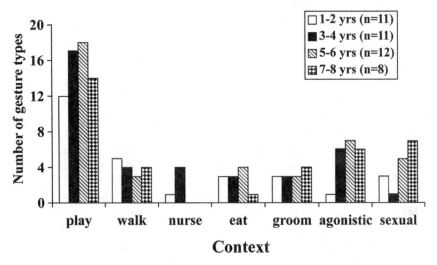

Figure 2.3. Number of gesture types per context as a function of age.

increased with age (Tomasello et al., 1994), the length of the combinations decreased with age with adults producing the shortest combinations and juveniles the longest combinations (Liebal et al., 2004).

3.3.3. Sex Differences

We did not investigate this topic.

3.3.4. Group Differences

Comparisons Between Groups. Tomasello et al. (1997) directly compared the gestures used by chimpanzees between two groups with similar group compositions and living conditions. They found that the most frequent gestures at one group were also more frequent at the other group. Focusing on commonly used gestures such as ground slap and throw stuff, Tomasello et al. (1997), found no striking differences between groups in the type of object gestures were directed to or the style of the action. When differences existed, in most cases they could be related to the existence of particular environmental features such as vertical poles or loose material such as wood chips covering the ground (Tomasello et al., 1989). In fact, Tomasello et al. (1989) documented the emergence of gestures such as throw stuff with the introduction of wood chips as ground cover in the original study group. Throw stuff was not a prominent gesture in the first study observation period but became one of the main gestures after the introduction of wood chips in the chimpanzees outdoor area.

Despite these similarities between groups in the most commonly used gestures, an analysis of the concordance between gesture types of the entire gestural repertoire (rather than their frequency of use) produced a relatively low level of between-group concordance (Cohen's kappa = 0.24). Incidentally, the concordance values for each of the within-group analyses were also comparatively low (0.29 and 0.38). Taken together, these data suggest that the main gestures in terms of frequency of use were comparable across groups but that important differences existed when the whole gestural repertoire was considered. Some of these differences could be traced back to specific environmental features present in one location but not in the other or to the use of idiosyncratic gestures.

Comparisons Across Generations. The longitudinal nature of these studies allowed us to observe the original group in four consecutive periods with 4-year gaps that spanned a total of 16 years. We used the same concordance analyses alluded to earlier to carry out cross-generational comparisons. Tomasello et al. (1997) found that the within-generation concordance was higher than the between-generation comparisons (within = 0.34–0.48; between = 0.10–0.35). Moreover, the farther apart two generations were, the lower their concordance values became, even after controlling for age. Thus, those subjects observed in 1985 were more similar to those observed in 1989 than those observed in 1994, even though group composition was more similar between 1985 and 1994 than between 1985 and 1989. Nevertheless, the concordance levels were still rather low, which indicates that there was much variability across time periods.

3.4. Flexibility

3.4.1. Combinations

Approximately one-third of the gestures produced by chimpanzees occurred in combination with other gestures (Liebal et al., 2004; Tomasello et al., 1994). Two-gesture combinations were the most frequent ones accounting for almost two thirds of all combinations while 3-gesture combinations accounted for less than 20% of the sequences. In regard to the type of gestures involved in the combinations, they varied between studies. Tomasello et al. (1994) found that 61% of the combinations were formed by repetitions of the same gesture whereas the remaining 39% were combinations of two or more different gestures. Liebal et al. (2004) found that repetitions accounted for 45% of the combinations observed whereas 55% of combinations consisted of two or more distinct gestures.

In the vast majority of cases, the combination of gestures corresponded to the functions of the single gestures in the combination. In other words, combinations did not produce a different "meaning" than the preexisting "meaning" of the gesture components (Liebal et al., 2004; Tomasello et al., 1994). Instead, gesture combinations appeared to be the individual's attempt to engage unresponsive recipients. In fact, Liebal et al. (2004) found that responsiveness to single gestures was lower than to combinations of gestures. Upon failing to get a response from the recipient, chimpanzees repeated the same gesture more often that using another gesture.

3.4.2. Audience Effects

Chimpanzees use gestures of three sensory modalities (visual, auditory, and tactile) and adjust their gestures to the attentional state of recipients (Tomasello et al., 1994). Thus visual gestures are preferentially used when others are facing them but tactile gestures are deployed irrespective of the recipient's body orientation (see Fig. 2.4). Chimpanzees also deploy auditory gestures, which also have a visual component, preferentially when others are oriented to them although the effect of body orientation is not as marked as with visual gestures. We replicated these initial findings in a second study and with an additional group of youngsters (Tomasello et al., 1997). This suggests that chimpanzees are sensitive to the body orientation of recipients when deploying their gestures.

In a recent study, we probed this ability further and we investigated whether they would also use auditory gestures to modify the attentional state of the recipient. For instance, when the recipient is not looking and the individual wants to invite her to play with an arm raise gesture, would chimpanzees use an auditory gesture (to make the recipient look) before they used the visual gesture? We compared the distribution of combinations of gestures from different sensory modalities. Contrary to our expectations, we found a small number of combinations (that did not exceed chance levels) consisting of an auditory gesture followed by a visual gesture when the recipient was not attending to the individual

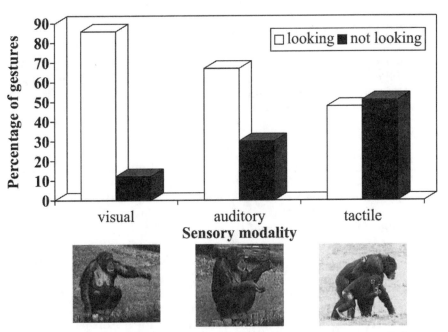

Figure 2.4. Mean percentage of gestures in each sensory modality produced when the recipient was facing toward the signaler.

at the beginning of the sequence. Instead, chimpanzees either used tactile gestures, which bypassed the problem of the recipient having the wrong body orientation, or they put themselves in a position where they could be seen by the recipient, by for instance, walking around an inattentive recipient until they were facing each other. Thus, we found no evidence that chimpanzees used auditory gestures to modify the attentional state of the recipient prior to using a visual gesture. Instead, they used other means to get the attention of inattentive recipients.

3.4.3. One Gesture for Multiple Contexts

Tomasello et al. (1994, 1997) documented that young chimpanzees used particular gestures for more than one context. In particular, between 38% and 48% of the gestures in their ethogram, depending on the study, were used in more than one context by individuals. The number of contexts served by a single gesture varied from five to one depending on the individuals. The context with more gestures was play ($M = 8$) followed by agonistic and travel ($M = 3$), nurse ($M = 2.8$), and eat ($M = 1.8$). Tomasello et al. (1997) confirmed the predominance of play as the context serviced by more gestures followed by the other contexts with comparable lower numbers ranging from 1 to 1.6 gestures per context.

3.4.4. Multiple Contexts for One Gesture

Tomasello et al. (1994) also found that chimpanzees used single gestures for multiple contexts. The number of multi-context gestures varied from six to zero across individuals (Tomasello et al., 1994). Only two out of eight subjects lacked multi-context gestures.

4. DISCUSSION

Chimpanzees have a varied repertoire of about 40 gestures belonging to three sensory modalities; visual, auditory and tactile. Visual gestures rely solely on visual information, auditory gestures rely mainly on sound production (although they also have an important visual component), and tactile gestures depend mainly on establishing physical contact with the recipient. Individuals use these gestures in multiple contexts to obtain a number of goals such as food, physical contact, transportation, reassurance, or support in agonistic encounters.

There are important individual differences in the use of gestures both in the kinds of gestures employed and also in their precise topography. In fact, all previously published ethograms invariably report some gestures seemingly unique to the observed individuals. The gestural repertoire of chimpanzees changes with age. At around one year of age, infant chimpanzees use about 12 gestures that increase steadily until about 3 to 4 years of age, when it reaches a plateau. The size of the gestural repertoire of the individual does not increase further because some gestures disappear as some contexts of use also disappear (e.g., nursing or travel). Thus, a key feature in the development of the gestural repertoire of chimpanzees is replacement rather than accumulation. Individual variability is the basis for the within- and between-group variability. Taking the gestural repertoire as a whole, there is a low index of concordance between the gestures used by individuals within the group compared to the gestures used by other groups. Nevertheless, concordance across generations decreases proportionally to the distance between generations. Thus, cohorts of individuals closest in time show higher concordance rates than cohorts farthest apart in time.

Gestures occur in combinations about one third of the time, mostly as a consequence for not receiving a response from recipients after single or multiple attempts. These combinations, however, appear to fulfill the same functions as the single gestures that form them. In a sense, combinations of gestures could be construed as an emphatic device, not a semantic one. Chimpanzees take into account the attentional state of the recipient when they use gestures. Thus, they use visual gestures when potential recipients are oriented to them, and therefore can see them. In contrast, they disregard the state of the recipient when they use tactile gestures. Faced with an individual that is not oriented to them, chimpanzees will either walk to a position where the recipient can see them and then use a visual gesture, or they use a tactile gesture directly without moving within the visual field of the recipient. We found no evidence that chimpanzees used auditory gestures to modify the attentional state of the recipient in their natural communication. Finally, chimpanzee gestural communication shows a clear dissociation between signals and functions (or contexts) because they use a single gesture for multiple contexts and a single context is served by multiple gestures.

5. CONCLUSION

There is one word that accurately captures the essence of chimpanzee gestural communication; flexibility. Chimpanzees use multiple gestures for a single context and conversely a single gesture is applied to multiple contexts. Besides contextual flexibility, chimpanzees often create new gestures for specific purposes and they can also adopt human gestures such as distal pointing to request items or activities. Furthermore, chimpanzees often produce strings of gestures, mostly consisting of repetitions of a single gesture. Chimpanzees also adapt their gesture production to the attentional state of the recipient, using visual gestures mostly when others are facing them and tactile gestures regardless of the attentional state of the recipient.

Gesture use develops with age through a combination of social learning and certain hardwired predispositions. Thus, some gestures such as ground slap appear regardless of the social context (individuals reared without adults also produce them) whereas others seemingly develop through mutual shaping by repeated interaction—a process called ontogenetic ritualization. In contrast, there is little evidence that chimpanzees learn gestures via imitation. This could explain the great within- and between-group variability observed in gesture use.

6. REFERENCES

Bailey, W. J., Hayasaka, K., Skinner, C. G., Kehoe, S., Sieu, L. C., Slightom, J. L., & Goodman, M. (1992). Reexamination of the African hominoid trichotomy with additional sequences from the primate ß-globin gene cluster. *Molecular Phylogenetics and Evolution, 1*, 97–135.

Berdecio, S., & Nash, L. T. (1981). Chimpanzee visual communication. *Anthropological research papers, No. 26*, (pp. 1–159). Arizona State University.

Bradley, B. J., & Vigilant, L. (2002). The evolutionary genetics and molecular ecology of chimpanzees and bonobos. In L. F. Marchant (Ed.), *Behavioural diversity in chimpanzees and bonobos* (pp. 259–276). Cambridge, England: Cambridge University Press.

Butynski, T. M. (2003). The robust chimpanzee *Pan troglodytes*: Taxonomy, distribution, abundance, and conservation status. In R. Kormos, C. Boesch, M. I. Bakarr, & T. M. Butynski (Eds.), *West African chimpanzees: Status survey and conservation* (pp. 5–12). Cambridge, England: IUCN/SSC Primate Specialist Group.

Byrne, R. W., & Whiten, A. (1988). *Machiavellian intelligence: Social expertise and the evolution of intellect in monkeys, apes and humans*. Oxford, England: Clarendon Press.

Call, J. (in press). Chimpocentrism: A continuing problem in ape cognition research. In C. Casanova & C. Sousa (Eds.), *Advances in primatology*. Lisbon: University of Lisbon.

Call, J. (2005). Chimpanzees are sensitive to some of the psychological states of others. *Interaction Studies, 6*, 413–427.

Call, J., & Carpenter, M. (2003). On imitation in apes and children. *Infancia y Aprendizaje, 26*, 325–349.

Call, J., & Tomasello, M. (2005). Reasoning and thinking in nonhuman primates. In K. J. Holyoak & R. G. Morrison (Eds.), *Cambridge handbook on thinking and reasoning* (pp. 607–632). Cambridge, England: Cambridge University Press.

Custance, D. M., Whiten, A., & Bard, K. A. (1995). Can young chimpanzees (*Pan troglodytes*) imitate arbitrary actions? Hayes & Hayes (1952) revisited. *Behaviour, 132*(11–12), 837–859.

De Waal, F. B. M. (1988). The communicative repertoire of captive bonobos (*Pan paniscus*) compared to that of chimpanzees. *Behaviour, 106*(3–4), 183–251.

Goodall, J. (1986). *The chimpanzees of Gombe.* Cambridge, MA: Harvard University Press.

Hayes, K. J., & Hayes, C. (1952). Imitation in a home-raised chimpanzee. *Journal of Comparative Psychology, 45,* 450–459.

Kaessmann, H., & Pääbo, S. (2002). The genetical history of humans and the great apes. *Journal of Internal Medicine, 251,* 1–18.

Liebal, K., Call, J., & Tomasello, M. (2004). The use of gesture sequences in chimpanzees. *American Journal of Primatology, 64,* 377–396.

Nishida, T., Kano, T., Goodall, J., McGrew, W. C., & Nakamura, M. (1999). Ethogram and ethnography of Mahale chimpanzees. *Anthropological Science, 107*(2), 141–188.

Parr, L. A., Hopkins, W. D., & De Waal, F. B. M. (1998). The perception of facial expressions by chimpanzees, *Pan troglodytes. Evolution of Communication, 2*(1), 1–23.

Plooij, F. X. (1984). *The behavioral development of free-living chimpanzee babies and infants.* Norwood, NJ: Ablex.

Povinelli, D. J. (2000). *Folk physics for apes.* Oxford, England: Oxford University Press.

Rowe, N. (1996). *The pictorial guide to the living primates.* East Hampton, NY: Pogonias Press.

Tomasello, M. (1996). Do apes ape? In C. M. Heyes & B. G. Galef, Jr. (Eds.), *Social learning in animals: The roots of culture* (pp. 319–346). San Diego: Academic Press.

Tomasello, M., & Call, J. (1997). *Primate cognition.* New York: Oxford University Press.

Tomasello, M., & Call, J. (2006). Do chimpanzees know what others see—or only what they are looking at? In S. Hurley & M. Nudds (Eds.), *Rational animals* (pp. 371–384). Oxford: Oxford University Press.

Tomasello, M., & Call, J. (in press). Do chimpanzees know what others see—or only what they are looking at? In S. Hurley & M. Nudds (Eds.), *Rational animals.* Oxford, England: Oxford University Press.

Tomasello, M., Call, J., Nagell, K., Olguin, R., & Carpenter, M. (1994). The learning and the use of gestural signals by young chimpanzees: A trans-generational study. *Primates, 35,* 137–154.

Tomasello, M., Call, J., Warren, J., Frost, T., Carpenter, M., & Nagell, K. (1997). The ontogeny of chimpanzee gestural signals: A comparison across groups and generations. *Evolution of Communication, 1,* 223–253.

Tomasello, M., George, B. L., Kruger, A. C., Farrar, M. J., & Evans, A. (1985). The development of gestural communication in young chimpanzees. *Journal of Human Evolution, 14,* 175–186.

Tomasello, M., Gust, D., & Frost, G. T. (1989). A longitudinal investigation of gestural communication in young chimpanzees. *Primates, 30*(1), 35–50.

van Hooff, J. A. R. A. M. (1973). A structural analysis of the social behaviour of a semi-captive group of chimpanzees. In M. von Cranach & I. Vine (Eds.), *Social communication and movement: Studies of interaction and expression in man and chimpanzee* (pp. 75–162). New York: Academic Press.

van Lawick-Goodall, J. (1968). The behaviour of free-living chimpanzees in the Gombe Stream Reserve. *Animal Behaviour Monographs, 1,* 165–311.

Whiten, A., Horner, V., Litchfield, C. A., & Marshall-Pescini, S. (2004). How do apes ape? *Learning and Behavior, 32*(1), 36–52.

CHAPTER 3

Gestures in Subadult Bonobos (Pan paniscus)

Simone Pika
University of St. Andrews

Figure 3.1.   Bonobos.

1. INTRODUCTION TO THE SPECIES

1.1. Taxonomy

Bonobos (*Pan paniscus*), along with common chimpanzees (*Pan troglodytes*), belong to the genus *Pan*. Molecular analysis of both nuclear and mitochondrial DNA confirms these closely related species (Bradley & Vigilant, 2002) to have been separated around 1.2–2.7 million years ago (Kaessmann & Pääbo, 2002).

1.2. Morphology

Bonobos constitute the least sexually dimorphic ape species with the males having longer canines than the females. In addition, adult male bonobos weigh on average 39 kg and have an average body length of 730–830 mm (Wrangham, 1985). Adult female bonobos weigh on average 30 kg and have an average body length of 700–760 mm (Wrangham, 1985). The pelage color is black and may turn more of a grayish color with age.

*Bonobos are also sometimes called *pygmy* or *dwarf* chimpanzees (e.g., Kano, 1992), these names originating from the fact that bonobos were thought to be smaller than chimpanzees (Boesch, Hohmann, & Marchant, 2002; White, 1989). Comparisons of anatomical features, however, show bonobos not to be smaller than chimpanzees, but to differ in distinct body proportions: Their upper limbs are shorter and their lower limbs are longer than those of chimpanzees, they have a narrower chest, and their skull is more gracile (Fleagle, 1988; Jungers & Susman, 1984; Zihlmann, 1996). The face of bonobos is black from birth and a white tail tuft is seen in adults and infants.

1.3. Distribution and Ecology

Bonobos exist only in the Congo Basin of the Democratic Republic of Congo (DRC, formerly Zaire), and population estimates range from only 5,000 to 100,000 individuals. Bonobos are thought to be restricted by the Congo-Zualaba River in the west, north, and east, and by the Kasai-Sankuru River in the south. Preferred habitats include primary, secondary, and swamp forests (Kano, 1992). Their precise distribution within the Congo Basin and their variety of habitats is, however, still unclear (Boesch et al., 2002; Kano, 1992). Bonobos of the Lukuru region in the south, for instance, have recently been observed foraging on savannas and in swamp areas (Myers-Thompson, 2002), habitats previously

---

*The name bonobo probably derived from a misspelling on a shipping crate going to 'Bolobo,' a town in the Democratic Republic of Congo (DRC). This town is in the area which bonobos were first discovered by scientists in the 1920s. The German zoo director H. Heck

thought not to be used by bonobos. These observations indicate greater behavioral flexibility and diversity in bonobos than was previously assumed (Boesch et al., 2002).

Like chimpanzees, bonobos subsist primarily on plant food, including fruits, seeds, sprouts, leaves, flowers, bark, stems, pith, roots, and mushrooms (Badrian & Malenky, 1984; Kano & Mulavwa, 1984).

Fruits form the core of their diet (50%; pulp and seeds), and although bonobos at Wamba and Lomako are thought to use a smaller diversity of foods than chimpanzees, their daily fruit intake is higher (although there are exceptions such as the Mahale M-group and the Budongo Forest residents; Kano, 1992; Wrangham, 1977). In addition to plant food, bonobos feed on insect larvae, earthworms, honey, eggs, and soil (Badrian & Malenky, 1984; Kano & Mulavwa, 1984), and have been observed to hunt mammalian prey such as flying squirrels (Ihobe, 1992; species unknown, Kano & Mulavwa, 1984) and duikers (*Cephalophus spp.*, Hohmann & Fruth, 1993a). Carnivory is reported from Wamba (Ihobe, 1992) and Lomako (Badrian & Malenky, 1984), but only at Lomako is the consumption of meat accompanied by food sharing, due to the large size of prey (Fruth & Hohmann, 2002). Contrary to common chimpanzees, which commonly hunt monkeys for food (e.g., Mitani & Watts, 2001), bonobos have never been directly observed to hunt, kill, or eat monkeys (Sabater-Pi, Bermejo, Illera, & Vea, 1993). They have only been observed, and merely anecdotally, to be in possession of and to handle monkeys (Sabater-Pi et al., 1993).

Bonobos divide the time they spent feeding and traveling between the ground and trees (Susman, 1984a), and build their sleeping nests in trees (Fruth & Hohmann, 1996). The average day range of bonobos is 1,200–2,400 m with a home range of around 20.5 km^2 (Hashimoto et al., 1998; Thompson-Handler, Malenky, & Reinartz, 1995). Home ranges of neighboring communities overlap extensively (Fruth, 1995).

A number of studies emphasized interspecific differences between bonobos and chimpanzees in terms of ecology and social behavior (see paragraph on social system). Explanations focus on presumed differences in the availability and distribution of food resources, resulting in differences between the species in feeding competition (Kano, 1992; Wrangham, 1986). Badrian and Badrian (1984), for instance, suggested that relaxed feeding competition in bonobos might be related to the consumption of herbaceous vegetation. Alternatively, White and Wrangham (1988) hypothesized that bonobos use food patches that are larger or more densely distributed than those used by chimpanzees. Another explanation suggests that the availability of high-quality food is supposed to be less affected by seasonal variation for bonobos than for chimpanzees (Malenky & Wrangham, 1994). A comparative study at a

bought two bonobos in 1936 from an African dealer and then coined this word as a German species name (Kemf & Wilson, 1997; Kortlandt, 1998).

newly established study site, Lui Kotale in the vicinity of Salonga National Park, addresses this question, focusing on species differences in diet due to protein levels and energy consumption (Hohmann & Fruth, in preparation).

1.4. Social Structure and Behavior

Similar to common chimpanzees, bonobos live in fission-fusion polygynous societies composed of several males, several females, and their offspring (e.g., Boesch et al., 2002; Thompson-Handler, Malenky & Badrian, 1984; White, 1996). In contrast to the more patrilineal society of chimpanzees—that consists of a flexible community of strongly bonded adult males and "individualistic" (Nishida, 1979) and less "gregarious" females (Wrangham & Smuts, 1980)—the society of bonobos centers around the adult females (Kano, 1992; Susman, 1984b; White, 1989). Furthermore, it can be characterized by egalitarian relationships between the sexes and large parties (e.g., Boesch et al., 2002; Kano, 1992; Thompson-Handler et al., 1984; White, 1996). These parties are biased toward females (Boesch et al., 2002), and the community ranges are shared equally between the sexes (Thompson-Handler et al., 1984). Females spend more time in parties with other females, whereas males often leave or join parties as lone animals (White, 1988). Males establish dominance relationships with each other, but aggression among males and between the sexes is less intense than in chimpanzees, and conflicts are often settled in non-agonistic ways (Furuichi, 1997; but also see, Hohmann & Fruth, 2003b; Kano, 1992). As young females approach adolescence, they become less social than males and disperse (Furuichi, 1989; Kano, 1992). In contrast, males stay in their natal groups, and mother and mature son are linked together by continuing strong bonds (Kano, 1992).

1.5. Cognition

Due to the natural distribution of bonobos and their limited numbers in zoos, investigations of their cognitive skills are scarce. The following paragraph follows the structure of the gorilla chapter (see chapter on gorilla) and reviews the available data on physical and social cognition in bonobos.

1.5.1. Physical Cognition

Savage-Rumbaugh and colleagues (Savage-Rumbaugh, McDonald, Sevcic, Hopkins, & Rupert, 1986) reported that the human-raised bonobo Kanzi easily learned to navigate to and communicate about several different locations in a large outdoor environment. Observations that he was able to choose novel and efficient travel routes throughout the forest imply spatial memory and cognitive mapping skills. To investigate sensorimotor skills (Piaget, 1954; see gorilla chapter), Vauclair and Bard (1983) focused on object manipulation in captive bonobos. They observed secondary circular reactions to repeat object effects (actions directed at objects outside the body), and tertiary circular reactions (relation of objects to one another; involve relations among objects, for instance stacking objects of different sizes). In a study by Spinozzi and Langer (1999), a bonobo spontaneously combined manipulations into routines to generate class-consistent categories of objects. These routines featured much reproduction of the same manipulations, but also included *planful* acts that anticipated follow-up manipulations.

Contrary to chimpanzees, which use a wide range of tools while feeding (e.g., Boesch & Boesch-Achermann, 2000; Goodall, 1986), bonobos in the wild rarely use tools, and they have never been observed using tools to procure or process food (Hohmann & Fruth, 2003a; Ingmanson, 1996; Kano, 1982). In Lomako, a stick was found thrust into a termite mound, but it was not possible to definitely attribute this to the bonobos in the area (Badrian, Badrian, & Susman, 1981).

Kano (1982) and Ingmanson (1996) describe individuals at Wamba using rain hats made out of a variety of materials such as leafy branches, and small twigs or sticks that had been frayed by chewing before use. In addition, Ingmanson (1996) reports that bonobos at Wamba use leaves as wipers or napkins, use small twigs as toothpicks after eating sugar cane (two observations of one adult male), use sticks to swat bees (one observation) and also to scratch their own backs, and incorporate objects into their play. In captivity, however, bonobos use tools in many contexts; for example, to (a) obtain out-of-reach objects, (b) probe crevices for food, (c) perform agonistic displays, (d) hit or prod conspecifics, (e) sponge water (leaves), (f) clean the body, (g) swing (using long twigs), (h) cross a moat (observed once; Ingmanson, 1996; Jordan, 1982; Walraven, 1998), and crack palm nuts using big stones as anvils and smaller ones as hammers (Pika, personal observation). In addition, a female bonobo was observed several times eating a piece of bread after first dipping it in the flesh of an avocado (Pika, personal observation). Furthermore, a wild-born adult female used fallen branches as ladders to bypass protective sheaths and gain access to trees. She even used a branch as a weapon to beat to death a peahen (*Pavo christatus*; Gold, 2002).

In addition, the bonobo Kanzi, raised in a humanlike cultural environment with some training in a humanlike system of communication, shows a wide variety of tool-use skills with a wide variety of human tools and artifacts, including tool manufacture (Savage-Rumbaugh, 1991). Recently, Kanzi learned from a human to make stone flakes by striking one stone against another or by throwing the stone against a concrete floor. He then used the flakes to cut a rope that prevented his access to food—arguably an instance of metatool use (Schick, Toth, & Garufi,1999; Toth, Schick, Savage-Rumbaugh, Sevcic, & Rumbaugh, 1993).

1.5.2. Social Cognition

A recent study on social attention provides evidence that bonobos are able to follow the visual gaze of humans to external phenomena in an apparent attempt to take the visual perspective of the experimenter (Bräuer, Call, & Tomasello, 2005). In addition, Kaminski and colleagues (Kaminski, Call, & Tomasello, 2004) investigated whether bonobos (and also chimpanzees and orangutans) are sensitive to the attentional state of humans. They found that all individuals were sensitive to the body and face orientation of the experimenter. Specifically, all apes gestured more to the human when her face was oriented toward them than when it was oriented away, but only if her body was in a position to deliver the food. Kaminski and colleagues therefore argued that two different types of information were being conveyed to the chimpanzees: Face orientation indicated the human's perceptual access to the signal, whereas body orientation indicated the human's ability and disposition to provide food. In addition, Liebal and colleagues (Liebal, Pika, Call, & Tomasello, 2004) showed that great apes used visual gestures preferentially to beg for food when they were facing a human experimenter. Contrary to gorillas and orangutans, however, bonobos and chimpanzees produced their gestures in front of the experimenter in all experimental conditions, including that in which they had to leave the food to communicate with the experimenter. The authors argued that these findings might indicate a special sensitivity in the genus *Pan* for directing visual signals to a human with the appropriate body orientation.

With regard to intentional communication, only anecdotal evidence is available. Kanzi, for instance, was observed to hand a nut to a person who was supposed to crack it open (Savage-Rumbaugh et al., 1986).

Furthermore, Hyatt and Hopkins (1994; but see also, Walraven, 1998) provide evidence of mirror self-recognition in bonobos (but see also gorilla chapter). Ten bonobos out of two groups, both of which were naive to mirror and language training, engaged in higher frequencies of self-directed behaviors with the mirror than without it, and they also showed several instances of mirror-aided self-grooming.

The most impressive results regarding human language comprehension and symbol use have come from the bonobo Kanzi, who spent the first 2½ years of his life observing his adopted mother Matata while she was interacting with humans around a computerized keyboard (e.g., Greenfield & Savage-Rumbaugh, 1990; Savage-Rumbaugh & Brakke, 1992; Savage- Rumbaugh, Shanker, & Taylor, 1998). From the first tasks on, Kanzi understood the symbols bidirectionally, which means that he was able to both produce and comprehend them without any specific training. In many ways, his early vocabulary matched the early vocabularies of human children, including names for individuals, labels for common objects, and words for actions, locations, and properties. It even included a few function words such as no and yes. Although no other linguistic ape has reached a similar level of competency, Kanzi's abilities suggest that apes raised in more humanlike cultural environments may also use their symbols in a more humanlike manner.

1.6. Communication: State of the Art

Only limited information is available on the communicative behavior of bonobos (e.g., Bermejo & Omedes, 1999; de Waal, 1988; Hohmann & Fruth, 1993b; Van Krankelsven, Dupain, Van Elsacker, & Verheyen, 1996). Bermejo and Omedes (1999) investigated the vocal repertoire of wild bonobos at Lilingu and described 15 vocal units and 19 sequences, indicating high variability. Hohmann and Fruth (1993b) focused on a particular vocalization, the *high hoots,* and found that these calls are part of a system of signals that facilitate communication between members of different parties and might affect movement. Furthermore, de Waal (1988) and de Waal and Lanting (1997) suggest that the vocal repertoire of bonobos is similar to that of the chimpanzees, but that bonobos are more vocal than chimpanzees.

Concerning the use of communicative gestures, Nishida and colleagues' (1999) ethogram of the Mahale chimpanzees provides the most complete ethogram of the genus *Pan.* Researchers of wild populations at Lomako and Wamba describe some gestures such as *begging, branch dragging, drumming, embracing, presenting, rocking,* and *staring* that are performed in different contexts (Badrian & Badrian, 1984; Ingmanson, 1996; Kano, 1980; Kuroda, 1984b). For captive bonobos, Savage-Rumbaugh and colleagues (Savage & Bakeman, 1978; Savage-Rumbaugh, Wilkerson, & Bakeman, 1977) report the use of 20 gestures in the sexual context. In addition, de Waal (1988) provides a comparison of the gestural signaling of bonobos and chimpanzees, based on the gestural signaling of one bonobo group. He describes 15 distinct gestures for bonobos that are merely imperative (meaning that they are used to get another individual to help in attaining a goal) and are linked to particular situations.

Referential gestures such as imperative pointing or declarative gestures, however, have only been described anecdotally for one individual in the wild (Vea & Sabater-Pi, 1998) and one human-raised bonobo (Savage-Rumbaugh et al., 1986). Interestingly, Savage-Rumbaugh and colleagues (Savage & Bakeman, 1978; Savage-Rumbaugh et al., 1977) report some gestures that they consider to be iconic uses of gestures (depict motion in space). These gestures were performed by a bonobo male that moved his hand across a female's body, indicating the action he wanted her to perform or the position he wanted her to take. Roth (1995) tried to replicate these findings with a follow-up study on 20 bonobos from three different groups but did not find evidence for either the iconic use of gestures or for gestures that were correlated with positioning or utilized to negotiate a copulatory position. According to Roth (1995), gestures during sexual encounters only determine whether a sexual interaction will or will not take place.

However, all of the above-mentioned studies lack a clear definition of the term *gesture*, and none investigated the flexibility of gestures (e.g., Bruner, 1981; Tomasello, et al., 1989).

The main goal of the present study therefore was to provide such information, focusing on the following three aspects; (1) gestural inventory, (2) learning of gestures, and (3) gestural use. First, we compiled the gestural repertoire of bonobos to enable a comparison with the findings of Savage-Rumbaugh and colleagues (Savage & Bakeman, 1978; Savage-Rumbaugh et al., 1977) and de Waal (1988). The second goal concerned the learning of gestures, and we focused on individual and group variability to distinguish between underlying social and individual learning processes. Third, we investigated how bonobos use their gestures, by focusing on (a) adjustment to audience effects, (b) means–ends dissociation, and (c) the responses of recipients toward gestures.

Our study is based on the following definition: A gesture is an expressive movement of limbs or head and body postures that appears to transfer a communicative message, such as a request and/or a desired action/event (e.g., play, nurse, or ride), is directed to a recipient, and is accompanied by the following criteria; gazing at the recipient and/or waiting after the signal has been produced (e.g., Bruner, 1981; Tomasello et al., 1989). Therefore, gestures that appear to have components of ritualized morphology (e.g., *swagger quadrupedal*) are included in this definition only if they meet the criteria outlined earlier.

2. METHODS

2.1. Individuals

Seven subadult captive-born bonobos raised by their mothers were observed in (1) the Dierenpark Apenheul, the Netherlands, and (2) the Wild Animal Park Planckendael, Belgium. (The subadult subjects of this study, their age, and their sex are listed in Table 3.2.)

2.2. Data Collection

We used focal-animal sampling (Altmann, 1974) to establish a complete inventory of gestures for each of the seven subjects (20h/individual). After that, videotaping was done using a digital camera (behavior sampling: 15h/subadult bonobo). This design resulted in a total of 245 hours of observation (35h/individual) and 33 hours of videotape. We analyzed 1,290 different gestures.

2.3. Description of the Gestural Inventory

2.3.1. Visual Gestures

- *Bow*–Raise and lower the torso by alternately stretching and flexing its limbs; also includes gestures like *head nod, head shake* or *head turn*.
- *Gallop*–Run in an exaggerated, dashing manner toward or close to another animal.
- *Ice skating*–Make a pirouette with hands on the ground or in the air.
- *Jump*–Spring from or over an object close to another animal or onto another animal.
- *Look*–Relatively long gaze at the partner in a very direct manner.
- *Move*–Displace an object in front of another animal, for instance a branch, straw, and so forth, mainly on the ground.
- *Peer*–Sit or stand very close to another animal and put her lips/face very close to the lips/face or hand of a feeding partner. Another form is begging with a hand that is outstretched with palm facing upward toward another animal.
- *Present*–Offer the genital region, rump, belly, or penis.
- *Reach*–Stretch out a limb toward another animal, palm facing sideways or downward.

- *Shake*–Hang upside down from a branch or rope and move legs/arms from side to side in front of another animal.
- *Somersault*–Make a flip.

2.3.2. Tactile Gestures

- *Grab*–Grasp another animal with the whole hand; fingers are bent.
- *Grab-push-pull*–Grasp another animal and directly pull it or push it.
- *Kick*–Use the legs to forcefully move another animal away.
- *Pull*–Grasp another animal and forcefully bring it closer.
- *Punch*–Performs a brief forward or downward thrust on or against another animal with the fist, knuckles, or fingers.
- *Push*–Use the arms to forcefully displace another animal away.
- *Slap*–Hit another animal forcefully with the palm of the hand.
- *Touch*–Gentle and short (< 5 sec) contact with flat hands, body part or feet.

2.3.3. Auditory Gestures

- *Stomp*–Bring the sole or heel of the foot suddenly and forcibly against the ground or an object, or walk in a pounding manner, either in a bipedal or quadrupedal stance.

3. GESTURAL REPERTOIRE

3.1. Overview

Overall we observed 20 distinct gestures (see Table 3.1), which consisted of 1 auditory (5%), 8 tactile (40%), and 11 visual gestures (55%). These gestures do not belong in the category of idiosyncratic gestures and were used toward conspecifics. We did not observe any iconic uses of gestures. In Table 3.1, we compiled a gestural inventory of bonobos based on the results of the present study and also on descriptions of gestures in the studies by Savage-Rumbaugh and colleagues (Savage & Bakeman, 1978; Savage-Rumbaugh et al., 1977) and de Waal (1988). To investigate the function of each gestural signal, we did a quantitative contextual analysis of the response of the recipient.

Table 3.1

Gestural Inventory (Same Gestures or Similar Behaviors Named with Different Terms)

Current study	(Savage & Bakeman, 1978; Savage-Rumbaugh et al., 1977)	De Waal (1988)
Auditory gestures		
Clap (was only observed towards visitors)		Chest beat
		Clap
Slap ground (idiosyncratic gesture). Response: Play: 83.3%; affiliative: 16.6%.		
Stomp: Response: Travel: 100%.		Rhythmic movements; stomping
Tactile gestures		
Grab: Response: Play: 41.5%; agonistic: 30.8%; travel: 23.2%; affiliative: 1.5%; ride: 1.5%; other: 1.5%.		Lateral embrace
		Ventral embrace
		Grab
Special form: Grab penis (idiosyncratic). Response: Travel: 50%; play: 25%; agonistic: 25%.		
Grab-push-pull: Response: Agonistic: 50%; nurse: 16.7%; ride: 16.7%; other: 16.6%.		
Kick: Response: Play: 54.5%; agonistic: 27%; travel: 9%; other: 9%.		Hunch over

(continued)

TABLE 3.1 (continued)

Current study	(Savage & Bakeman, 1978; Savage-Rumbaugh et al., 1977)	De Waal (1988)
Tactile gestures (con't.)		Mouth kiss; tongue kissing was observed in a quarter of the instances
	Move hand and arm across body. Move hand toward another portion of cage.	
Pull: Response: Play: 50%; sex: 25%; other: 25%.	Pull toward self by putting arm around partner's back; pull limb toward self.	*Pat*
Punch: Response: Play: 50%; travel: 25%; agonistic: 25%.		*Punch:* 2 out of 10 individuals.
Push: Response: Travel: 53.8%; play: 30.8%; food: 7.7%; agonistic: 7.7%.	*Push:* Differentiation between push limb across body; push leg or arm out from body; push under chin. Rest knuckles on arm or back.	
Slap: Response: Play: 50%; travel: 19.2%; agonistic: 15.4%; sex: 7.7%; other: 15.4%.		
Touch: Response: Play: 28.5%; travel: 28.5%; agonistic: 10.7%; other: 7.1%; ride: 10.7%; sex: 7.1%; affiliative: 3.6%; nurse: 3.6%.	*Touch* outside of partner's shoulder, hip or thigh and motion across body with hand and forearm movement; *Touch* hand or arm and motion outward from partner's body; *Touch* shoulder or back and move hand toward self; *Touch* head, chin or inside of shoulder and lift hand upward; *Touch* partner and walk to other end of cage; Rest knuckles on arm or back and move arm toward self; Move hand and forearm across body.	

Visual gestures

Gesture (Response)	Description	
Bow: Response: Play: 58.3%; travel: 16.6%.	Bipedal stand; raise body up and back up while standing bipedal. Body shake, raise head back, sway; shake head horizontally or circularly.	Arm up
Gallop: Response: Play: 44.5%; agonistic: 33.3%; travel: 22.2%.		
Ice skate: Response: Play: 100%.		
Jump: Response: Play: 62.5%; travel: 25%; agonistic: 12.5%.	Jump-stamp	
Look: Response: Travel: 37.5%; ride: 25%; affiliative: 12.5%; sex: 12.%; other: 12.5%.	Look at	
Move: Response: Affiliative: 40%; play: 30%; agonistic: 20%; sex: 10%.		Hand-up begging, hand-side begging, leg-out begging, flexing.
Peer: Response: Food: 28.6%; travel: 28.6%; agonistic: 14.3%; play: 14.3%; other: 14.2%.	Peer/beg	Present: Differentiation between concave back, ventrally present and rump present.
Present: Response: Affiliative: 60%; sex: 20%; other: 20%.		
Reach: Response: Travel: 50%; play: 30%; agonistic: 10%; affiliative: 10%.	Raise arm; raise arm and flip; move hand toward another portion of cage; raise up.	
Shake: Response: Play: 66.6%; agonistic: 33.3%.		Stretch over
Somersault: Response: Play: 83.3%; affiliative: 16.6%.		
Swagger quadrupedal: Response: Nurse: 50%; travel: 50%.	Stand bipedal and wave arms out from body. Wrist shake	Wrist shake: 3 out of 10 individuals. Wave

3.2. Context

These gestures were performed mainly in the play context (55%), but also in the food (14%), travel (10%), nurse (5%), ride (5%), sex (5%), affiliative (3%), and agonistic (3%) contexts.

3.3. Variability

3.3.1. Individual Differences

The tactile gestures *grab, slap,* and *touch,* were performed by all seven individuals, whereas the performance of the other 17 gestures showed a high degree of variability (see Table 3.2). On average, each individual used 11 (± 2.8) gestures.

3.3.2. Age Differences

Due to the small sample size ($N = 7$), age differences were not analyzed.

3.3.3. Group Differences

To investigate whether group-specific differences could be found, we performed two sets of analyses, reported in the two following subsections. First, we investigated the similarities of gestural repertoires within a group (between individuals of the group) and between groups. The second analysis examined whether we could detect group-specific gestures that could not be explained by environmental differences or social settings.

To assess the degree of concordance in the performance of gestures between and within the two groups, we used Cohen's kappa statistics (see methods/coding procedures). The between-group ($M = 0.45, ± 0.13$) and within-group kappas ($M = 0.46, ± 0.2$, for Apenheul group; $M = 0.55$, ± 0.18, for the Planckendael group) did show very low degrees of concordance (Altmann, 1991) and were highly similar. Although the within-group kappas were slightly higher than the between-group kappas, an analysis of the individual kappas of average concordance with group members and with members of the other group did not show a significant difference (Wilcoxon-test: $Z = -0.845, p = .398, N = 6$).

In addition, we observed three idiosyncratic gestures, which were performed by three different individuals: Zamba from the Planckendael group performed the gesture *slap ground,* Tarishi from the Apenheul

TABLE 3.2
Individual Differences in Gesture Use

	Unga (8.5, F)	Vifijo (6, M)	Zomi (3.6, F)	Liboso (3.5, F)	Zamba (3.3, M)	Tarishi (2.8, M)	Kumbuka (1.10, F)	%
Grab	x	x	x	x	x	x	x	100% (N=7)
Slap	x	x	x	x	x	x	x	100% (N=7)
Touch	x	x	x	x	x	x	x	100% (N=7)
Peer		x	x	x	x	x	x	86% (N=6)
Jump		x	x	x	x		x	71% (N=5)
Move	x			x	x	x	x	71% (N=5)
Push		x	x	x		x	x	71% (N=5)
Gallop		x	x		x	x		57% (N=4)
Reach arm			x		x	x	x	57% (N=4)
Kick			x		x	x	x	57% (N=4)
Ice skating		x			x	x		43% (N=3)
Somersault		x	x		x			43% (N=3)
Look at					x	x	x	43% (N=3)
Punch	x	x			x			43% (N=3)
Shake	x		x					29% (N=2)
Stomp					x	x		29% (N=2)
Bob		x			x			29% (N=2)
Pull		x			x			29% (N=2)
Grab-pull-push	x				x			29% (N=2)
Present				x	x			29% (N=2)

Note. Names of individuals, age (years and months), sex (M: male, F: female), and gestures used.

group performed *swagger quadrupedal*, and Kumbuka also from the Apenheul group performed *grab penis*.

We found group-specific differences in the performance of two distinct gestures. The gesture *punch* was exclusive to bonobos in the Apenheul group, whereas the gesture *somersault* was only performed in the Planckendael group. *Punch* was performed by all three subadults and *somersault* by three of four individuals in that group.

We did not observe any instances of iconic uses of gestures.

3.4. Flexibility

3.4.1. Combinations

We did not analyze gesture combinations.

3.4.2. Audience Effects

We found a significant difference between the use of tactile and visual gestures among all individuals based on a variation in the degree of visual attention of the recipient (Wilcoxon-test: $Z = -2.366, p = .018, N = 7$). On average, 79% (± 10%) of visual gestures were performed when the recipient was looking, whereas only 50% (± 10%) of tactile gestures were directed to an attending recipient (see Fig. 3.2).

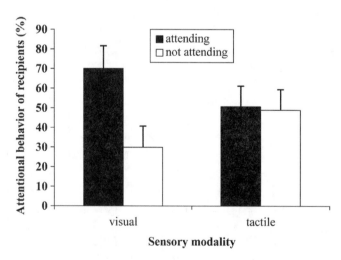

Figure 3.2. Audience effects: Percentage of visual and tactile gestures used toward an attending and nonattending recipient, error bars indicate the SD.

3.4.3. Means–Ends Dissociation

To make inferences about the flexibility of gestural signals, we analyzed whether they were used in different contexts and whether several signals were used within the same context.

3.4.3.1. One Gesture for Multiple Contexts. Figure 3.3a shows that with respect to the number of all gestures performed, 50% (10 of 20 gestures) were performed in only one context and the other 50% were observed in more than one context, with 35% (seven gestures) performed in two contexts, 10% (two gestures) performed in three contexts, and 5% (one gesture) performed in five contexts. Tactile gestures occurred more frequently in two contexts (mean of 2.13 contexts/individual, ± 1.36; see Fig. 3.3b) than visual gestures ($M = 1.55$ contexts/ individual, ± 0.69), but the differences were not significant (MWU TAC>/<VIS: $Z = -9.431$, 2-tailed, $p = .395$, $_{Ntac} = 8$; $N_{vis} = 11$). Overall, each individual used an average of 2.7 (± 1.48) gestures in more than one context (Fig. 3.3c).

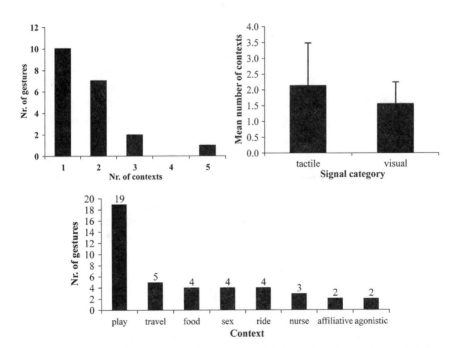

Figure 3.3. Flexibility of use: (a; top left) Number of gestures observed in different numbers of contexts; (b; top right) mean number of contexts for tactile and visual gestures, and (c; bottom) number of gestures per context. Error bars indicate the SD.

3.4.3.2. One Context With Multiple Gestures.   The results indicate that in every context, on average approximately 2 (± 0.6) different gestures were used. Figure 3.3c displays that, overall, in the play context, 19 different gestures (95%) were observed, whereas in the agonistic and affiliative contexts, only 10% of all gestures occurred. In the travel context, 25% (5) of all gestures were used; in the food, sex and ride contexts 20% (4) of all gestures were used; and in the nurse context 15% (3) were used. These differences between the occurrence of signals in different contexts were significant for the play context versus all other contexts (Friedman: $\chi_7^2 = 89.876$, $p = .001$; for Z-values of the Wilcoxon-test see Pika, Liebal & Tomasello, 2005).

3.5. Function of Gestures

We analyzed the responses of recipients toward gestural signals (see Fig. 3.4a). On average, 23.5% (± 8.93) of the gestures did not receive a response, 13.5% (± 3.15) led to a change in the attentional state of the recipient (not attending changed to attending), 15.5% (± 4.62) received a response in the form of a gesture, and 40% (± 11.94) led to an interaction between the signaler and the recipient. These interactions could be grouped into the following contextual categories (see Fig. 3.4b); overall play: 40%; travel: 24%; agonistic: 14%; affiliative: 6.5%; other: 5%; sex: 4%; nurse: 3%; ride: 2%; and food: 1.5%. In 30% of the cases in which a gesture did not receive a response, the signaler used a second gesture.

4. DISCUSSION

The three main goals of this chapter are (1) to compile a gestural inventory of bonobos based on the present and previous studies, (2) to investigate how they learn their communicative gestures, and (3) to examine how they use these gestures.

Overall, we describe 20 distinct auditory, tactile, and visual gestures. Concerning auditory gestures, we observed the gestures *slap ground* and *stomp*, which are combined in de Waal's (1988) term *rhythmic movement.* Interestingly, for the bonobo group at the San Diego Zoo, de Waal cites the auditory gestures *clap* and *chest beat. Chest beat* is a species-typical gesture for gorillas (Pika et al., 2003) and has not yet been described for other captive or wild bonobo groups.

Concerning tactile gestures, we observed the gestures *grab* and *punch,* which are listed using the same terms in other studies (Kano, 1998;

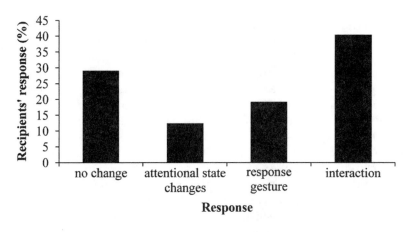

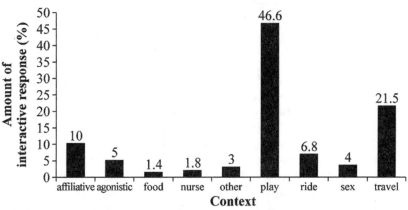

Figure 3.4. (a; top) Recipients' response per observed gesture in percent, and (b; bottom) recipients' type of interactive response per interaction in percent.

Kuroda, 1984a, 1984b, 1980; Nishida et al., 1999; Savage & Bakeman, 1978; Savage-Rumbaugh et al., 1977; Tratz & Heck, 1954). The tactile gestures *pull, push,* and *touch* are subclassified in other studies to provide further details, for instance *pull limb toward self, pull toward self by putting arm around partner's back*; and so forth (e.g., Savage-Rumbaugh et al., 1977). The gestures *kick, slap,* and *grab, push-pull,* however, were not described in the other studies. We did not observe tactile gestures such as *hunch over* and *mouth kiss,* and *pat* (de Waal, 1988), as well as the gesture *embrace,* which was subclassified by de Waal (1988) in *lateral* and *ventral embrace.*

Concerning visual gestures, the gestures *peer* and *present* are either de-scribed in other studies using the same terms (Kano, 1998; Kuroda, 1984a, 1984b, 1980; Nishida et al., 1999; Savage & Bakeman, 1978; Savage-Rumbaugh et al., 1977; Tratz & Heck, 1954) or are subclassified. For in-stance *peer* is subclassified as *hand up begging, hand side begging, leg out beg-ging,* and *flexing* (de Waal, 1988); and *present* is subclassified as *ventrally present* and *rump present* (de Waal, 1988). The gesture *reach* is described as *raise arm, out, raise up, extend,* and so forth (Roth, 1995; Savage & Bakeman, 1978; Savage-Rumbaugh et al., 1977). We observed the gesture *bow,* which is subclassified in other studies (Savage & Bakeman, 1978; Savage-Rumbaugh et al., 1977) in terms such as *bipedal stand, raise body up and back up while standing bipedal, body shake, raise head back,* and *sway, shake head hor-izontally or circularly.* The visual gesture *jump* resembles an element of the gesture *jump stamp* (Savage & Bakeman, 1978; Savage-Rumbaugh et al., 1977), and a resembling term for the gesture *look* is the gesture *look at* (Savage & Bakeman, 1978; Savage-Rumbaugh et al., 1977). However, *look at* seems to be a special version of *look,* because *look at* involves a specific distance from the partner (other end of the cage). We did not observe ges-tures such as *arm up, stretch over, wave,* and *wrist shake,* which were de-scribed in other studies (Kano, 1998; Kuroda, 1984a, 1984b, 1980; Nishida et al., 1999; Savage & Bakeman, 1978; Savage-Rumbaugh et al., 1977; Tratz & Heck, 1954). However, we recorded gestures that were not observed in any other study such as *gallop, ice skate, move, shake, swagger quadrupedal,* and *somersault.* Some of these differences might be due to different obser-vation designs. In some cases (gestures *clap* and *chest beat*), the differences compared to other studies may be due to different rearing histories or demonstrate clear group-specific differences. In addition, Savage-Rumbaugh and colleagues (Savage & Bakeman, 1978; Savage-Rumbaugh et al., 1977) focused on communicative gesturing in the sexual context be-tween adult bonobos. Our differences with these studies may therefore be explained by age differences and imply that some gestures achieve a par-ticular function after the animals reach maturity.

Furthermore, contrary to the studies by Savage-Rumbaugh and col-leagues, we did not observe any instances of iconic use of gestures. It is possible that our analysis did not focus in sufficient detail on the receiv-ers' responses to detect these. However, the results of the present study might support the findings of Roth (1995) and strengthen the hypothesis of Tomasello and Zuberbühler (2002) that some data have been overin-terpreted. A role for iconicity in the performance and comprehension of gestures by bonobos and other apes has therefore not yet been properly demonstrated (Tomasello & Call, 1997).

To make inferences about the role gestures play in the communication of bonobos, we analyzed the responses of the recipients toward gestures. This approach enabled us to investigate if bonobos use gestures to achieve a certain goal that is understood by the receiver. The results showed that bonobos respond to the majority of all performed gestures by either looking at the signaler, performing a response gesture, or interacting with the signaler. In addition, in a third of the cases the signaler continued performing additional gestures if the recipient did not react.

To investigate whether bonobos acquire their gestures via a social or an individual learning process, we focused on concordances in the gestural repertoires within and between groups, idiosyncratic as well as group-specific gestures. We found three idiosyncratic gestures, and showed that the concordances between and within groups were similar. These results are taken as indicators against a social learning process involved, which is consistent with findings on chimpanzees (Tomasello, Call, Nagell, Olguin, & Carpenter, 1994) and gorillas (Pika et al., 2003). Furthermore, they extend the theory of Tomasello and Call (2002) regarding chimpanzees by confirming that bonobos also acquire the majority of their gestures via ontogenetic ritualization.

We observed two group-specific gestures, *somersault* and *punch*, that cannot be easily explained by different physical or social settings. The findings of the present study are therefore consistent with observations on group-specific gestures in wild chimpanzees, such as *leaf clipping* (Nishida, 1980), the *grooming hand clasp* (McGrew & Tutin, 1978), and the just recently recorded *social scratch* (Nakamura, McGrew, Marchandt, & Nishida, 2000). In addition, they support the findings of de Waal (1988) and Ingmanson (1987), who observed two group-specific gestures, *clap* and *chest beat*, in the bonobo group at the San Diego Zoo in the context of grooming. The gesture *clap* was used between conspecifics and was observed in seven animals out of three different groups. Interestingly, this behavior only occurred in animals that were human raised, implying that the gesture *clap* might have been transmitted from humans to bonobos. In addition, Thompson (1994) showed that this gesture spread from the San Diego group to other zoos by transfer of San Diego individuals to these zoos (see for similar results on common chimpanzees, de Waal & Seres, 1997), suggesting that a social learning process was involved. In addition, for a captive gorilla group at Apenheul Zoo, the Netherlands, Pika and colleagues (2003) recently described the group-specific gesture *arm shake*. Although the present data are limited due to the small sample size, these results imply the involvement of a social learning process in the acquisition of specific gestures (but see Tomasello & Call, 1997 for a different opinion). They therefore add fuel to the ongoing debate concerning population-specific differences and culture in apes (e.g., Boesch, 2003; McGrew & Tutin, 1978; Nakamura et al., 2000; Nishida, 1980; Tomasello, 1990).

Concerning the flexibility of use, we showed that bonobos used around 10 gestures in at least two or more functional categories and utilized on average two different gestural signals within a single context. In addition, bonobos adjusted their use of gestures to the attentional state of the recipient, performing visual gestures most often when the recipient was looking than when she was not. These findings are consistent with studies on chimpanzees (Tomasello & Call, 1997; Tomasello et al., 1994) and gorillas (Pika et al., 2003). Similar to findings with gorillas, the present study demonstrated that tactile gestures also represent the most flexible gestures in bonobos, showing the highest variety of functional categories, whereas auditory gestures and visual gestures are linked to fewer contexts, mainly play.

5. CONCLUSION

In conclusion, the data indicate that the gestural repertoire of subadult bonobos is characterized by flexibility, with adjustments to communicative circumstances such as a nonresponding recipient and the attentional state of the receiver. Furthermore, the results imply (1) that signalers use gestures to achieve a certain goal, show persistence toward the goal, and understand the way their signals function and, (2) that gestures are received as important means of communication by receivers. These results therefore provide strong evidence that gestures function as important communicative means for bonobos.

ACKNOWLEDGMENTS

I am grateful to all the keepers and collaborators of the Wild Animal Park Planckendael, Belgium and the Dierenpark Apenheul, the Netherlands for their friendliness and helpfulness. The advice on statistics given by Daniel Stahl is gratefully acknowledged. For comments on an earlier draft, I thank Jonas Eriksson.

REFERENCES

Altmann, D. (1991). *Practical statistics for medical research.* CRC: Chapman & Hall.
Altmann, J. (1974). Observational study of behaviour: Sampling methods. *Behaviour,* *49,* 227–267.

Badrian, A., & Badrian, N. (1984). Social organization of *Pan paniscus* in the Lomako Forest, Zaire. In R. L. Susman (Ed.), *The pygmy chimpanzee: Evolutionary biology and behavior* (pp. 325–346). New York: Plenum Press.

Badrian, N., Badrian, A., & Susman, R. L. (1981). *Preliminary observations on the feeding behavior of Pan paniscus in the Lomako forest, Zaire.* New York: Plenum Press.

Badrian, N., & Malenky, R. K. (1984). Feeding ecology of *Pan paniscus* in the Lomako forest, Zaire. In R. Susman (Ed.), *The pygmy chimpanzee* (pp. 275–299). New York: Plenum Press.

Bermejo, M., & Omedes, A. (1999). Preliminary vocal repertoire and vocal communication of wild bonobos (*Pan paniscus*) at Lilungu (Democratic Republic of Congo). *Folia Primatologica, 70*(6), 328–357.

Boesch, C. (2003). Is culture a golden barrier between humans and chimpanzees? *Evolutionary Anthropology, 12,* 82–91.

Boesch, C., & Boesch-Achermann, H. (2000). *The chimpanzees of the Tai forest.* Oxford, England: Oxford University Press.

Boesch, C., Hohmann, G., & Marchant, L. F. (2002). *Behavioral diversity in chimpanzees and bonobos.* Cambridge, England: Cambridge University Press.

Bradley, B. J., & Vigilant, L. (2002). The evolutionary genetics and molecular ecology of chimpanzees and bonobos. In C. Boesch, G. Hohmann, & L. F. Marchandt (Eds.), *Behavioural diversity in chimpanzees and bonobos* (pp. 259–276). Cambridge, England: Cambridge University Press.

Bräuer, J., Call, J., & Tomasello, M. (2005). All great ape species follow gaze to distant locations and around barriers. *Journal of Comparative Psychology, 119*(2), 145–154.

Bruner, J. (1981). Intention in the structure of action and interaction. In L. Lipsitt (Ed.), *Advances in infancy research* (Vol. 1, pp. 41–56). Norwood, NJ: Ablex.

de Waal, F. B. M. (1988). The communicative repertoire of captive bonobos (*Pan paniscus*) compared to that of chimpanzees. *Behaviour, 106*(3–4), 183–251.

de Waal, F. B. M., & Lanting, F. (1997). *The forgotten ape.* Cambridge, England: Cambridge University Press.

de Waal, F. B. M., & Seres, M. (1997). Propagation of handclasp grooming among captive chimpanzees. *American Journal of Primatology, 43,* 339–346.

Fleagle, J. G. (1988). *Primate adaptation and evolution.* New York: Academic Press.

Fruth, B. (1995). *Nests and nest groups in wild bonobos (Pan paniscus): Ecological and behavioural correlates.* Aachen: Verlag Shaker.

Fruth, B., & Hohmann, G. (1996). Nest building behavior in the great apes: The great leap forward? In T. Nishida (Ed.), *Great apes societies* (pp. 225–240). Cambridge, England: Cambridge University Press.

Fruth, B., & Hohmann, G. (2002). How bonobos handle hunts and harvests: Why share food? In C. Boesch, G. Hohmann, & L. F. Marchandt (Eds.), *Behavioral diversity in chimpanzees and bonobos* (pp. 231–243). Cambridge, England: Cambridge University Press.

Furuichi, T. (1989). Social interactions and the life history of female *Pan paniscus* in Wamba, Zaire. *International Journal of Primatology, 10*(3), 173–197.

Furuichi, T. (1997). Agonistic interactions and matrifocal dominance rank of wild bonobos (*Pan paniscus*) at Wamba. *International Journal of Primatology, 18*(6), 855–875.

Gold, K. C. (2002). Ladder use and clubbing by a bonobo (*Pan paniscus*) in Apenheul Primate Park. *Zoo Biology, 21,* 607–611.

Goodall, J. (1986). *The chimpanzees of Gombe, patterns of behaviour*. Cambridge, England: Harvard University Press.

Greenfield, P. M., & Savage-Rumbaugh, E. S. (1990). Grammatical combination in *Pan paniscus*: Processes of learning and invention in the evolution and development of language. In S. T. Parker & K. R. Gibson (Eds.), *'Language' and intelligence in monkeys and apes* (pp. 540–578). Cambridge, England: Cambridge University Press.

Hashimoto, C., Tashiro, Y., Kimura, D., Enomoto, T., Ingmanson, E. J., Idani, G., & Furuichi, T. (1998). Habitat use and ranging of wild bonobos (*Pan paniscus*) at Wamba. *International Journal of Primatology, 19*(6), 1045–1061.

Hohmann, G., & Fruth, B. (1993a). Field observations on meat sharing among bonobos (*Pan paniscus*). *Folia Primatologica, 60*, 225–229.

Hohmann, G., & Fruth, B. (1993b). Structure and use of distance calls in wild bonobos (*Pan paniscus*). *International Journal of Primatology, 15*(5), 767–782.

Hohmann, G., & Fruth, B. (2003a). Culture in bonobos? Between-species and with-species variation in behavior. *Current Anthropology, 44*(4), 563–571.

Hohmann, G., & Fruth, B. (2003b). Intra- and inter-sexual aggression by bonobos in the context of mating. *Behaviour, 140*, 1389–1413.

Hyatt, C. W., & Hopkins, W. D. (1994). Self-awareness in bonobos and chimpanzees: A comparative perspective. In S. T. Parker, R. W. Mitchell, & M. L. Boccia (Eds.), *Self-awareness in animals and humans* (pp. 248–253). Cambridge, England: Cambridge University Press.

Ihobe, H. (1992). Observations on the meat-eating behavior of wild bonobos (*Pan paniscus*) at Wambe, Republic of Zaire. *Primates, 31*, 109–112.

Ingmanson, E. J. (1987). Clapping behavior: Non-verbal communication during grooming in a group of captive pygmy chimpanzees. *American Journal of Physical Anthropology, 72*, 214.

Ingmanson, E. J. (1996). Tool-using behavior in wild *Pan paniscus*: Social and ecological considerations. In A. E. Russon & K. A. Bard (Eds.), *Reaching into thought: The minds of the great apes* (pp. 190–210). Cambridge, England: Cambridge University Press.

Jordan, C. (1982). Object manipulation and tool-use in captive pygmy chimpanzees (*Pan paniscus*). *Journal of Human Evolution, 11*, 35–39.

Jungers, W. L., & Susman, R. L. (1984). Body size and skeletal allometry in African apes. In R. L. Susman (Ed.), *The pygmy chimpanzee: Evolutionary biology and behavior* (pp. 131–177). New York: Plenum Press.

Kaessmann, H., & Pääbo, S. (2002). The genetical history of humans and the great apes. *Journal of Internal Medicine, 251*, 1–18.

Kaminski, J., Call, J., & Tomasello, M. (2004). Body orientation and face orientation: Two factors controlling apes' begging behavior from humans. *Animal Cognition, 7*, 216–223.

Kano, T. (1980). Social behaviour of wild pygmy chimpanzees (*Pan paniscus*) of Wamba: A preliminary report. *Journal of Human Evolution, 9*, 243–260.

Kano, T. (1982). The use of leafy twigs for rain cover by the pygmy chimpanzees of Wamba. *Primates, 23*(3), 453–457.

Kano, T. (1992). *The last ape: Pygmy chimpanzee behavior and ecology*. Stanford, CA: Stanford University Press.

Kano, T. (1998). A preliminary glossary of bonobo behaviors at Wamba. In T. Nishida (Ed.), *Comparative study of the behavior of the genus Pan by compiling video ethogram* (pp. 39–81). Kyoto: Nissho Printer.

Kano, T., & Mulavwa, M. (1984). Feeding ecology of the pygmy chimpanzee (*Pan paniscus*) of Wamba. In R. L. Susman (Ed.), *The pygmy chimpanzee* (pp. 233–274). New York: Plenum Press.

Kemf, E., & Wilson, A. (1997). *Great apes in the wild*. Gland: World Wide Fund for Nature.

Kortlandt, A. (1998). Pygmy chimpanzee, bonobo or gracile chimpanzee: What's in a name. *African Primates, 3*, 13.

Kuroda, S. (1984a). Interaction over food among pygmy chimpanzees. In R. L. Susman (Ed.), *The pygmy chimpanzee, evolutionary biology and behavior* (pp. 301–324). New York: Plenum Press.

Kuroda, S. (1984b). Rocking gesture as communicative behavior in the wild pygmy chimpanzee in Wamba, Central Zaire. *Journal of Ethology, 2*, 127–137.

Kuroda, S. J. (1980). Social behavior of the Pygmy chimpanzees. *Primates, 21*(2), 181–197.

Liebal, K., Pika, S., Call, J., & Tomasello, M. (2004). Great ape communicators move in front of recipients before producing visual gestures. *Interaction studies, 5*(2), 199–219.

Malenky, R. K., & Wrangham, R. W. (1994). A quantitative comparison of terrestrial herbaceous food consumption by *Pan paniscus* in the Lomako Forest, Zaire, and *Pan troglodytes* in the Kibale Forest, Uganda. *American Journal of Primatology, 19*, 999–1011.

McGrew, W. C., & Tutin, C. E. G. (1978). Evidence for a social custom in wild chimpanzees? *Man, 13*, 234–251.

Mitani, J. C., & Watts, D. P. (2001). Why do chimpanzees hunt and share meat? *Animal Behaviour, 61*(5), 915–924.

Myers-Thompson, J. (2002). Bonobos of the Lukuru Wildlife Research Project. In C. Boesch, G. Hohmann, & L. F. Marchandt (Eds.), *Behavioral diversity in chimpanzees and bonobos* (pp. 61–70). Cambridge, England: Cambridge University Press.

Nakamura, M., McGrew, C., Marchandt, L. F., & Nishida, T. (2000). Social scratch: Another custom in wild chimpanzees? *Primates, 41*(3), 237–248.

Nishida, T. (1979). The social structure of chimpanzees of the Mahale mountains. In D. A. Hamburg & E. R. McCown (Eds.), *The great apes* (pp. 72–121). Menlo Park, CA: Benjamin/Cummings.

Nishida, T. (1980). The leaf-clipping display: A newly discovered expressive gesture in wild chimpanzees. *Journal of Human Evolution, 9*, 117–128.

Nishida, T., Kano, T., Goodall, J., McGrew, W. C., & Nakamura, M. (1999). Ethogram and ethnography of Mahale chimpanzees. *Anthropological Science, 107*(2), 141–188.

Piaget, J. (1954). *The construction of reality in a child*. New York: Norton.

Pika, S., Liebal, K., & Tomasello, M. (2003). Gestural communication in young gorillas (*Gorilla gorilla*): Gestural repertoire, learning and use. *American Journal of Primatology, 60*(3), 95–111.

Roth, R. R. (1995). *A study of gestural communication during sexual behavior in bonobo (Pan paniscus, Schwartz)*. Unpublished PhD dissertation. University of Calgary, Calgary.

Sabater-Pi, J., Bermejo, M., Illera, G., & Vea, J. J. (1993). Behavior of bonobos (*Pan paniscus*) following their capture of monkeys in Zaire. *International Journal of Primatology, 14*, 797–804.

Savage, S., & Bakeman, R. (1978). Sexual morphology and behavior in *Pan paniscus, Proceedings of the Sixth International Congress of Primatology* (pp. 613–616). New York: Academic Press.

Savage-Rumbaugh, E. S. (1991). Multi-tasking: The Pan-human rubicon. *Neurosciences, 3,* 417–422.

Savage-Rumbaugh, E. S., & Brakke, K. E. (1992). Linguistic development: Contrasts between co-reared *Pan troglodytes* and *Pan paniscus.* In T. Nishida, W. C. McGrew, P. Marler, M. Pickford, & F. B. M. de Waal (Eds.), *Topics in primatology: Human Origins* (Vol. 1, pp. 51–66). Tokyo: University of Tokyo Press.

Savage-Rumbaugh, E. S., McDonald, K., Sevcic, R. A., Hopkins, W. D., & Rupert, E. (1986). Spontaneous symbol acquisition and communicative use by pygmy chimpanzees (*Pan paniscus*). *Journal of Experimental Psychology: General, 115,* 211–235.

Savage-Rumbaugh, E. S., Shanker, S. G., & Taylor, T. J. (1998). *Apes, language, and the human mind.* New York: Oxford University Press.

Savage-Rumbaugh, E. S., Wilkerson, B. J., & Bakeman, R. (1977). Spontaneous gestural communication among conspecifics in the pygmy chimpanzee (*Pan paniscus*). In G. H. Bourne (Ed.), *Progress in ape research* (pp. 97–116). New York: Academic Press.

Schick, K. D., Toth, N., & Garufi, G. (1999). Continuing investigations into the stone tool-making and tool-using capabilities of a bonobo (*Pan paniscus*). *Journal of Archaeological Science, 26,* 821–832.

Spinozzi, G., & Langer, J. (1999). Spontaneous classification in cation by a human-enculturated and language-reared bonobo (*Pan paniscus*) and common chimpanzee (*Pan troglodytes*). *Journal of Comparative Psychology, 113*(3), 286–296.

Susman, R. L. (1984a). Locomotor behavior of *Pan paniscus.* In R. L. Susman (Ed.), *The pygmy chimpanzee evolutionary biology and behavior* (pp. 369–393). New York: Plenum Press.

Susman, R. L. (1984b). *The pygmy chimpanzee: Evolutionary biology and behavior.* New York: Plenum Press.

Thompson, J. A. M. (1994). Cultural diversity in the behavior of *Pan.* In D. Quiatt & J. Itani (Eds.), *Hominid culture in primate perspective* (pp. 95–115). Niwot, CO: University Press of Colorado.

Thompson-Handler, N. T., Malenky, R. K., & Badrian, N. (1984). Sexual behavior of *Pan paniscus.* In R. L. Susman (Ed.), *The pygmy chimpanzee: Evolutionary biology and behavior* (pp. 347–368). New York: Plenum Press.

Thompson-Handler, N. T., Malenky, R. K., & Reinartz, G. E. (1995). *Action plan for Pan paniscus: Report on free ranging populations and proposal for their preservation.* Milwaukee, WI: Zoological Society of Milwaukee County.

Tomasello, M. (1990). Cultural transmission in the tool use and communicatory signalling of chimpanzees. In S. Parker & K. Gibson (Eds.), *'Language' and intelligence in monkeys and apes: Comparative developmental perspectives* (pp. 274–311). Cambridge, England: Cambridge University Press.

Tomasello, M., & Call, J. (1997). *Primate cognition.* New York: Oxford University Press.

Tomasello, M., Call, J., Nagell, K., Olguin, R., & Carpenter, M. (1994). The learning and use of gestural signals by young chimpanzees: A trans-generational study. *Primates, 35*(2), 137–154.

Tomasello, M., Call, J., Warren, J., Frost, T., Carpenter, M., & Nagell, K. (1997). The ontogeny of chimpanzee gestural signals. In S. Wilcox, B. King, & L. Steels (Eds.),

Evolution of Communication (pp. 224–259). Amsterdam/Philadelphia: John Benjamins Publishing Company.

Tomasello, M., Gust, D., & Frost, G. T. (1989). A longitudinal investigation of gestural communication in young chimpanzees. *Primates, 30*(1), 35–50.

Tomasello, M., & Zuberbühler, K. (2002). Primate vocal and gestural communication. In M. Bekoff & C. S. Allen & G. Burghardt (Eds.), *The cognitive animal: empirical and theoretical perspectives on animal cognition* (pp. 293–299). Cambridge: MIT Press.

Toth, N., Schick, K. D., Savage-Rumbaugh, E. S., Sevcic, R. A., & Rumbaugh, D. M. (1993). *Pan* the tool-maker: Investigations into the stone tool-making and tool-using capabilities of a bonobo (*Pan paniscus*). *Journal of Archaeological Science, 20*, 81–91.

Tratz, E., & Heck, H. (1954). Der africkanische Anthropoids 'Bonobo' eine neue Menschenaffengattring. *Säugetierkundliche Mitteilungen, 2*, 97–101.

Van Krankelsven, E., Dupain, J., Van Elsacker, L., & Verheyen, R. F. (1996). Food calling by captive bonobos (*Pan paniscus*). *International Journal of Primatology, 17*(2), 207–217.

Vauclair, J., & Bard, K. (1983). Development of manipulation with objects in apes and human infants. *Journal of Human Evolution, 12*, 631—645.

Vea, J. J., & Sabater-Pi, J. (1998). Spontaneous pointing behaviour in the wild pygmy chimpanzee (*Pan paniscus*). *Folia Primatologica, 69*(5), 289–290.

Walraven, V. M. (1998). *Tool use, social learning and mirror-self recognition: A study of the cognitive capacities of bonobos.* Belgium: Universitaire Instelling Antwerpen.

White, F. J. (1988). Party composition and dynamics in *Pan paniscus*. *International Journal of Primatology, 9*, 179–193.

White, F. J. (1989). Social organization of pygmy chimpanzee. In P. G. Heltne & L. A. Marquardt (Eds.), *Understanding chimpanzees* (pp. 194–207). Cambridge, MA: Harvard University Press.

White, F. J. (1996). Comparative socio-ecology of *Pan paniscus*. In W. C. McGrew, L. F. Marchandt, & T. Nishida (Eds.), *Great ape societies* (pp. 29–41). Cambridge, England: Cambridge University Press.

White, F. J., & Wrangham, R. W. (1988). Feeding competition and patch size in the chimpanzee species *Pan paniscus* and *Pan troglodytes*. *Behaviour, 105*, 148–163.

Wrangham, R. W. (1977). Feeding behaviour of chimpanzees in Gombe National Park, Tanzania. In T. H. Clutton-Brock (Ed.), *Primate ecology* (pp. 503–538). London: Academic Press.

Wrangham, R. W. (1985). Chimpanzees. In D. Macdonald (Ed.), *Primates* (pp. 126–131). New York: Torstar Books.

Wrangham, R. W. (1986). Ecology and social relationships in two species of chimpanzees. In D. I. Rubenstein & R. W. Wrangham (Eds.), *Ecological aspects of social evolution: Birds and mammals* (pp. 352–278). Princeton, NJ: Princeton University Press.

Wrangham, R. W., & Smuts, B. B. (1980). Sex differences in the behavioral ecology of chimpanzees in the Gombe National Park, Tanzania. *Journal for Reproductive Fertility, 28*, 13–31.

Zihlmann, A. (1996). Reconstructions reconsidered: Chimpanzee models and human evolution. In C. McGrew, L. F. Marchandt, & T. Nishida (Eds.), *Great ape societies* (pp. 293–304). Cambridge, England: Cambridge University Press.

CHAPTER 4

Gestures in Orangutans (Pongo pygmaeus)

Katja Liebal
University of Portsmouth

Figure 4.1. Orangutan.

1.INTRODUCTION TO THE SPECIES

1.1. Taxonomy

Orangutans diverged from the human lineage approximately 12–15 million years ago (Glazko & Nei, 2003) and therefore represent the most ancient living great ape species. According to Groves (2001), the orangutan populations on the islands of Sumatra and Borneo represent two distinct species; the Sumatran orangutan (*Pongo abelii*) and the Bornean orangutan (*Pongo pygmaeus*), with the latter split into three subspecies that are morphologically distinguishable. Both populations have been geographically isolated since at least 10,000 years ago. Although this resulted in a genetic and morphological differentiation, both Bornean and Sumatran orangutans readily breed and produce offspring in captivity (Rijksen & Meijaard, 1999). Furthermore, the behavioral repertoire of Bornean and Sumatran orangutans is basically identical, although there might be a difference in sociability. Due to the variability in both the morphology and social behavior within Bornean and Sumatran orangutans (Rodman, 1988), the taxonomy of orangutans is still disputed (see also Enard & Pääbo, 2004).

1.2. Morphology

Orangutans are an arboreal species and practice a variety of different locomotor modes (Tuttle, 1970), although they mainly climb quadrumanously (Rodman & Mitani, 1987). Their long forelimbs with long hooklike fingers and their short but mobile hind limbs represent specializations for their suspensory type of locomotion (Fleagle, 1999).

Although the Bornean and Sumatran orangutan differ in morphological features such as length and color of their hair, shape of the males' cheek pads, size and shape of the throat pouch, and body build (Rodman, 1988), there is a high degree of variability within the populations of the two islands (Rijksen & Meijaard, 1999; Tuttle, 1986).

Orangutans are characterized by a strong sexual dimorphism. With a weight between 60–80 kg, males are twice as heavy as females (Rowe, 1996). In addition, there are two different sexually mature male morphs (which is sometimes referred to as *bimaturism*; Bennett, 1998) that are distinguished by both morphological features and behavioral traits (Delgado & van Schaik, 2000). Fully developed or flanged males develop a number of secondary sexual characteristics, such as wide cheek pads, long hair, and a large laryngeal sac (Knott, 1999; Rodman, 1988).

Unflanged males are about the same size as adult females (Galdikas, 1985) and do not show these secondary sexual features, but they are sexually fully mature and able to sire offspring (Rijksen & Meijaard, 1999). Although the causes of the males' bimaturism are not fully understood, the two morphs seem to represent different developmental phases rather than alternative strategies, reflecting the variability of the long maturation period of males that may finally develop into flanged males (Delgado & van Schaik, 2000).

1.3. Distribution and Ecology

Orangutans represent the only Asian species of great ape and live exclusively in restricted areas on the islands of Sumatra and Borneo (Rijksen & Meijaard, 1999). They mainly inhabit lowland tropical forest close to rivers or swamps between 200 and 400 meters in altitude (Rijksen & Meijaard, 1999), but their distribution in space and time can vary depending on the abundance of food (Djojosudharmo & van Schaik, 1992). Orangutans are characterized by an almost exclusively arboreal lifestyle in the canopy of the tropical rain forest, but adult Bornean male orangutans sometimes travel on the ground because large terrestrial predators such as tigers are absent on that island (MacKinnon, 1989; Sugardjito, 1986).

The orangutan population density varies between 2 to 7 individuals per km^2 close to rivers, and less than 1 individual per km^2 in higher altitudes (Rijksen & Meijaard, 1999).

Orangutans are a frugivorous species feeding mainly on a wide range of different species of fruit, supplemented by leaves and animal protein such as insects and eggs (Djojosudharmo & van Schaik, 1992; Rijksen, 1978). The quantitative and qualitative distribution of the orangutan's fruit diet in time and space is one major determinant of its ranging behavior, population density, and social organization (Rijksen & Meijaard, 1999). In this regard, the density of strangling figs and topsoil pH seem to be reliable predictors for orangutan density in undisturbed dryland forests (Wich, Buij, & van Schaik, 2004).

The daily activity patterns of wild orangutans vary depending on age and sex of the individuals (Rijksen, 1978). Following Rodman (1979), they spend most of their daily activity feeding (45.9%) and resting (39.2%). Besides traveling (11.1%) and nest building (1%), less than 2% of their time is spent in social activities, such as mating and vocalizing (Knott, 1999).

Orangutans represent a highly endangered primate species. Current population estimates refer to 23,500 orangutans in Borneo (Rijksen &

Meijaard, 1999) and 3,500 in Sumatra (Wich et al., 2003). Because of habitat destruction and hunting, they are vulnerable to extinction. The low population densities and large home ranges require extended and undisturbed forest formations (Rijksen & Meijaard, 1999; Singleton & van Schaik, 2001). Under the impact of logging, the population density can decline to less than 40% of that in undisturbed forests (Rao & van Schaik, 1997).

1.4. Social Structure and Behavior

Previously, orangutans were considered a solitary species, but this view has changed as more information has been gathered about their social organization (Rijksen & Meijaard, 1999). Overall, there are three basic social units, including (a) adult females with their offspring, (b) adolescent and/or subadult individuals of both sexes, and (c) solitary, adult males (Horr, 1975, 1977; MacKinnon, 1974; Rijksen, 1978; Rodman, 1973). Resident males and females are mostly high-ranking individuals, which results in their occupying high-quality ranges. Female ranges vary in size from between 0.6 and 1 km², whereas adult males can cover ranges larger then 10 km² (Horr, 1975; Rijksen, 1978). However, residents represent the minority of orangutan populations; the majority are commuters characterized by a nomadic existence and regularly present in a certain area for only several weeks or months a year over several years. In addition, there are a few wanderers that are seen in given areas only once or infrequently (Rijksen & Meijaard, 1999). The status of an individual may change with ontogeny; young orangutans are residents as long as they are dependent on their mothers, but they may aggregate into groups of social commuters when they become adolescents or subadults. As adults, they may occupy a range and therefore become resident again. Because the ranges of individuals can overlap, different social units can aggregate to form temporary associations or social groups during feeding in the same fruit tree or while traveling (MacKinnon, 1974; Rijksen, 1978; Rijksen & Meijaard, 1999). It is most often immature orangutans that initiate contact with other orangutans and participate in a variety of groupings varying in degree and frequency of interaction (Galdikas & Vasey, 1992). The behavior of orangutans in such encounters is described as tolerant but it only rarely involves social interactions, and friendly greeting gestures are particularly lacking (Galdikas & Vasey, 1992; MacKinnon, 1974). Similar observations are described for captive orangutans, which can be kept in groups consisting of several adult individuals and their offspring. Although they usually tolerate each other (with the exception of adult males) and aggressive encounters are rare, the orangutans do not seem to seek social contact with others (Becker, 1984; Jantschke, 1972).

In general, adult males are intolerant of other adult males and, except during periods of sexual consortship, they are truly solitary, spending less than 2% of their time with other individuals (Galdikas, 1985). They usually avoid each other, but observations of various injuries or other physical anomalies indicate the occurrence of overt fighting between adult males, in particular if females are present (Galdikas, 1985). Unflanged males travel widely to enforce copulations with females. Their ascent to a higher sociosexual status appears to be associated with the establishment of long-lasting sexual relationships (Rijksen & Meijaard, 1999).

To summarize, the social structure of orangutans is characterized by a high degree of variation in individual social behavior and ecology depending on sex, age, reproductive state, and social status. Different social units can aggregate if food is abundant, but a certain interindividual distance is always maintained except in sexual consortships and between young orangutans (Rijksen & Meijaard, 1999). Thus, the semisolitary social organization of orangutans can be described as an individual-based fission-fusion system that is highly variable over space and time (van Schaik, 1999).

1.5. Cognition

Yerkes and Yerkes (1970) described orangutans as "lethargic, reserved, and cautious, but curious and exploratory" apes. Although these characteristics vary depending on age, sex, and individuality (Yerkes & Yerkes, 1970), orangutans' temperament together with their arboreal morphology seem to be the major reasons for the low number of studies investigating their cognitive skills, compared to chimpanzees (Lethmate, 1977). However, a number of studies do refer to orangutans' extraordinary abilities in regard to learning, deduction, and invention (Lethmate, 1977; Rumbaugh, 1970).

1.5.1. Physical Cognition

Orangutans are forced to travel when searching for distributed food patches. Their distribution, quality, and quantity varies over time and space (Rijksen & Meijaard, 1999). There is some evidence that they utilize cognitive mapping strategies, together with their highly developed spatial memory, to find irregularly distributed food patches and to systematically check the productive state of different food sources (Galdikas & Vasey, 1992).

In terms of tool use and manufacturing, there are very few reports from the wild (Galdikas, 1982a, 1982b; van Schaik & Knott, 2001; van Schaik, Fox, & Fechtman, 2003; van Schaik, Fox, & Sitompul, 1996). Wild orangutans use leaves to protect their hands and feet from thorny branches while feeding (Fox & bin'Muhammad, 2002) or to rub and clean their fur (MacKinnon, 1974; Rijksen, 1978). Sticks are used to extract edible seeds from fruits and to retrieve social insects and their products from tree holes, although these behaviors are limited to few sites (van Schaik et al., 1996). Depending on the requirements of the task, orangutans manufacture different stick tools varying in length and diameter (van Schaik et al., 1996). In contrast to wild chimpanzees, there are very few examples of tool use by orangutans outside of the feeding context, for example, the use of branch "hooks" during locomotion (Fox & bin'Muhammad, 2002), the dropping of branches (Galdikas, 1982b), or the use of leaves to protect themselves from rain (Rijksen, 1978). The lack of tool use at most study sites in the orangutan's natural habitat is explained by the lack of suitable conditions for the transmission of tool use (Delgado & van Schaik, 2000). Paradoxically, captive orangutans and rehabilitants deploy sophisticated skills that are at least as complex as those of chimpanzees (Lethmate, 1977; van Schaik, 1996). For example, sticks are used to extract objects, to bring objects within reach, or to hit other individuals (Call & Tomasello, 1994a; Chevalier-Skolnikoff, 1983; Lethmate, 1982). Wright (1972) reported the use of stones for hitting and cutting. Lethmate (1977) provided a detailed description of the use and manipulation of a variety of different objects, and Parker (1969) concluded that captive orangutans use a wider range of specific behaviors to manipulate objects than do gorillas and chimpanzees. Applying Piaget's model of cognitive development, captive orangutans' sophisticated skills in using and manufacturing tools, as well as in manipulating objects, represent a sensorimotor stage of at least 5 or higher (Chevalier-Skolnikoff, 1983). The manipulation of objects has also been observed in wild orangutans (Bard, 1995; Galdikas, 1982a), but it is difficult to determine from those reports the extent to which the manipulations involved exploring the effects of actions on objects or relating objects to one another systematically (Tomasello & Call, 1997). The instrumental skills involved in tool use, object manipulation, and/or problem solving seem to be acquired by different learning mechanisms. Both individual and social learning are described in this context (Shepherd, 1923; Wright, 1972; Yerkes, 1916). The intelligent and creative tool use of orangutans may be the reason for a powerful manifestation of emulation learning in this species, whereas there is no evidence that instrumental skills are acquired via imitation (Call & Tomasello, 1994a; Tomasello & Call, 1997).

Studies relating to orangutans' performance in object permanence tasks suggest that their object tracking skills correspond to at least Stage 4, and maybe to Stage 5, according to Piaget's model (Call & Tomasello, 1994b). The same conclusions were drawn from a delayed-response test by Fischer and Kitchener (1965).

In terms of quantities, orangutans can distinguish different numbers of food pieces up to a quantity of ten, as demonstrated in a study by Hanus and Call (in review) employing an object-choice task. Although the orangutans' choice between two containers holding different numbers of food items was influenced by the ratio of the quantities, they mostly chose the container with the greater number of food pieces. Furthermore, they did so even when the containers were presented consecutively rather than concurrently. Orangutans also show some understanding that an object retains its properties regardless of changes in its appearance in a Piagetian liquid-conservation task (Suda & Call, 2004). Although they relied to a greater extent on visual estimation than on having some appreciation of the constancy of liquid quantities as it was found for the other great apes, they outperformed the bonobos and chimpanzees in this task.

1.5.2. Social Cognition

Most primates live in complex social groups where they recognize other individual members of their group. They understand and predict at least some of the behavior of others, remember their previous interactions with others, and form direct relationships with other members of the group (Tomasello & Call, 1997). This social complexity of primate groups is suggested as one possible reason for the sophisticated cognitive skills of social primates, in particular great apes (Whiten & Byrne, 1997).

Orangutans recognize other members of their species as individuals and know the personal relationships they share with them (Galdikas & Vasey, 1992). They show some understanding of third-party relationships, sometimes redirecting aggression they received from a particular individual toward that aggressor's kin or close associates, and occasionally engaging in coalitions and alliances (Galdikas & Vasey, 1992).

They also show sensitivity to the attentional state of conspecifics during communicative interactions (Liebal, Pika, & Tomasello, 2006), although Kaplan and Rogers (2002) found that orangutans avoid gazing directly at conspecifics. However, orangutans do follow the gaze of a human experimenter upward toward the ceiling or around a barrier, suggesting they do not simply orient to the same target as the gazer but actually attempt to take his/her visual perspective (Bräuer, Call, & Tomasello, 2005).

Thus, orangutans understand conspecifics (and humans) as animate and directed beings. In particular, they have some understanding of the visual perception of others, as indicated by others' bodily orientation together with their eye gaze direction. Those cues influence their subsequent behavior and are used for discovering objects and events at other locations in their environment (Kaminski, Call & Tomasello, 2004; Tomasello & Call, 1997).

Studies using the mirror self-recognition paradigm found that orangutans behave in the same manner as chimpanzees, suggesting that orangutans recognize their own bodies and therefore have some knowledge of self (Lethmate & Dücker, 1973; Miles, 1994; Suarez & Gallup, 1981).

However, given that sophisticated social cognitive skills are usually correlated with the social complexity of primate groups (Whiten & Byrne, 1997), the extraordinary intelligence of orangutans seems to be paradoxical, considering their semisolitary lifestyle (Delgado & van Schaik, 2000).

1.6. Communication: State of the Art

There are only a few studies on orangutan vocalizations, and most of them report only a more general description of vocal utterances within the orangutan's behavioral repertoire (e.g., Jantschke, 1970). MacKinnon (1974) describes 16 vocalizations of wild orangutans and Rijksen (1978) offers a list of 13 vocalizations. Mitani (1984) focused on *long calls,* which are important for intraspecies interactions and enable orangutans to communicate over large distances. Both the attraction of females and the spacing of males are discussed as possible functions for this vocalization (Galdikas, 1983; MacKinnon, 1971, 1974; Mitani, 1984, 1985).

With regard to facial expressions, MacKinnon (1974) describes a *pout face, fear face,* and *bare teeth threat,* also reported by Rijksen (1978), which appear to be very similar to the facial expressions observed in chimpanzees (van Hooff, 1971; van Lawick-Goodall, 1968).

The gestural communication of orangutans is only poorly investigated, in contrast to the African great ape species (de Waal, 1988; Goodall, 1986; Kano, 1992; Pika, Liebal, & Tomasello, 2003; Tanner & Byrne, 1996; Tomasello et al., 1985, 1989, 1994, 1997). Some authors suggest that despite their semisolitary lifestyle, orangutans use a wide range of vocal signals and gestures (Kaplan & Rogers, 2000; MacKinnon, 1974), whereas others speculate that their social organization may result in less complex communication skills (Bennett, 1998).

MacKinnon (1974) established a repertoire of tactile and visual gestures of wild Bornean and Sumatran orangutans and describes *embrace, kiss, branch shaking, arm waving,* and *lunge.* Rijksen (1978) mentions a number of "gestures and postures involving a clear taxis component with reference to a social partner" in both wild and rehabilitant Sumatran orangutans. For example, *look at mouth* or *peer begging* are gestures used in the food context and are always performed by the younger or lower ranking individual. Bard (1992) describes some gestures involved in food sharing between mothers and their offspring with a focus on the ontogeny of these signals. Like MacKinnon (1974), Rijksen (1978) observed an *arm wave,* but in addition, observed *throwing, hold out hand, hit away,* and *presenting* as well as several tactile gestures including *touch, mouth to mouth contact,* and *grasp* are mentioned. For captive individuals, Maple (1980) described *hand extension, slapping,* and *hair pulling,* and Jantschke (1972) refers to the use of *slap with objects, arm wave, pull,* and *stare* in the context of play behavior. In aggressive encounters, Jantschke (1972) observed *hit* and *bite intentions* together with *lunge* and *stare* as described for wild individuals (MacKinnon, 1974; Rijksen, 1978).

To summarize, most references to orangutans' gestural communication are restricted to a listing within a general ethogram of orangutans. Therefore, it is difficult to decide whether these behaviors can be identified as intentional and directed behaviors according to the definition of gesture used in this book. Sometimes there are comments on the context in which some gestures are performed, but with the exception of Bard's (1990) approach to gestures as tools to manipulate animate objects, nothing is known about cognitive aspects of gestural communication in orangutans, such as the flexible use and learning of gestures.

Therefore, the focus of this chapter is on the use of gestures in orangutans with the goal of documenting (1) the number and kind of gestures used in general, (2) the variability of the individual repertoires as a function of group, age class, and sex, and (3) the flexibility of use in terms of means–ends dissociation and audience effects.

The findings are interpreted with regard to the ecology, social structure, and cognitive skills of orangutans. First, it was expected that orangutans, being arboreal, would utilize a smaller gestural repertoire—in particular fewer visual gestures, given the restricted range of vision in arboreal habitats—compared to the terrestrial great ape species (Marler, 1965). Second, their gestural repertoire should be characterized by a higher degree of variability compared to the repertoires of species living in small and stable groups, because of their more egalitarian, individualistic society characterized by changing and unpredictable interactions with other individuals. Third, advanced cognitive skills should be reflected in a rich repertoire of complex gestures, including the incorporation of objects, and a high degree of flexibility in terms of the use of gestures across different functional contexts.

2.METHODS

2.1. Individuals

Sixteen individuals of two different groups were observed (as shown in Table 4.2). The classification of age classes was largely adopted from Rijksen (1978). However, there was no distinction made between subadult and adult males; both flanged and unflanged males older than 10 years of age were considered as adults. The group at Leipzig Zoo consisted of 7 individuals ranging from 11 months to 28 years old. There were 2 adult males (> 10 years) including a fully developed male and an undeveloped male, 2 adult females (> 10 years), 1 subadult female (5–10 years), 1 juvenile (2½–5 years) and 1 infant female (0–2½ years). The group at Zürich Zoo consisted of 9 individuals ranging from 4.5 to approximately 41 years old. The group consisted of 2 adult males, including a fully developed male and an undeveloped male, 4 adult females, 2 subadult females, and 1 juvenile female. All together, there were 10 adult orangutans, 3 subadults, 2 juveniles, and 1 infant, representing 4 males and 12 females. All individuals except 1 (Pongo) were born in captivity.

2.2. Data Collection

Focal-animal sampling (Altmann, 1974) was applied to calculate the total frequencies of particular gestures and to therefore enable comparisons across individuals, groups, age classes, and sex. A digital video camera (SONY DCR-TRV900E) was used to record a total of 10 hours per individual, resulting in a total of 160 hours of observation on tape. Every focal animal was selected in a random order and was videotaped in 15-min bouts.

The methods of data analysis and the corresponding statistical tests are reported in Liebal et al. (2006), and therefore no detailed information is reported in this chapter. If not otherwise mentioned, the results are presented as median numbers or proportions of individual performance. Differences are reported only if they were significant.

2.3. Description of the Gestural Inventory

The observed gestures are listed according to their sensory modality with their total frequency shown in brackets. A total of 29 gestures were observed, including 14 tactile and 15 visual gestures. No auditory gestures were observed.

2.3.1. Visual Gestures

- *Approach face*—Stare at another individual's mouth, rarely at the eyes, in close proximity (149).
- *Bite intention*—Perform a rapid movement with the upper part of the body together with an *open mouth* toward the recipient, but stop in this forward movement without physical contact (38).
- *Extend arm*—Direct the arm toward the recipient (30).
- *Hand shake*—Rotate hands around the wrists (9).
- *Headstand*—Turn vertically and stand on head and shoulders (2).
- *Hit intention*—Perform an arm movement as if to hit but without making physical contact with the recipient (12).
- *Hold hand in front of the mouth*—Put an extended arm with the palm open upward in front of the mouth of another individual (2).
- *Jerking body movements*—Hang in front of the recipient while moving the body up and down by angling the arms repeatedly (2).
- *Offer arm with food pieces*—Chew leaves or fruits into the arm's fur and then present the food to another individual (15).
- *Offer body part*—Present another body part for grooming (33).
- *Offer food*—Extend the arm with a piece of food in the hand and hold it in front of the mouth of the recipient (24).
- *Present genitals*—Sit or hang in front of the recipient, raise and offer the genital region to another individual (28).
- *Present object*—Extend the arm with an object (other than food) in the hand or hide under an object (11).
- *Shake object*—Push an object rapidly back and forth (30).
- *Wave arm*—Extend an arm and shake it horizontally in front of the body (4).

2.3.2 Tactile Gestures

- *Bite in hand*—Contact the recipient's hand with an open mouth and gently bit it (15).
- *Embrace*—Approach the recipient frontally or laterally and put one or two arms around the other's body (6).

- *Formal bite*—Touch some part of the recipient's body with an open mouth and gently bite it (97).
- *Gentle touch*—Put the hand or foot on any body part of the recipient (123).
- *Hold tight*—Seize the hand or foot of the recipient (26).
- *Lip touch*—Approach the recipient's mouth and touch it with the lips; can be accompanied by surrounding the recipient's head with one arm (94).
- *Nudge*—Touch the recipient with single fingers, knuckles, or a fist (as opposed to *slap*, which is performed by using the flat hand or rear palm of the hand) (49).
- *Pull*—Grasp some part of the recipient's body with a hand or foot and perform a short forceful movement with it (258).
- *Push*—Apply pressure against the recipient's body with a rapid and vigorous movement of the hands, feet, or head. (144).
- *Put face on face*—Approach the face of the recipient and make mouth to mouth (slightly open) contact (3).
- *Put hand on head*—Place a flat hand on the head or back of the recipient (as opposed to *gently touch*) and leave it there (5).
- *Slap*—Hit the recipient with a flat hand on any body part (170).
- *Throw object*—Toss an object at another individual (5).
- *Touch with genital region*—Hang in front of the recipient and contact its face with the genitals; it may derive from *present genitals* (7).

3. GESTURAL REPERTOIRE

3.1. Overview

A total of 1,343 gestures was observed, representing a median number of 0.5 gestures per hour and per individual. Frequent tactile gestures were *pull* (258), *slap* (170) and *push* (144; see section 2.3). *Approach face* (149) was the most frequent visual gesture. Other signals, for example *headstand, hold hand in front of the mouth,* and *jerking body movements,* were each observed only twice. Some of the gestures, for example *shake object, throw object,* and *present object,* were object based and involved the use of ropes, branches, or other objects. Occasionally, individuals used branches or sticks to *slap* or *nudge* another orangutan. Although the overall observed repertoire consisted of nearly the same amount of visual and tactile gestures, individuals used a higher variety of different tactile gestures as compared to visual gestures. Furthermore, tactile gestures were the most frequent gesture modality, representing almost three quarters of all gestures observed (72.6%).

Table 4.1 provides a summary of the terms used in the current chapter in comparison to other studies with both wild and captive orangutans, supplemented by the functional contexts in which the gestures were used.

3.2. Context

With respect to the frequency distribution of gestures across the different functional contexts, individuals used their gestures 25.6% of the time in the context of ingestion, followed by play (21.9%), the agonistic context (16%), and affiliation (10.9%). All other contexts (grooming, sexual behavior, access, nursing, and walking) represented less than 5%.

When comparing the use of tactile and visual gestures in the different functional contexts (Fig. 4.2), only tactile gestures were utilized in the context of nursing and walking. Furthermore, in the context of access, affiliation, agonistic behavior, and play, tactile gestures represented the majority of gestures observed (80.6–95.1%). However, in the contexts of sexual behavior, ingestion and grooming, more than 50% of the signals observed were visual gestures.

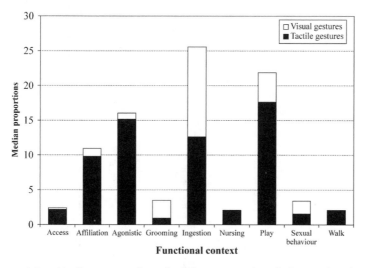

Figure 4.2. Median proportion of tactile gestures in relation to visual gestures in the different functional contexts.

TABLE 4.1

Terms Used in the Current Chapter in Comparison to Other Studies With Both Wild and Captive Orangutans, Supplemented by Their Functional Context

Liebal, Pika and Tomasello		Other Captive Studies		Studies in the Wild	
Tactile gestures	Functional context	Signal [Translation] (reference)	Functional context	Gesture	Functional context
Bite in hand	affiliation, play	Biting hands/feet (Maple, 1980)	play		
Embrace	affiliation, parental care			Embrace (MacKinnon, 1974; Rijksen, 1978)	affiliation, parental care
Formal bite	access, agonistic, play, sexual			Mock bite (Rijksen, 1978)	play
Gentle touch		Anfassen [touch] (Becker, 1984)	play	Touch (Rijksen, 1978)	contact/affiliation
Lip touch	ingestion, play, affiliation			Kiss (?) (MacKinnon, 1974) Mouth-mouth contact (Rijksen, 1978)	food, play
Pull	all contexts except submissive	Ziehen [pull] (Becker, 1984; Jantschke, 1972)	play	Grasp (Rijksen, 1978)	play
Push	all contexts except submissive	Hair pulling (Zucker et al., 1978) Push/dragging (Zucker et al., 1978)	play play		
Put face to face	affiliation, play	Head butting (Maple, 1980)	play	Muzzle-pushing (?) (Rijksen, 1978)	
Slap	agonism, ingestion, play, sexual	Schlagen [hit] (Becker, 1984) Slapping (Maple, 1980) Face-stroking (Zucker et al., 1978)	play play play	Hitting (Rijksen, 1978)	play, food

Visual gestures	Functional context	Gesture [Translation] (reference)	Functional context	Gesture	Functional context
Throw object	affiliation, play	Objekt werfen [throw object] (Becker, 1984)	play	Throwing (Rijksen, 1978)	play
Approach the face	affiliation, grooming, ingestion		Look at mouth (Rijksen, 1978)	ingestion/food	
Bite intention	agonistic, grooming, play	Beißintention [bite intention] (Jantschke, 1972)	agonism	Lunge (MacKinnon,1974)	intimidation/agonism
Extend arm	affiliation, ingestion play	Hand extension (Maple, 1980) Handausstrecken [hand extension] (Becker, 1984)	play play	Hold out hand (Rijksen, 1978)	parental care, affiliation, submission
Hit intention	agonistic, play	Schlagintention [hit intention] (Jantschke, 1972)	agonism	Hit away (?) (Rijksen, 1978)	walking
Present genitals	sexual			Presenting (Rijksen, 1978)	sexual behavior
Present object	play	Object vorzeigen [present object] (Becker, 1988, Jantschke, 1972)	play	Self decorate (Rijksen, 1978)	play
Wave arm	play			Arm (leg) waving (MacKinnon, 1974) Arm wave (Rijksen, 1978)	intimidation/agonism play

3.3. Variability

3.3.1. Individual Differences

Table 4.2 gives an overview of the individual use of the different gestures along with corresponding information regarding the age class and sex of the orangutans. It also summarizes the results with regard to how many of the individuals were using each of the gestures observed. None of the individuals produced all 29 gestures. The median number of gestures used was 14, corresponding to 48% of the total repertoire. Depending on the individual, the number of gestures ranged from 6 to 19. Only 2 gestures (*push* and *slap*) were performed by all individuals (Table 4.2).

3.3.2. Age Differences

The median number of gestures increased from nine in the infant, to 17.5 and 17 in the juveniles and subadults, respectively; and it decreased in adults to 12.5 gestures. In terms of gesture modality, adults used a lower number of visual gestures (*Mdn* = 4) compared to their offspring (*Mdn* = 8.5), but no difference was found with regard to the number of tactile gestures used ($Mdn_{adult} = 7$, $Mdn_{youngster} = 8.5$) (see Fig. 4.3). In terms of frequency, both young and adult orangutans used tactile gestures more often than visual gestures.

Regarding the use of gestures across the functional contexts, young orangutans performed the highest variety of gestures in the play context, whereas adults used the highest number of gestures in the agonistic context, followed by the contexts of play, ingestion, and affiliation.

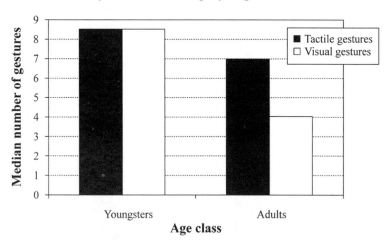

Figure 4.3. Median number of gestures used depending on age.

TABLE 4.2

Distribution of Gestures Among Individuals Arranged According to Their Age Class

	Individuals																Percent of individuals using it
Group	Kila	Xira	Padana	Salih	Tuah	Toba	Pongo	Bimbo	Walter	Djaro	Lea	Pini	Dunja	Timor	Selatan	Oceh	
Age and sex class	i/f	j/f	j/f	s/f	s/f	s/f	a/m	a/m	a/m	a/m	a/f	a/f	a/f	a/f	a/f	a/f	
	L	Z	L	Z	Z	L	Z	L	L	Z	Z	L	L	Z	Z	Z	
Tactile gestures																	
Bite in hand	–	–	x	–	–	x	–	–	–	–	–	x	x	–	–	–	25
Embrace	–	–	x	–	–	x	–	–	–	–	–	x	x	–	–	–	25
Formal bite	–	x	x	x	X	x	x	–	x	x	x	x	x	x	x	x	88
Gentle touch	x	x	x	x	x	x	x	–	x	x	x	x	x	x	x	x	94
Hold tight	–	–	–	x	x	–	x	–	–	–	x	–	x	–	–	–	31
Lip touch	x	x	x	x	x	x	x	–	x	x	x	x	x	–	x	x	88
Nudge	x	x	x	x	x	x	x	x	x	–	x	x	x	x	x	–	88
Pull	x	x	x	x	x	x	x	–	x	x	x	x	x	x	x	x	94
Push	x	x	x	x	x	x	x	x	x	x	x	x	x	x	x	x	100
Put face on face	–	–	–	–	–	–	x	–	–	x	–	–	–	–	–	–	13
Put hand on head	–	–	–	–	–	–	–	–	–	–	x	–	–	–	–	–	6
Slap	x	x	x	x	x	x	x	x	x	x	x	x	x	x	x	x	100
Throw object	–	x	–	x	–	–	–	–	–	–	x	–	–	–	–	–	19
Touch with genital region	–	–	–	x	–	x	–	–	–	–	–	x	–	–	–	x	25

(continued)

TABLE 4.2 (continued)

	Individuals																Percent of individuals using it
	Kila	Xira	Padana	Salih	Tuah	Toba	Pongo	Bimbo	Walter	Djaro	Lea	Pini	Dunja	Timor	Selatan	Oceh	
Age and sex class	ilf	ilf	jlf	slf	slf	slf	alm	alm	alm	alm	alf	alf	alf	alf	alf	alf	
Group	L	Z	L	Z	Z	L	Z	L	L	Z	Z	L	L	Z	Z	Z	
Visual gestures																	
Approach the face	x	x	x	x	x	x	–	–	x	x	x	x	–	x	x	x	81
Bite intention	–	–	x	x	–	x	x	–	x	x	–	x	x	x	x	x	63
Extend arm	x	x	x	x	x	x	–	x	–	x	–	x	x	–	x	x	69
Hand shake	–	x	–	x	x	x	–	–	x	–	–	x	–	–	–	x	38
Headstand	–	–	–	–	–	x	–	x	–	–	–	–	–	–	–	–	13
Hit intention	–	x	x	–	x	–	x	–	–	–	–	x	–	x	x	–	44
Hold hand in front of the mouth	–	–	–	–	–	–	–	–	–	–	x	–	–	–	–	–	6
Jerking body movements	–	–	–	x	–	–	–	–	–	–	–	–	–	–	–	–	6
Offer arm with food pieces	–	–	–	–	–	x	–	–	x	–	–	x	–	–	–	–	19
Offer body part	x	x	x	x	–	–	–	–	–	–	–	–	–	–	x	x	38
Offer food	–	x	x	–	x	x	–	–	x	–	x	–	–	–	–	–	38
Present genitals	–	x	x	x	x	x	–	–	–	–	x	–	–	x	–	x	44
Present object	–	–	x	–	x	–	–	–	–	–	x	–	–	x	–	–	25
Shake object	–	x	x	x	x	x	–	x	x	–	–	–	–	–	–	x	56
Wave arm	–	x	x	–	–	–	–	–	–	–	–	–	–	–	x	–	13
Total of gestures	9	17	18	18	16	19	11	6	13	9	15	17	12	9	13	14	

Note. (i = infant; j = juvenile; s = subadult; a = adult) and sex (f = female; m = male). Group affiliation refers to Leipzig (L) and Zürich (Z). In addition, for each gesture, it is shown what percentage of all individuals used it.

3.3.3. Group Differences

Excluding the three gestures performed by single individuals, the gestures *headstand, offer arm with food pieces, bite in hand,* and *embrace* were observed only in the Leipzig group, whereas *put face on face, wave arm,* and *throw object* occurred only in the Zürich group. However, because all those gestures were performed generally by a low number of individuals (2–4) it is difficult to draw any conclusions about whether those gestures can be classified as group specific. At least the gesture *offer arm with food pieces* seems to represent such a case, because the individuals of the Leipzig group frequently chewed food pieces in their fur to suck on it by themselves or to offer it to another individual. A similar behavior was never observed in the Zürich group.

Cohen's kappa was used to measure the degree of concordance between the individual repertoires within each group and between groups according to the method of Bakeman and Gottman (1986). Within groups, the individuals' repertoires were very similar, representing "good" (Leipzig group = .60) and "moderate" (Zürich group = .59) levels of agreement. Between groups, the degree of concordance of the individuals' repertoires was only .55. These results suggest that the individuals' repertoires within groups were more concordant than the repertoires between groups.

3.3.4. Sex Differences

Because all offspring in the present study were females, only adult males and females were compared with respect to the number of gestures used. Males performed a median number of 10 different gestures as opposed to 13.5 in females. In terms of gesture modality, adult females performed a higher variety of visual gestures than males (5.5 compared to 2.5) and slightly more tactile gestures than males (8.5 compared to 7).

3.4. Flexibility

3.4.1. Combinations

Figure 4.4 shows the proportion of sequences as a function of the number of gestures combined. Approximately 17.6 % ($N = 236$) of all observed gestures were combined in 1 of 93 gesture sequences. The majority (70%) represented two-gesture sequences; the proportions of the other various gesture sequences declined steadily as the number of gestures in a sequence increased. The highest number of gestures produced

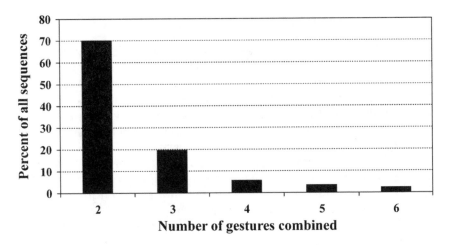

Figure 4.4. Proportion of sequences as a function of the number of gestures combined.

in a sequence was six. With the exception of two individuals that never performed any gesture sequences, the orangutans performed on average 4.5 gesture sequences. The highest numbers of sequences occurred within the functional contexts of play and ingestion ($N = 28$), whereas no gesture sequence was observed within the context of grooming.

3.4.2. Audience Effects

Tactile gestures were directed toward an attending recipient 77.4% of the time, whereas visual gestures were only used if the recipient was attending (100%). Thus, although both gesture modalities were performed more often toward an attending recipient, the proportion of visual gestures directed toward an attending recipient was higher compared to tactile gestures.

3.4.3. Means–Ends Dissociation

3.4.3.1. One Gesture for Multiple Contexts.   Overall, four-fifths of the observed gesture repertoire were used in more than one functional context, with the majority (31%) observed in two different contexts (Table 4.3). Two gestures were performed in all nine functional contexts. One-fifth of all gestures were used in only one functional context; these were all visual gestures. For example, *offer body part* was only

TABLE 4.3
Use of Gestures Across the Different Functional Contexts

Gesture	Access	Affiliation	Agonistic	Grooming	Ingestion	Nursing	Play	Sexual behavior	Walk	Sum of contexts per gesture
					Functional context					
Approach face	x	x		x	x					4
Bite in hand		x			x		x			3
Bite intention			x	x	x		x	x		5
Embrace		x				x				2
Extend arm					x		x			3
Formal bite	x		x	x	x	x	x	x		7
Gentle touch	x	x	x	x	x	x	x	x	x	9
Hand shake			x		x		x	x		4
Headstand		x					x			2
Hit intention			x				x		x	2
Hold hand in front of the mouth					x					1
Hold tight		x	x				x			3
Jerking body movements								x		1
Lip touch	x	x		x	x		x			5
Nudge	x	x	x		x	x	x			6
Offer arm with food pieces					x					1
Offer body part				x						1
Offer food			x	x						2
Present genitals								x		1
Present object		x					x			2
Pull	x	x	x	x	x	x	x	x	x	9
Push	x	x	x	x	x	x	x	x		8
Put face on face		x					x			2
Put hand on head		x	x							2
Shake object			x				x			2
Slap	x		x	x			x	x		5
Throw object		x					x			2
Touch with genital region		x	x					x		3
Wave arm							x			1
Sum of gestures per context	**8**	**16**	**14**	**8**	**15**	**6**	**19**	**10**	**2**	

observed in the context of grooming, *jerking body movements* and *present genitals* in the sexual context, *wave arm* exclusively during play, and *offer arm with food pieces* and *hold hand in front of the mouth* in the context of ingestion. Individuals performed tactile gestures in a higher variety of functional contexts (*Mdn* = 1.7) than visual gestures (*Mdn* = 1.1).

3.4.3.2. One Context With Multiple Gestures. The highest variety of gestures occurred in the play context (65.5%) followed by affiliation (55.1%) and ingestion (51.7%) contexts. Only 2 gestures (6.9%) were observed in the context of walking. For 78.1% of all contexts, more than one gesture was used.

On average, individuals performed 2.8 different gestures per context. In terms of gesture modality, 2.1 different tactile gestures per context were used compared to 0.7 visual gestures. The highest variety of tactile gestures was observed in the agonistic context (3.9), whereas the highest variety of visual gestures was performed during ingestion (1.8) and play (1.7).

3.5. Function of Gestures

Individuals did not respond to a sender's gesture 41.2% of the time, or they left without any overt reaction 4.4% of the time. Nonresponses were most common in the context of ingestion, during which receivers failed to respond almost 50% of the time to senders' gestures (mostly *approach face* or *lip touch*). When there was a response, 18.6% of the time, a sender's gesture changed the recipient's attentional state from not attending to attending. The majority of gestures caused an unspecified response in the recipient (45%), or the recipient responded with another gesture (14.3%). Eight percent of the time, the recipient responded with an action, for example play (64.8%), walk (13.8%), or food sharing (8%).

3.6. Handedness

There was a preference for the use of the right hand (57%) for the performance of manual gestures, for example *slap, pull,* and *extend arm.* No differences were found with respect to the use of hands in the different functional contexts.

4. DISCUSSION

With respect to gestures, the most important findings are that captive orangutans use a variety of different tactile and visual gestures flexibly across several functional contexts, whereas they do not perform any auditory gestures. Although the gestural repertoire consisted of basically the same number of tactile and visual gestures, the most frequent gesture modality used was tactile, representing almost three-quarters of all observed gestures. Tactile gestures were used mainly in the context of access, affiliation, agonistic behavior, and play whereas visual gestures were prominent in the contexts of sexual behavior, ingestion, and grooming. Although this study investigated captive individuals, orangutans' greater reliance on tactile as opposed to visual gestures is apparently a reflection of adaptation to an arboreal lifestyle (Maestripieri, 1999; Marler, 1965).

Orangutans incorporate objects into their communicative interaction. For example, they throw or present objects or use branches to hit another individual. The use of objects within communicative interactions is also described in wild orangutan males that throw tree branches to alert those within hearing distance to the male's presence (Galdikas, 1983).

In terms of functional context, the majority of gestures were produced in the context of ingestion, followed by play and then by agonistic behavior. The importance of gestures in the context of ingestion is also described for wild and rehabilitant orangutans. Bard (1992) observed that young orangutans began to use intentional gestures at an age of approximately 2½ years, but only later produced them on a regular basis, at 3½ years of age. Gestures used in the play context have been reported for rehabilitant and captive orangutans, mainly referring to interactions between peers (Becker, 1984; Jantschke, 1970; Rijksen, 1978). However, in wild orangutans the frequency of interactions in the play context depends on the presence of siblings or other peers (Rodman, 1988). Almost no interactions in the context of grooming were observed in the present study, consistent with reports on wild orangutans, in which grooming is "not very thorough" (MacKinnon, 1974). The same is reported for captive individuals, where grooming bouts last only several minutes, although females groom slightly more often and longer than do males (Maple, 1980). The individuals in the present study also performed a number of gestures in the affiliation context. However, although wild orangutans may use some affiliative gestures when feeding or traveling together (Galdikas & Vasey, 1992), there is an apparent lack of greeting gestures and other behaviors initiating social interactions (MacKinnon, 1974). Thus, the less frequent interactions among orangutans in the play and grooming contexts compared to other ape species seem to reflect their semisolitary nature.

In terms of age, the number of gestures increased throughout adolescence but dropped again in adulthood. Considering gesture modalities, young orangutans used a higher variety of visual gestures compared to adults, whereas no differences were found for the number of tactile gestures. With respect to frequency, both young and adult orangutans used tactile gestures more often than visual gestures.

There was a high degree of variability in the individuals' repertoires depending on age, group, and sex. Less than one-third of all gestures were used by more than 75% of all individuals, including only two gestures performed by all individuals. However, the majority of gestures were used by only a few individuals. Two gestures, *hold hand in front of the mouth* and *put hand on head*, were performed by only one individual female. However, because she was raised in a human environment, it is difficult to draw any conclusions about whether those gestures can be called idiosyncratic or whether they relate to her rearing history.

Regarding the variability between groups, the individuals' repertoires within a group were more similar than the repertoires of individuals from the two different groups. However, there was a higher degree of variability both within and between groups compared to siamangs and gorillas (Liebal, Pika, & Tomasello, 2004; Pika et al., 2003). However, because the majority of gestures were performed by a generally low number of individuals, it is difficult to draw any conclusions in terms of group-specific gestures or with regard to the learning mechanisms involved. The high degree of variability, both within and between groups as well as between age classes, seems to reflect the very individualistic and variable nature of orangutan behavior. The social system of orangutans is comparable to the fission-fusion system of chimpanzees (Delgado & van Schaik, 2000). This social organization seems to be the major force selecting for a highly variable communicative repertoire used flexibly in a number of different functional contexts (Maestripieri, 1999). The high degree of variability of gestures in orangutans supports this hypothesis.

In terms of flexibility, the majority of gestures were used in two or more functional contexts, and multiple gestures were used for one context. Furthermore, visual gestures were only performed if the recipient was visually attending to the sender, similar to the results found for other ape species. These results indicate that gestural communication in orangutans is characterized by means–ends dissociation as it is described for other ape species and that they are able to adjust their gestures depending on the behavior of the recipient. Orangutans also used their gestures in a goal-directed manner to influence the recipient's behavior. The majority of the gestures caused a response in the recipient, such as a change in attentional state or engagement in play, food sharing, or another interaction in one of the nine functional contexts. However, if the recipient did not respond at all or did not show an appropriate reaction, the sender persisted in communicating by performing several gestures one after another. Thus, the combination of gestures seems to represent a way to persist in communication and to consider the recipient's previous behavior (Liebal, Call, & Tomasello, 2004).

Another aspect of gesture use reflecting the cognitive skills of a species might be the use of objects within communicative interactions (Chevalier-Skolnikoff, 1976). In contrast to siamangs, both wild and captive orangutans incorporate objects into their production of gestures, for example *throwing objects, slapping with sticks, shaking branches* or other objects, and *presenting an object* (MacKinnon, 1974; Maple, 1980; Rijksen, 1978). Furthermore, many of their signals were manual gestures rather than body postures and facial expressions (see Liebal et al., 2006), which seem to be more prominent in monkey species such as *macaques* and *baboons* (Hinde & Rowell, 1962; Kummer, 1968; Maestripieri, 1999) as well as in siamangs (Liebal et al., 2004). This clearly differentiates the orangutan's signal repertoire from that of monkeys and siamangs, which is therefore more similar to the gesture repertoires of other great ape species. Similar to the African great apes (Pika et al., 2003; Pika, Liebal, & Tomasello, 2005; Tomasello et al., 1997), the orangutans' repertoire comprised a higher variety of visual gestures than that of siamangs (Liebal et al., 2004). However, with regard to the frequency of use, both siamangs and orangutans most often produced tactile gestures, supporting the idea that arboreal species should use mainly tactile gestures, rather than visual gestures, because of the restricted range of vision in their habitat (Marler, 1965).

5. CONCLUSIONS

Orangutans used a remarkable gestural repertoire consisting of both tactile and visual gestures. Although they performed approximately the same number of tactile and visual gestures, tactile gestures represented the dominant gesture modality with regard to frequency of use. No auditory gestures were observed. A quarter of all gestures were observed in the context of ingestion, followed by the gestures used in the play context.

The communication of orangutans is characterized by a considerable degree of variability in the individual repertoires. The number of gestures increased with age, but dropped after the individuals reached adulthood, similar to the other ape species. The variability of the individual repertoires was basically the same within each of the two groups, but between groups, the degree of variability was slightly higher. Orangutans showed sensitivity to the attentional state of others, in that they used visual gestures only if the recipient was attending. They also performed the majority of their gestures for more than one functional context and used multiple gestures in one context.

Thus, the gestural communication of orangutans is characterized by a high degree of variability in the individuals' gestural repertoires, which may reflect their variable social structure and behavior. The lack of auditory gestures and the greater frequency of tactile gestures seem to be related to orangutans' arboreal nature. Their cognitive skills are reflected in a rich repertoire of mainly manual gestures, the incorporation of objects into their communicative signals, and a high degree of flexibility, reflected in their sensitivity to the behavior of the recipient and their use of gestures in a number of different functional contexts.

REFERENCES

Altmann, J. (1974). Observational study of behavior: Sampling methods. *Behaviour, 49*, 227–267.

Bakeman, R., & Gottman, J. (1986). *Observing interaction: An introduction to sequential analysis.* Cambridge, England: University Press.

Bard, K. A. (1990). "Social tool use" by free-ranging orangutans: A Piagetian and developmental perspective on the manipulation of an animal object. In S. T. Parker & K. R. Gibson (Eds.), *"Language" and intelligence in monkeys and apes: Comparative developmental perspectives* (pp. 356–378). New York: Cambridge University Press.

Bard, K. A. (1992). Intentional behaviour and intentional communication in young free-ranging orangutans. *Child Development, 63*, 1186–1197.

Bard, K. A. (1995). Sensorimotor cognition in young feral orangutans (*Pongo pygmaeus*). *Primates, 36*(3), 297–321.

Becker, C. (1984). *Orangutans und Bonobos im Spiel* [Play behavior of Orangutans and Bonobos]. Munich: Profil-Verlag.

Bennett, E. L. (1998). *The natural history of orangutan.* Kota Kinabalu: Natural History Publishers.

Bräuer, J., Call, J., & Tomasello, M. (2005). *All great apes follow gaze to distant locations and around barriers.* Unpublished manuscript.

Call, J., & Tomasello, M. (1994a). The social learning of tool use by orangutans (*Pongo pygmaeus*). *Human Evolution, 9*(4), 297–313.

Call, J., & Tomasello, M. (1994b). Production and comprehension of referential pointing by orangutans (*Pongo pygmaeus*). *Journal of Comparative Psychology, 108*(4), 307–317.

Chevalier-Skolnikoff, S. (1976). The ontogeny of primate intelligence and its implications for communicative potential: A preliminary report. *Annals of the New York Academy of Sciences*, 173–211.

Chevalier-Skolnikoff, S. (1983). Sensorimotor development in orangutans and other primates. *Journal of Human Evolution, 12*(6), 545–561.

Delgado, R. A., Jr., & van Schaik, C. P. (2000). The behavioral ecology and conservation of the orangutan (*Pongo pygmaeus*): A tale of two islands. *Evolutionary Anthropology, 9*(5), 201–218.

De Waal, F. B. M. (1988). The communicative repertoire of captive bonobos (*Pan paniscus*) compared to that of chimpanzees. *Behaviour, 106*(3–4), 183–251.

Djojosudharmo, S., & van Schaik, C. P. (1992). Why are orangutans so rare in the highlands? Altitudinal changes in a Sumatran forest. *Tropical Biodiversity, 1*, 11–22.

Enard, W., & Pääbo, S. (2004). Comparative primate genomics. *Annual Review of Genomics and Human Genetics, 5*, 351–378.

Fischer, G. J., & Kitchener, S. L. (1965). Comparative learning in young gorillas and orangutans. *Journal of Genetic Psychology, 107*, 337–348.

Fleagle, J. G. (1999). *Primate adaptation and evolution* (2nd ed.). San Diego: Academic Press.

Fox, E. A., & bin'Muhammad, I. (2002). New tool use by wild Sumatran orangutans (*Pongo pygmaeus abelii*). *American Journal of Physical Anthropology, 119*(2), 186–188.

Galdikas, B. M. F. (1982a). An unusual instance of tool-use among wild orangutans in Tanjung Puting Reserve, Indonesian Borneo. *Primates, 23*, 138–139.

Galdikas, B. M. F. (1982b). Orangutan tool-use at Tanjung Puting Reserve, Central Indonesian Borneo (Kalimantan Tengah). *Journal of Human Evolution, 11*, 19–33.

Galdikas, B. M. F. (1983). The orangutan long call and snag crashing at Tanjung Puting Reserve. *Primates, 24*(3), 371–384.

Galdikas, B. M. F. (1985). Adult male sociality and reproductive tactics among orangutans at Tanjung Puting. *Folia Primatologica, 45*(1), 9–24.

Galdikas B. M. F., & Vasey, P. (1992). Why are orangutans so smart? Ecological and social hypothesis. In F. D. Burton (Ed.), *Social processes and mental abilities in nonhuman primates* (pp. 183–224). Lewiston, NY: Edwin Mellen Press.

Glazko, G., & Nei, M. (2003). Estimation of divergence times for major lineages of primate species. *Molecular Biology and Evolution, 20*, 424–434.

Goodall, J. (1986). *The chimpanzees of Gombe: Patterns of behavior.* Cambridge, MA: Harvard University Press.

Groves, C. P. (2001). *Primate taxonomy.* Washington, DC: Smithsonian Institution Press.

Hanus, D., & Call, J. *Quantity based discrimination in great apes (Gorilla gorilla Pan paniscus, Pan troglodytes, Pongo pygmaeus).* Manuscript in review.

Hinde, R. A., & Rowell, T. E. (1962). Communication by postures and facial expressions in the rhesus monkey, *Macaca mulatta. Proceedings of the Zoological Society of London, 138*, 1–21.

Horr, D. A. (1975). The Borneo orangutan: Population structure and dynamics in relationship to ecology and reproductive strategy. In L. A. Rosenblum (Ed.), *Primate behavior: Developments in field and laboratory research* (pp. 307–323). New York: Academic Press.

Jantschke, F. (1972). *Orangutans in Zoologischen Gaerten* [Orangutans in zoos]. Munich: R. Piper & Company.

Kaminski, J., Call, J., & Tomasello, M. (2004). Body orientation and face orientation: Two factors controlling apes' begging behaviour from humans. *Animal Cognition, 7*, 216–223.

Kano, T. (1992). *The last ape: Pygmy chimpanzee behavior and ecology.* Stanford, CA: Stanford University Press.

Kaplan, G., & Rogers, L. J. (2000). *The orangutans: Their evolution, behavior, and future.* Cambridge, MA: Perseus Publication.

Kaplan, G., & Rogers, L. J. (2002). Patterns of gazing in orangutans (*Pongo pygmaeus*). *International Journal of Primatology, 23*(3), 501–526.

Knott, C. D. (1999). Orangutan behavior. In P. Dolhinow & A. Fuentes (Eds.), *The nonhuman primates* (pp. 50–57). Mountain View: Mayfield Publishing.

Kummer, H. (1968). *Social organization of hamadryas baboons. A field study.* Basel: Karger.

Lethmate, J. (1977). Problem solving behavior of orangutans (*Pongo pygmaeus*). *Fortschritte der Verhaltensforschung, 10*, 1–69.

Lethmate, J. (1982). Tool-using skills of orangutans. *Journal of Human Evolution, 11,* 49–64.

Lethmate J., & Dücker, G. (1973). Experiments on self-recognition in a mirror in orangutans, chimpanzees, gibbons and several monkey species. *Zeitschrift für Tierpsychologie, 33,* 248–269.

Liebal, K., Call, J., & Tomasello, M. (2004). The use of gesture sequences in chimpanzees. *American Journal of Primatology, 64,* 377–396.

Liebal, K., Pika, S., & Tomasello, M. (2004). Social communication in siamangs (*Symphalangus syndactylus*): Use of gestures and facial expressions. *Primates, 45,* 41–57.

Liebal, K., Pika, S., & Tomasello, M. (2006). Gestural communication of orangutans (*Pongo pygmaeus*). *Gesture, 6,* 1–38.

MacKinnon, J. (1971). The orangutan in Sabah today: A study of a wild population in the Ulu Segama reserve. *Oryx, 11,* 141–191.

MacKinnon, J. R (1974). The behaviour and ecology of wild orangutans (*Pongo pygmaeus*). *Animal Behaviour, 22,* 3–74.

MacKinnon, J. R. (1989). Field studies of wild orangutans: Current state of knowledge. In P. K. Seth & S. Seth (Eds.), *Perspectives in primate biology* (pp. 173–186). New Delhi, India: Today and Tomorrow's Printers & Publishers.

Maestripieri, D. (1999). Primate social organization, gestural repertoire size, and communication dynamics: A comparative study of macaques. In B. J. King (Ed.), *The evolution of language: Assessing the evidence from nonhuman primates* (pp. 55–77). Santa Fe, NM: School of American Research.

Maple, T. L. (1980). *Orangutan behavior.* New York: Van Nostrand Reinhold Company.

Marler, P. (1965). Communication in monkeys and apes. In I. DeVore (Ed.), *Primate behavior: Field studies of monkeys and apes* (pp. 544–584). New York: Holt, Rinehart & Winston.

Miles, H. L. W. (1994). Me Chantek: The development of self-awareness in a signing orangutan. In S. T. Parker, R. W. Mitchell, & M. L. Boccia (Eds.), *Self-awareness in animals and humans: Developmental perspectives* (pp. 254–272). Cambridge, England: Cambridge University Press.

Mitani, J. C. (1984). *Experimental field studies of orangutan and gibbon vocalizations.* Unpublished doctoral dissertation, University of California, Davis.

Mitani, J. C. (1985). Mating behaviour of male orangutans in the Kutai Game Reserve, Indonesia. *Animal Behaviour, 33*(2), 392–402.

Parker, C. E. (1969). Responsiveness, manipulation, and implementation behavior in chimpanzees, gorillas, and orangutans. In C. R. Carpenter (Ed.), *Proceedings of the Second International Congress of Primatology: Vol. 1. Behavior,* (pp. 160–166). Basel: S. Karger.

Pika, S., Liebal, K., & Tomasello, M. (2003). Gestural communication in young gorillas (*Gorilla gorilla*): Gestural repertoire, learning, and use. *American Journal of Primatology, 60*(3), 95–111.

Pika, S., Liebal, K., Call, J., & Tomasello, M. (2005). Gestural communication in subadult bonobos (*Pan paniseus*): Repertoire and use. *American Journal of Primatology, 65*, 39–61.

Rao, M. & van Schaik, C. P. (1997). The behavioral ecology of Sumateran orangutans in logged and unlogged forest. *Tropical Biodiversity, 4*(2), 173–185.

Rijksen, H. D. (1978). *A field study on Sumatran orangutans (Pongo pygmaeus abelli Lesson 1827): Ecology, behaviour and conservation.* Wageningen, The Netherlands: H. Veenman & Zonen.

Rijksen, H., & Meijaard, E. (1999). *Our vanishing relative: The status of wild orangutans at the close of the twentieth century.* Dordrecht, The Netherlands: Kluwer.

Rodman, P. S. (1973). Population composition and adaptive organisation among orangutans of the Kutai Reserve. In R. P. Michael & J. H. Crook (Eds.), *Comparative ecology and behaviour of primates* (pp. 171–209). London: Academic Press.

Rodman, P. S. (1979). Individual activity patterns and the solitary nature of orangutans. In D. A. Hamburg & E. R. McCown (Eds.), *Perspectives on human evolution: Vol. 5. The great apes* (pp. 235–255). Menlo Park, CA: Benjamin/Cummings Publishing Company.

Rodman P. S. (1988). Diversity and consistency in ecology and behavior. In J. H. Schwartz (Ed.), *Orangutan biology* (pp. 31–51). New York: Oxford University Press.

Rodman, P. S., & Mitani, J. C. (1987). Orangutans: Sexual dimorphism in a solitary species. In B. Smuts, D. I. Cheney, R. Seyfarth, T. Struhsaker, & R. W. Wrangham (Eds.), *Primate societies* (pp. 146–154). Chicago: University of Chicago Press.

Rowe, N., Goodall, J., & Mittermeier, R. A. (1996). *The pictorial guide to the living primates.* East Hampton, New York: Pogonias Press.

Rumbaugh, D. M. (1970). Learning skills of anthropoids. In L. A. Rosenblum (Ed.), *Primate behavior: Developments in field and laboratory research* (pp. 1–70). New York: Academic Press.

Shepherd, W. T. (1923). Some observations and experiments of the intelligence of the chimpanzee and orang. *American Journal of Psychology, 34*, 590–591.

Singleton, I., & van Schaik, C. P. (2001). Orangutan home range size and its determinants in a Sumatran swamp forest. *International Journal of Primatology, 22*, 877–911.

Suarez, S. D., & Gallup, G. G., Jr. (1981). Self-recognition in chimpanzees and orangutans, but not gorillas. *Journal of Human Evolution, 10*, 175–188.

Suda, C., & Call, J. (2004). Piagetian liquid conservation in the great apes. *Journal of Comparative Psychology, 118*(3), 265–279.

Sugardjito, J. (1986). *Ecological constraints on the behavior of Sumatran orangutans in the Gunung Leuser National Park, Indonesia.* Unpublished doctoral dissertation. Utrecht University, The Netherlands.

Tanner, J. E., & Byrne R. W. (1996). Representation of action through iconic gesture in a captive lowland gorilla. *Current Anthropology, 37*(1), 162–173.

Tomasello, M., & Call, J. (1997). *Primate cognition.* New York: Oxford University Press.

Tomasello, M., Call, J., Nagell, K., Olguin, R., & Carpenter, M. (1994). The learning and the use of gestural signals by young chimpanzees: A trans-generational study. *Primates, 35*, 137–154.

Tomasello, M., Call, J., Warren, J., Frost, T., Carpenter, M., & Nagell, K. (1997). The ontogeny of chimpanzee gestural signals: A comparison across groups and generations. *Evolution of Communication, 1,* 223–253.

Tomasello, M., George, B. L., Kruger, A. C., Farrar, M. J., & Evans, A. (1985). The development of gestural communication in young chimpanzees. *Journal of Human Evolution, 14,* 175–186.

Tomasello, M., Gust, D., & Frost, G. T. (1989). A longitudinal investigation of gestural communication in young chimpanzees. *Primates, 30,* 35–50.

Tuttle, R. H. (1986). *Apes of the world: Their social behaviour, communication, mentality, and ecology.* Park Ridge, NJ: Noyes.

Tuttle, R. H. (1970). Postural, propulsive, and prehensile capabilities in the cheiridia of chimpanzees and other great apes. In G. H. Bourne (Ed.), *The Chimpanzee: Vol. 2. Physiology, behavior, serology, and diseases of chimpanzees* (pp. 167–253). Baltimore, MD: University Park Press.

van Hooff, J. A. R. A. M. (1971). *Aspects of the social behaviour and communication in human and higher non-human primates.* Unpublished doctoral dissertation, Bronder-Offset, Rotterdam.

van Lawick-Goodall, J. (1968). The behaviour of free-living chimpanzees in the Gombe Stream Reserve. *Animal Behaviour Monographs, 1,* 165–311.

van Schaik, C. P. (1996). Toward an understanding of the orangutan's social system. In W. C. McGrew, L. F. Marchant, & T. Nishida (Eds.), *Great apes societies* (pp. 3–15). Cambridge, England: Cambridge University Press.

van Schaik, C. P. (1999). The socioecology of fission-fusion sociality in orangutans. *Primates, 40*(1), 69–86.

van Schaik, C. P., Fox, E. A. & Fechtman, L. T. (2003). Individual variation in the rate of use of tree-hole tools among wild orangutans: Implications for hominin evolution. *Journal of Human Evolution, 44*(1), 11–23.

van Schaik, C. P., Fox, E. A., & Sitompul, A. F. (1996). Manufacture and use of tools in wild Sumatran orangutans: Implications for human evolution. *Naturwissenschaften, 83*(4), 186–188.

van Schaik, C. P., & Knott, C. D. (2001). Geographic variation in tool use on Neesia fruits in orangutans. *American Journal of Physical Anthropology, 114*(4), 331–342.

Whiten, A., & Byrne, R. W. (Eds.). (1997). *Machiavellian intelligence II: Extensions and evaluations.* Cambridge, England: Cambridge University Press.

Wich, S., Buij, R., & van Schaik, C. P. (2004). Determinants of orangutan density in the dryland forests of the Leuser Ecosystem. *Primates, 45,* 177–182.

Wich, S., Singleton, I., Utami-Atmoko, S. S., Geurts, M. L., Rijksen, H. D., & van Schaik, C. P. (2003). The status of the Sumatran orangutan *Pongo abelii*: An update. *Oryx, 1,* 49–54.

Wright, R. V. S. (1972). Imitative learning of a flaked stone technology: The case of an orangutan. *Mankind, 8,* 296–306.

Yerkes, R. M. (1916). *The mental life of monkeys and apes.* Delmar, NY: Scholars' Facsimiles & Reprints.

Yerkes, R. M., & Yerkes, A. W. (1970). *The great apes: A study of anthropoid life* (Reprint of 1929). New York: Johnson.

CHAPTER 5

Gestures in Subadult Gorillas (Gorilla gorilla)

Simone Pika
University of St. Andrews

Figure 5.1. Gorillas.

1. INTRODUCTION TO THE SPECIES

1.1. Taxonomy

Gorillas (genus *Gorilla*) are as genetically distant from chimpanzees (genus *Pan*) as they are from humans (genus *Homo*) (Kaessmann, Wiebe, Weiss, & Pääbo, 2001). Following the taxonomy of Groves (2001), gorillas are currently classified as two species: western and eastern gorillas (*Gorilla gorilla* and *Gorilla beringei*, respectively) and five subspecies: the western lowland gorillas (*Gorilla gorilla gorilla*) in West Africa, the Cross River gorillas (*Gorilla gorilla diehli*) at the Nigerian/Cameroonian border, the Virunga gorillas (*Gorilla beringei beringei*) at the Virunga volcanoes, the Bwindi gorillas (no scientific name) in Uganda, and the Grauer's gorillas or eastern lowland gorillas (*Gorilla beringei graueri*) in the eastern Democratic Republic of Congo.

1.2. Morphology

Gorillas are the largest and the most sexually dimorphic[1] of all extant primate species. Adult male gorillas weigh on average 140 kg (western lowland gorillas) to 175 kg (eastern lowland gorillas) and have an average body length ranging from 170 cm (western lowland gorillas) to 175 cm (eastern lowland gorillas; Gregory, 1950). Adult females weigh on average 75 kg (western lowland gorillas) to 85 kg (Virunga gorillas; Estes, 1992) and have an average body length of 150 cm (Harcourt, 1985). Adult males have an enlarged sagittal crest and develop a silvery color on the back that extends with age to the rump and thighs (Harcourt, 1985). Like all great apes, gorillas have a laryngeal sac (Gregory, 1950), which functions as a resonance organ during chest beating (Meder, 1993).

The color of the pelage varies across subspecies, from brownish-gray with reddish highlights in western gorillas to black in eastern gorillas (Harcourt, 1985). Virunga and Bwindi gorillas have longer hair than the other subspecies. Each gorilla has a unique nose pattern, as with the human fingerprint.

1.3. Distribution and Ecology

Gorillas occur in two widely separated regions in Central Africa—one in the west and one in the east—and they are found in a variety of forest habitats including primary lowland rainforest, secondary forest, swamp forest, marshy clearings (bays), and even montane forest.

The Cross River gorillas (circa 250 individuals), the Bwindi gorillas (circa 300 individuals), and the Virunga gorillas (circa 360 individuals) are the rarest and most endangered subspecies (Butynski, 2001). More numerous but less known are the eastern lowland gorillas, which make up 8–9% of the total gorilla population (circa 3,000 individuals) and the western lowland gorillas, which constitute the most common gorilla subspecies (circa 100,000 individuals; Butynski, 2001).

The Virunga gorillas represent the most studied gorilla population, due to the landmark studies of George Schaller (1965, 1963, 1964a), Dian Fossey (1983), and other researchers at the Karisoke Research Center in Rwanda (e.g., Harcourt, 1979b; Robbins, 2001; Watts, 1996). Studies of other gorilla populations (e.g., Casimir, 1975; Doran & McNeilage, 1998; Tutin, 1996; Yamagiwa, 1983) began later and have not achieved the same level of behavioral detail because habituation has proven difficult (Taylor & Goldsmith, 2003). However, comparisons of gorilla ecology are becoming increasingly possible across the geographical range of the genus (Tutin, 2003).

Gorillas live primarily on the ground, spend 5–20% of the day in trees (Fossey & Harcourt, 1977; Schaller, 1963; Watts, 1996), and sleep mainly in ground nests (Fruth & Hohmann, 1996; Yamagiwa & Kahekwa, 2001). The average day range of western lowland gorillas (200–5,500 m) is 2–3 times greater than that of eastern gorillas (500–1,100 m; for an overview, see Doran & McNeilage, 2001). In addition, the annual home range size of western lowland gorillas (7–23 km; Doran & McNeilage, 2001) is at least double that reported for mountain gorillas (Watts, 1996). These home ranges frequently overlap with those of other groups (Tutin, 1996; Watts, 1998a). Traditionally, gorillas have been characterized as folivores[2]—based on long-term studies of the Virunga gorillas whose diet is herbivorous[3]—and characterized by little diversity or seasonal variation as well as low feeding competition (Fossey & Harcourt, 1977; Schaller, 1963; Watts, 1996; 1998b). Recent research, however, has emphasized the importance of fruit consumption and dietary flexibility of gorillas at most study sites in lower altitudes (Doran et al., 2002; Goldsmith, 2003; Nishihara, 1995; Remis, 1997; Rogers, Williamson, Tutin, & Fernandez, 1990; Tutin, Fernandez, Rogers, Williamson, & McGrew, 1991). Their fruit consumption varies seasonally, and there is increased arboreal behavior when fruit is abundant (Remis, 1997). When fruit is scarce, however, gorillas tend to increase both the folivorous portion of their diet (Remis, 2003; Tutin & Fernandez, 1993; Yamagiwa et al., 2003), and their daily path length (Doran & McNeilage, 2001; Goldsmith, 1999; Remis, 1997; Tutin, 1996; Yamagiwa, Basabose, Kaleme, & Yumoto,

2003). The most frugivorous[4] subspecies is the western lowland gorilla, which lives in the botanically diverse lowland tropical forests of the Congo basin and eats 80–120 different species of fruit (Tutin, 2003). This subspecies spans the frugivore–folivore divide between the Virunga gorillas and the bonobos (*Pan paniscus;* Goldsmith, 2003).

1.4. Social Structure and Behavior

The classic description of a gorilla group is that of one silverback with several females and their offspring, all of which stay together while moving and resting (Schaller, 1963). This description still holds for the western gorillas (Bradley, Doran-Sheehy, Lukas, Boesch, & Vigilant, 2004; Parnell, 2002). The Virunga gorillas, however, live in groups consisting of one (~60%) or several adult male silverbacks (~40%) that coexist for many years and are often related (Robbins, 1995, 2001). The formation of groups seems to be in part due to two factors; (a) females selecting males who can provide protection against infanticide, and (b) a strategy of long-term mate guarding by males (Harcourt, 1981; Watts, 1996). The social system is age graded, "nonfemale-bonded" (Harcourt, 1979a; Wrangham, 1980), with the strongest long-term relationships being formed between adult males and females; relationships between females are weak (Harcourt, 1979b; 1979c). Furthermore, the social system has been described by female transfer and male dispersal, although individuals of both sexes have been observed to stay in their natal groups (Harcourt, Stewart, & Fossey, 1976; Watts, 1996).

Although comparable detailed data on social behavior and life history are still lacking for western gorillas, researchers suggest that their grouping patterns and social behavior are similar to that found in the Virunga gorillas (i.e., groups are relatively cohesive and stable in size; Tutin, 1996). Others have proposed that lowland gorillas' social units are constrained by within-group feeding competition and are therefore less cohesive (i.e., they may form temporary subgroups on occasion; Goldsmith, 1996; Kuroda, 1996; Mitani, Moutsambote, & Oko, 1992). Interestingly, interactions between social groups seem to occur more frequently in western gorillas than in the Virunga gorillas, and these interactions are often (Doran, Greer, Mongo, & Schwindt, 2004; Tutin, 1996), although not always, nonaggressive (Cipoletta, 2003; Tutin, 1996). An investigation of the genetic relationships among western gorilla males at Mondika Research Center in the Central African Republic and Republic of Congo detected that group-leading silverbacks were usually related to one or more neighboring males (Bradley et al., 2004). Bradley and colleagues (2004) therefore suggested the existence of an unrecognized "dispersed male network" social structure in western gorillas, which could provide a basis for extra-group, kin-biased behaviors, and that might explain the peaceful intergroup encounters that have been observed in this species.

1.5. Cognition

To assess the cognitive skills of primates, studies and experiments have focused on physical and social cognition. Investigations of physical cognition have centered on four major domains; object permanence, object manipulation, tool use, and categorization (Call & Tomasello, 1996).

A number of scientists, however, have argued that the cognitive capacities of primates are most naturally deployed when solving social problems, not physical ones (Humphrey, 1976; Jolly, 1966). Investigations of primates' social cognition has therefore centered on five major domains; social attention, intentional communication, social learning, cooperation, and theory of mind (Call & Tomasello, 1996). In the following section, I review the available data on physical and social cognition in gorillas.

1.5.1. Physical Cognition

Gorillas show skills of cognitive mapping (MacDonald, 1994) and achieve the highest levels of sensorimotor intelligence (Stages 4, 5, and 6 based on Piaget's model of sensorimotor intelligence, 1954)[5] in problem solving, exploration, and object permanence tasks (e.g., Gomez, 1999; Natale, Antinucci, Spinozzi, & Poti, 1986; Redshaw, 1978).

Object manipulation, but especially tool use, often involves complex cognitive processes; it implies an understanding of the manipulated object (tool) in relation to another object (goal; (Tomasello & Call, 1997). Object manipulation has been studied extensively in gorillas in their natural environment (Byrne, 1999; Byrne & Byrne, 1993). Very well known are, for instance, the complex food processing techniques used by Virunga gorillas to disarm leaves of food plants that are protected by various kinds of stingers, tiny hooks, or spines (Byrne & Byrne, 1993). In addition, Pika and Tomasello (2001) reported a food processing technique in captive gorillas that is similar in function to the Japanese macaques' "wheat placer mining behavior" (Kawai, 1965). Namely, the technique involves blowing air to separate grain from chaff. A special category of object manipulation is symbolic or pretend play, which is difficult to identify unequivocally (Call & Tomasello, 1996). An anecdotal example was for instance described by Patterson and Linden

(1981): The human raised gorilla Koko pretended to be an elephant by using a rubber tube as a substitute for the trunk.

Surprisingly, until now, only captive gorillas have been observed to use or create tools (Boysen, Kuhlmeier, Halliday, & Halliday, 1999; Fontaine, Moisson, & Wickings, 1995; Gomez, 1990; Nakamichi, 1999; Parker, Kerr, Markowitz, & Gould, 1999). A wide variety of tool use behaviors have been reported, including *probing, scratching,* or *rubbing with an object, raking, levering, striking,* or *breaking with an object, aimed throwing,* using a ladder or a stool, using an object as a bridge, *digging,* using a container for water, using a stick as a fork to hold food, and using a stick to prop up a sore limb. Gorillas have also been observed modifying tools, for example adjusting sticks to retrieve food from a tray with holes in it (Nakamichi, 1999; Sue Taylor Parker et al., 1999).

1.5.2. Social Cognition

Investigations of social cognitive skills shed light on the abilities of species to understand the behavior of their conspecifics (Tomasello & Call, 1997). Gorillas are able to recognize individual conspecifics, form coalitions and alliances (for an overview see, Byrne, 1996; Harcourt & De Waal, 1992; Tomasello & Call, 1997), and intervene in conflicts (Sicotte, 1995; Watts, 1997). In addition, Mitchell (1999) reported four types of deceit in two adult males that were trying to get access to an infant that was being protected by its mother (for a definition of deceit see Whiten & Byrne, 1988). The males engaged in two forms of hiding; (a) *hiding from view* and (b) *inhibiting attention,* as well as two forms of deception: (c) *creating a neutral image,* and (d) *manipulating a target using a social tool.* Behaviors for category (a) *hiding from view* were, for instance, moving closer to the infant, touching the infant while parallel screening these from the view of the gorilla mother. In (b) *inhibiting attention,* the males avoided looking (e.g., watching peripherally, acting 'disinterested') at the infant when such looking would lead the mother's noticing it. Evidence for category (c) *present neutral image* was provided by a single observation in which one male acted as if foraging to get closer to the infant. Behaviors for category (d) *manipulating a target using a social tool* were, for instance, instances of teasing the gorilla mother to get in contact with the infant (see also, Patterson & Cohn, 1994). Several observations of deceptive communication were also reported by Tanner and Byrne (1993): A female gorilla at the San Francisco Zoo, deliberately hid her 'play face' by placing one hand over her mouth, presumably to conceal her playful intentions.

All social interactions, therefore, depend on the ability to learn about other group members and their behavior and to acquire social and communicative strategies to achieve desired goals.

A final possible source of social comprehension is social learning. Researchers discriminate four different types of social learning: mimicking (reproduction of sensorimotor acts), local enhancement (which involves an animal approaching or contacting an object or location more often due to common attraction to stimuli), emulation (reproduction of changes of state in the environment that others have produced), and imitative learning (attempting to reproduce or match the intentional strategies of others; Tomasello & Call, 1997). These four types of learning require different levels and different kinds of social cognition, with imitation representing the most complex type. The only example of imitation in a wild gorilla population might be the complex food processing skills of the Virunga gorillas (Byrne & Byrne, 1993). These manipulations consisted of complex sequences of behaviors that were reliably used with different plants by all noninfant individuals of the observed group (Byrne & Byrne, 1993). The researchers suggested that these skills are acquired by individual learning, whereas the logical organization of the strategy is copied from others using so called "program-level" imitation (for an alternative explanation, see Tomasello, 1999).

In an experimental setting, Stoinski and colleagues (2001) exposed six gorillas to an artificial fruit task, which represents a functional analogue of food-processing problems encountered in the wild. The task required gorillas to remove a series of defenses in order to reach an edible interior. Before handling the artificial fruit themselves, subjects watched a human model removing a series of three defenses using one of two alternative techniques. The gorillas used the observed technique significantly more often than the alternative one. Stoinski and colleagues (2001) interpreted these results as evidence for imitation in gorillas (for an alternative explanation, see Heyes, 1998; Tomasello, 1996). In addition, Patterson (1979) provided anecdotal evidence that imitation was common in a human-raised gorilla that was trained to use a human sign language (American Sign Language or ASL).

Furthermore, gorillas are able to use experimenter-given manual and facial cues in an object-choice task to obtain a food reward (Peignot & Anderson, 1999). Interestingly, performance levels were high when the experimenter tapped on or pointed to an object or gazed with the eyes and head oriented toward the correct object. However, when the only cue was the experimenter's eye orientation, the gorillas did not successfully complete the task (Peignot & Anderson, 1999).

Gorillas are able to follow the gaze of humans to external phenomena (Bräuer, Call, & Tomasello, 2005), use a variety of behavioral and attentional strategies to intentionally communicate a desired goal, and *use* other individuals as causal agents (Gomez, 1990, 1991). These social skills imply that gorillas may have some understanding of voluntary agency in other individuals, and they may know that others need to be visually oriented toward them in order to respond to their behavior. Interestingly, in a recent experimental study on all four great ape species (Liebal, Pika, Call, & Tomasello, 2004), gorillas used visual gestures preferentially to beg for food when they were facing a human experimenter as opposed to auditory and tactile gestures. In the experimental condition, however, in which the experimenter moved to an alternative location, left the food bowl in place (behind her) and did not face the gorillas anymore; they stayed with the food bowl. The authors suggested that these findings might indicate a special sensitivity in the genus *Pan* for directing visual signals to a human with the appropriate body orientation. They furthermore claimed that this study may have uncovered a possible difference in social cognition among the great apes (Liebal et al., 2004).

In addition, Gallup's (1970) experiment on mirror self-recognition has provided puzzling results. In this task, animals were (a) exposed to a mirror or, (b) first anesthetized and marked with bright color on visually inaccessible parts of the body (e.g., eyebrows, ears). Subsequently, the behavior of the animals toward a mirror was observed. Higher instances of touching inaccessible parts of the body in front of the mirror (Condition a and b) or marked areas (Condition b), as well as self- inspection behaviors compared to a control situation (without a mirror or/and marked body parts) were interpreted as awareness of one's own mental state and the implication of awareness of the mental states of others. Mirror self-recognition has therefore been viewed as a dimension of social cognition. Interestingly, contrary to all other great ape species, which have demonstrated fairly conclusive responses toward mirrors (for an overview, see Tomasello & Call, 1997), only two gorillas (Patterson & Cohn, 1994; Swartz & Evans, 1994) have passed the mirror-mark task. The human-raised and language-trained gorilla Koko, for instance, passed a mark test performed by stealth rather than anesthetic, and she explored parts of her body in a mirror that she could normally not see (Patterson & Tanner, 1988). Because Heyes (1994) criticized that the significant increase in face touching by the tested individuals may reflect only an artifact of recovery from anesthesia, the behavior of Koko, who was not anesthetized, provides the best evidence for mirror self-recognition in any great ape. However, whether this ability can be interpreted as the possession of a *self-concept* or *self-awareness* (e.g., Parker, Mitchell, & Boccia, 1994), or is instead just a form of body perception, remains an open question (Heyes, 1994; Tomasello & Call, 1997).

1.6. Communication: State of the Art

The majority of studies on gorilla communication have focused on vocalizations (Fossey, 1972; Harcourt & Stewart, 1986, 1994, 1996, 2001; Schaller, 1963). The vocal repertoire of gorillas consists of over a dozen different vocalizations, and one of the most frequent social behaviors is a vocalization, their so-called *close calling* (Harcourt & Stewart, 2001). Although the meaning and function of gorillas' loud long calls, alarm calls, antipredator calls, and threat calls seems to be understood (Fossey, 1972), the meaning and function of gorillas' close calls still remains a mystery (Harcourt & Stewart, 2001). Despite the fact that these calls are correlated with the rank of an individual (dominant individuals give more syllabled calls, especially *double grunts*; subordinate individuals give more nonsyllabled calls such as *grumbles* and *hums*), no behavioral reaction other than an answering call is observable (Fossey, 1972; Harcourt, Stewart, & Hauser, 1993). Harcourt and Stewart (2001) therefore suggest that vocal signaling and exchange might function to facilitate social interactions and relationships, and can therefore be thought of as servicing relationships. The servicing can be done both at a distance and while individuals are involved in other behaviors, for example, feeding and grooming (Dunbar, 1996).

Unlike vocalizations, the gestural communication of gorillas, especially in wild populations, is less well understood. First descriptions of tactile as well as auditory-visual gestures come from Schaller (1963, 1964b) and Fossey (1983) but are primarily anecdotal. Schaller, for instance, described the species-typical display of wild mountain gorillas and mentioned gestures such as *chest beat*, and *stiff stance*. Fossey (1983) reported *chest patting, clap*, and also described some idiosyncratic gestures. For western lowland gorillas, Parnell and Buchanan-Smith (2001) reported a specific gesture called the *splash display* that is used to intimidate other silverbacks, and Fay (1989) observed *hand-clapping* behavior in females. Ogden and Schildkraut (1991) mention in their compilation of gorilla ethograms several auditory gestures such as *backhand pound, bodybeat, chestbeat, chestpat, clap, knock*, and *slap surface*; tactile gestures such as *brush, nudge, poke, push, tag*, and *touch with hand*; and visual gestures such as *armcross, arm shake, armswing, extended palm, foot back, head shake, head turn, head twirl*, and *pat*.

Tanner and Byrne's study (Tanner, 1998; Tanner & Byrne, 1996, 1999), however, is the only study that focuses in detail on limb and head gestures in gorillas. They investigated the gestural behavior of a captive gorilla group at the San Francisco Zoo and observed about 30 different gestures. These gestures appeared to fall into three groups depending on variation in the degree of visual attention toward the recipient, ranging from 39–100%): (1) a high visual attention group of silent gestures, (2) a medium visual attention group of auditory gestures, and (3) a low visual attention group of tactile-close gestures. Each class of gestures had consistent but different communicative effects: Tactile-close gestures usually resulted in movements of the receiver's body in the direction indicated by the actor; silent visually received gestures lead to a high rate of bodily contact in play activity; and auditory gestures resulted in redirection of the attention or alteration of the locomotion of the recipient. The majority of these gestures were imperative, which means that they were used to get another individual to help in attaining a goal (cf., Bates, 1976). Declarative gestures, on the other hand, are used to draw another's attention to an object or entity merely for the sake of sharing attention (e.g., holding up an object and showing it, Bates, 1976). However, referential gestures such as imperative pointing or declarative gestures have only been described for a human-raised gorilla (Patterson, 1978).

Interestingly, Tanner and Byrne (1996) reported a number of cases that they consider to be iconic uses of gestures (i.e., depict motion in space). An adult gorilla male, for instance, seemed to signal to a female playmate with his hand, arm, or head, the direction in which he wanted her to move or the action he wanted her to perform.

The goal of the present study was to systematically compare the gestural communication of subadult gorillas (*Gorilla gorilla*) living in two different groups. We had three major goals: First, we compiled the gestural repertoire of gorillas to enhance the understanding of gestural communication in gorillas and to enable a comparison with the findings of Tanner and Byrne (Tanner, 1998; Tanner & Byrne, 1999).

Second, we were interested in how gorillas acquire their gestures; therefore, our data analysis centered on individual and group variability to distinguish between underlying social and individual learning processes.

Third, we examined how gorillas use their gestures by focusing on (a) adjustment to audience effects, (b) means–ends dissociation, and (c) the responses of recipients toward gestures.

Our study is based on the following definition: A gesture is an expressive movement of limbs or head and body postures that appear to transfer a communicative message, such as a request and/or a desired action/event (e.g., play, nurse, or ride), is directed to a recipient, and is accompanied by the following criteria; gazing at the recipient and/or waiting after the signal has been produced (e.g., Bruner, 1981; Tomasello, Gust, & Frost, 1989). Therefore, gestures that appear to have components of ritualized morphology (e.g., *stiff stance*) are included in this definition only if they meet the criteria outlined earlier.

2. METHODS

2.1. Individuals

We observed 13 subadult gorillas (see Table 5.1), 1–6 years old, from two family groups in two different European zoos (Dierenpark Apenheul, Netherlands; Howletts Wild Animal Park, United Kingdom). The gorilla group from Apenheul consisted of 1 silverback [age classes similar to those established by Fossey, (1974)], 1 blackback, 6 adult females, 2 nulliparous females, 1 adolescent, 5 infants (0–3½ years), and 2 juvenile gorillas (3½–6 years). The group at Howletts had 1 silverback, 5 adult females, 4 infants, and 2 juvenile gorillas.

TABLE 5.1
Gestural Inventory

Current Study	(Tanner, 1998; Tanner & Byrne, 1999)	Other Reports
Auditory gestures		
Body beat	Body beat	Body beat (3)
Body slap		Chest pat (1)
Chest beat	Chest beat, chest knock	Chest beat (3; 4)
Clap	Clap	Clap (2; 4; 5)
Slap ground	Backhand pound, knock, slap surface	Backhand pound (1; 3), knock (1), slap surface (1), slap (4)
Stomp		
		Splash display
Tactile gestures		
Embrace		
Grab		
Grab-push-pull		
Hand on	Hands on shoulders	
Long touch		
	Mouth/lips	
Pull	Tactile-close	
Punch	Tap other	
Prod		Poke, tagging (1)
Push	Tactile-close	Push (1; 3)
Slap	Tactile-close	
Touch	Pat off, tactile-close	Brush, nudge, touch with hand (1; 3)

(continued)

	TABLE 5.1 (continued)	
Current Study	*(Tanner, 1998; Tanner & Byrne, 1999)*	*Other Reports*
Visual gestures		
	Arm cross	*Arm cross* (1)
Arm shake	*Arm shake, circle hands, go*	*Arm shake* (1)
	Arm swing under	
	Beat sides of head	*Beat sides of head* (2)
Bow	*Head nod, head shake, head turn, head twirl*	*Head shake* (1), *head turn* (1; 3) *Head twirl* (1)
Chuck-up	*Chest pat*	*Chest pat* (1)
	Down	
	Extended palm	*Extended palm* (1)
	Face wipe	
	Finger down lips	
Formal bite	*Foot back*	*Foot back* (1)
Gallop	*Bite*	*Bite* (2)
	Hands behind back	
	Hands between legs	
Ice skating	*Hide play face*	
Jump		
Move		
Object shake		
Pee		
Reach	*Away, up*	*Arm swing, hitting out* (1), *up* (3)
Shake		
Somersault		
Stiff stance		
Straw wave		
	Teeth	
Throw		
	Wrist glance	

Note: Ogden and Schildkraut (1991), 2: Fossey (1983), 3: Schaller (1963), 4: Redshaw and Locke (1976), 5: Parnell and Buchanan-Smith (2001), 6: Fay (1989).

2.2. Data Collection

We used focal animal sampling (Altmann, 1974) to establish a complete inventory of gestures for each of the 13 subjects (20h/individual). Following that, we videotaped the communicative behavior using a digital camera (behavior sampling; 15h/subadult gorilla). This technique resulted in a total of 455 h of observation (35h/individual), and 75 h of videotape. We analyzed 2,556 different gestures.

2.3. Description of the Gestural Inventory

2.3.1. *Visual Gestures*

- *Arm shake*–Shake arms and hands loosely with a rotational motion; may vary from prolonged motion of entire upper body to minimal motion of hand(s) shaken from wrists.
- *Bow*–Raise and lower the torso by alternately stretching and flexing its limbs; also includes gestures like *head nod, head shake,* or *head turn*.
- *Chuck up*–Fling the arms upward.
- *Formal bite*–Intention to bite on hands, feet, or neck (open mouth and teeth are shown).
- *Gallop*–Run in an exaggerated manner toward or close to another animal.
- *Ice skating*–Make a pirouette with hands on the ground or in the air.
- *Jump*–Spring from or over an object close to another animal or onto another animal.
- *Move*–Displace an object in front of another animal, for instance a branch, straw, and so forth, mainly on the ground.
- *Object shake*–Jiggle an object.
- *Peer*–Sit or stand very close to another animal and bring the face very close to the partner's face (who is usually chewing).
- *Reach*–Stretch out a limb toward another animal, palm facing sideways or downward.
- *Shake*–Hang upside down from a branch or rope and move legs/arms from side to side in front of another animal.
- *Somersault*–Make a flip.
- *Stiff stance*–Stand with the legs held rigidly and the body stiff and erect; tight lipped face often accompanies.
- *Straw wave*–Throw straw in the air or on the body or on another animal.
- *Throw*–Toss an object toward or close to another animal.

2.3.2. *Tactile Gestures*

- *Embrace*–Wrap the arm(s) and/or leg(s) around the body of another animal.
- *Grab*–Grasp another animal with the whole hand; fingers are bent.
- *Grab-push-pull*–Grasp another animal and directly pull it or push it.

- *Hand on*–Place the palm(s) of the hand(s) on the head of another animal for more than 2 sec.
- *Long touch*–Gently contact some other animal's body part with flat hand(s) for more than 5 sec.
- *Pull*–Grasp another animal and forcefully bring it closer.
- *Punch*–Perform a brief forward or downward thrust on or against another animal with the fist, knuckles, or fingers.
- *Prod*–Tap lightly and repetitively on a body part of another animal with the palm(s) or the knuckle(s).
- *Push*–Use the arms to displace another animal away.
- *Slap*–Hit another animal with the palm of the hand.
- *Touch*–Gentle and short (< 5 sec) contact with flat hands, body part, or feet.

2.3.3. Auditory Gestures

- *Body beat*–Slap repetitively on some of its own body parts except the chest with knuckle(s) or palm(s) of hand(s).
- *Body slap*–Slap once on some of its own body parts except the chest with knuckle(s) or palm(s) of hand(s).
- *Chest beat*–Slap repetitively on its own chest with alternating open hand(s) or knuckle(s).
- *Clap*–Strike an open hand against the other in front of the body.
- *Slap ground*–Hit the ground, wall, or some object with the palm(s) of the hand(s) or the fist.
- *Stomp*–Bring the sole or heel of the foot suddenly and forcibly against the ground or an object, or walk in a pounding manner, either in a bipedal or quadrupedal stance.

3. GESTURAL REPERTOIRE

3.1. Overview

We observed 33 different distinct gestures that belong to three signal categories (see Table 5.1); 6 auditory (18%), 11 tactile (33%,) and 16 visual gestures (49%). We did not observe any iconic uses of gestures. In Table 5.1, we compiled a gestural inventory of gorillas based on the results of the present study and also on descriptions of gestures or similar behaviors from other publications of wild and captive groups.

3.2. Context

The gestures occurred mainly in the play (40%) context, but also in the food (15%), ride (10%), nurse (10%), travel (10%), affiliative (10%), and agonistic (5%) contexts.

3.3. Variability

3.3.1. Individual Differences

We observed eight gestures that were performed by all individuals; 9 were used by more than 75% of all individuals, 6 by 50–75%, and 10 by less than 50% of the individuals (see Table 5.2).

3.3.2. Age Differences

In a cluster analysis (for a detailed description of the analysis see, Pika, Liebal, & Tomasello, 2003) we investigated whether the variety of gestures increased with age or if we could detect age-related changes in gesture variety. This analysis did not reveal any evidence that age classes clustered according to similarities in the performance of gestures. Figure 5.2 displays the mean number of gestures according to three age classes. We found an increase of number of gestures at the age of 3–4 from 18.5 (± 5.8) to 24 (± 3) gestures, whereas the number of gestures decreased at the age of 5–6 to 20.6 (± 4.2) gestures.

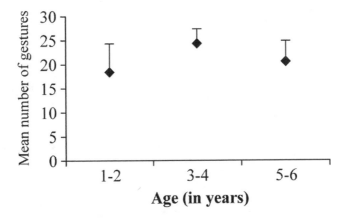

Figure 5.2.   Mean number of gestures as a function of age class: 1–2 years, 3–4 years 5–6 years. Error bars indicate the standard deviation.

TABLE 5.2
Individual Differences in Gestures Used: Names of Individuals,
Age (years and months), Sex (M=male, F=female), and Gestures Used

	Uzuri 6.2, M	Kumbo 5.4, M	Kihi 5.4, M	Bibi 3.7, F	M'Bewe 3.3, M	Komu 3.3, M	Kisiwa 2.10, F	Kidjoum 2.7, M	Kidogo 2.5, M	Kwimba 1.9, F	M'Kono 1.8, M	M'Tongue 1.7, M	Kdiki 1.3, F
Arm shake (39%, N: 5)					x	x			x		x	x	
Peer (100%, N: 13)	x	x	x	x	x	x	x	x	x	x	x	x	x
Bite intention (85%, N: 11)		x	x	x	x	x		x	x	x	x	x	x
Bodybeat (77%, N: 10)	x	x	x			x	x	x	x	x		x	x
Bodyslap (23%, N: 3)	x		x									x	
Bow (15%, N: 2)					x				x				
Chest beat (100%, N: 13)	x	x	x	x	x	x	x	x	x	x	x	x	x
Chuck up (23%, N: 3)					x	x	x						
Clap (62%, N: 8)		x	x	x			x	x	x	x		x	
Embrace (77%, N: 10)		x		x	x	x	x	x	x	x		x	x
Gallop (77%, N: 10)	x	x	x		x	x	x	x	x	x		x	
Grab (100%, N: 13)	x	x	x	x	x	x	x	x	x	x	x	x	x
Grab-pull-push (92%, N: 12)	x	x	x	x	x	x	x	x	x	x	x	x	
Hand on (54%, N: 7)	x	x			x	x	x	x	x				
Iceskating (77%, N: 10)		x	x		x	x	x	x	x	x	x	x	
Jump (77%, N: 10)		x	x	x	x	x	x	x	x	x		x	
Long touch (39%, N: 5)		x			x	x			x	x			
Move (62%, N: 8)		x	x		x	x	x	x	x			x	
Object shake (23%, N: 3)					x		x		x				
Prod (15%, N: 2)					x	x							
Pull (54%, N: 7)					x	x	x	x	x	x		x	
Punch (100%, N: 13)	x	x	x	x	x	x	x	x	x	x	x	x	x
Push (92%, N: 12)	x	x	x	x	x	x	x	x	x	x		x	x
Reach arm (100%, N: 13)	x	x	x	x	x	x	x	x	x	x	x	x	x
Shake (39%, N: 5)							x	x	x	x		x	
Slap (100%, N: 13)	x	x	x	x	x	x	x	x	x	x	x	x	x
Slap ground (100%, N: 13)	x	x	x	x	x	x	x	x	x	x	x	x	x
Somersault (62%, N: 8)		x	x	x		x	x	x	x	x			
Stiff stance (15%, N: 2)		x	x										
Stomp (69%, N: 9)	x	x	x	x		x	x	x	x	x			
Straw-wave (46%, N: 6)		x	x			x				x	x		x
Throw (77%, N: 10)	x	x	x			x	x	x	x	x	x	x	
Touch (100%, N: 13)	x	x	x	x	x	x	x	x	x	x	x	x	x
Total	16	24	22	23	19	27	25	25	27	24	14	23	13

3.3.3. Group Differences

The analysis (for a detailed description of the analysis see, Pika et al., 2003) of the degree of concordance in the performance of gestures between and within the two groups (Cohen's kappa statistics) showed an "excellent" strength of agreement (Altmann, 1991): The within-group kappas ($M = 0.73$ for Apenheul group, $M = 0.85$ for the Howletts group) were similar to the between-group kappas ($M = 0.72$). Although the within-group kappa was slightly higher than the between-group kappa, an analysis of the individual kappas of average concordance with group members and with members of the other group showed no significant difference (Wilcoxon test, $Z = -2.27$, $p = .23$, $N = 12$).

We observed three idiosyncratic gestures used to solicit play, performed by three different individuals in the Apenheul group: *object drum* (an animal drums repetitively on an object with alternating hands), *object on somebody* (an animal puts an object on another individual), and *break wood* (an animal breaks wood into pieces in an exaggerated movement). On average, 92.5% of the gestures observed occurred in the play context. In most cases, they received a response from the recipient in the form of an action (46.6%) such as play, or in the form of a responding gesture (20%).

We found group differences in the performance of two distinct gestures. The gesture *arm shake* and *chuck up* were specific to gorillas in the Apenheul group. *Arm shake* was performed by six of seven and *chuck up* by three of seven individuals.

3.4. Flexibility

3.4.1. Combinations

We did not analyze gesture combinations (however see, Tanner, 2004).

3.4.2. Audience Effects

To clarify whether gorillas adjust their use of gestures to the attentional state of the recipient, we analyzed the orientation of the sender toward the recipient. We detected a significant difference between the use of tactile and visual gestures (Wilcoxon-test; $Z = -2.22$, $p = .026$, $N = 13$). All gorillas adjusted their use of gestures to the attentional state of the recipient by using visual gestures mainly when the recipient was looking (89%). Tactile gestures however, were only used in 66% of the cases when the recipient was looking toward the sender (see Fig. 5.3). There were no significant differences between the use of auditory versus visual gestures and between auditory versus tactile gestures.

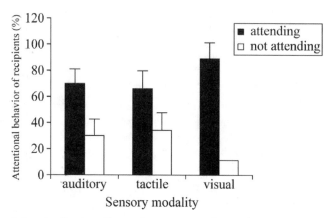

Figure 5.3. Audience effects: Percentage of visual and tactile gestures used toward an attending and nonattending recipient, error bars indicate the *SD*.

3.4.3. Means–Ends Dissociation

On average, each individual used 3.8 (± 1) gestures for more than one functional category, and an average of 3.3 (± 2.6) different gestures were used for the same end. With one exception, all of the animals used several of their signals for multiple ends and also used multiple signals for the same end. Only M'Bewe did not utilize any gesture for more than one functional category, although he did use multiple signals to request play from other conspecifics (see Table 5.3). The gestures *arm shake, body beat, body slap, bow, chuck up, prod, shake,* and *straw wave* were exclusively used in the context of play.

3.4.3.1. One Gesture for Multiple Contexts. With respect to the number of all performed gestures (Fig. 5.4a), more than 72% of all 33 gestures were observed in more than one context, 27% (9 gestures) were performed in only one context, 30% (10 gestures) in two and in three contexts, 9% (3 gestures) in five contexts, and 3% (1 gesture) in seven contexts. The number of different tactile gestures was significantly higher in several contexts than the number of different visual gesture types (KW: $\chi_2^2 = 6.108$, $p = .047$; MWU TAC>VIS: $Z = -2.203$, 2-tailed, $p = .028$, $N_{tac} = 11$; $N_{vis} = 16$; see Fig. 5.4b).

3.4.3.2. One Context With Multiple Gestures. Concerning the use of several gestures for one end, the results showed that in every context, on average, approximately 18 different gestures were used.

TABLE 5.3
Gestures Used for More Than One End Per Individual (3a) and Gestures Used for the Same End per Individual (3b)

3a)	Uzuri	Kumbo	Kihi	Bibi	M'Bewe	Komu	Kisiwa	Kidjoum	Kidogo	Kwimba	M'Kono	M'Tongue	Kidiki	Total
Chest beat	x					x		x	x					4
Clap						x								1
Gallop		x	x			x								3
Grab	x	x	x	x		x	x	x		x	x	x	x	11
Grab-push-pull						x						x		2
Hand on							x							1
Move		x	x						x			x		4
Peer										x				1
Punch						x	x							2
Push			x			x	x							3
Slap							x							1
Slap ground						x								1
Somersault							x							1
Stiff stance			x											1
Throw		x				x			x					3
Touch	x		x	x		x	x	x	x	x	x	x	x	11

3b)	Uzuri	Kumbo	Kihi	Bibi	M'Bewe	Komu	Kisiwa	Kidjoum	Kidogo	Kwimba	M'Kono	M'Tongue	Kidiki	Total (individual)
Affiliative									2					1
Agonistic	2	8	6			4	2	5	2			2		8
Food		3	3	3		4		6	2	4	2	3		9
Nurse						2								1
Play	16	17	19	17	21	23	13	22	19	21	11	20	9	13
Ride				3								2		2
Travel									3					1

Overall, in the context of play, all different gestures could be observed, whereas in the nurse context, only 24% of all gestures occurred (see Fig. 5.4c). In the agonistic and food contexts, 73% of all gestures were used, in the travel context 39%, in the affiliative context 36%, and in the ride context 30% were used. These differences between the occurrence of signals due to different contexts were significant for the context play versus all other contexts, and for the food and agonistic contexts versus the nurse, travel, ride, and affiliative contexts (Friedman: $\chi_7^2 = 121.471$, $p <$ .001; see Fig. 5.4c. For Z-values of the Wilcoxon-test, see Pika et al., 2003).

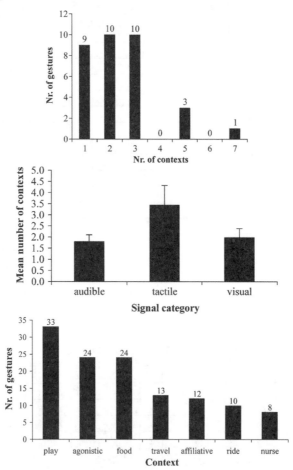

Figure 5.4. Means–ends dissociation: (a; top) One gesture is used for multiple contexts, (b; middle) mean number of contexts in relation to the three different signal categories of audible, tactile, and visual gestures, (c; bottom) multiple gestures are used for one context. Error bars indicate the standard deviation.

3.5. Function of Gestures

To investigate which functional role gestures play in the social communication of gorillas, we analyzed the response of recipients toward gestural signals. On average, 28% (± 10.23) of the gestures did not receive a
response, 12% (± 4.57) led to a change in the attentional state of the recipient (not attending changed to attending), 20% (± 4.53) received a response in the form of a gesture, and 40% (± 10.08) led to an interaction
between the signaler and the recipient (see Fig. 5.5).

These interactions could be grouped into the following contextual
categories (see Fig. 5.5); overall play = 40%; agonistic = 18%; travel =
16%; affiliative = 12%; other = 9%; ride = 3%, and nurse = 2%. In 57% (±
9.32) of cases in which a gesture did not receive a response, the signaler
used a second gesture.

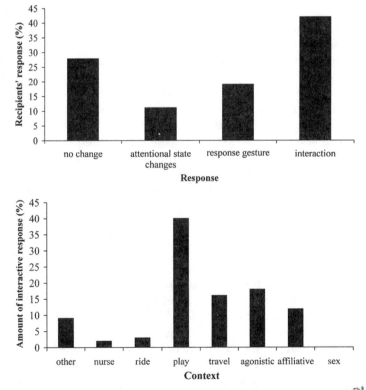

Figure 5.5.   Recipients' response per observed gesture in percent (a; top),
and (b; bottom) recipient's type of interactive response in percent.

4. DISCUSSION

The present study aimed to enhance the knowledge of gestural signaling in gorillas, focusing on the compilation of the gestural repertoire, as well as on the learning and use of gestures. We provided strong evidence that gestures play an important role in the communication of gorillas, with subadult gorillas using around 30 distinct auditory, tactile, and visual gestural signals in a variety of contexts such as affiliative, agonistic, food, nurse, play, ride, and travel. Gorillas responded to the majority of all performed gestures either by looking at the signaler, by performing a response gesture, or by interacting with the signaler. In addition, in more than half of the cases, the signaler continued to perform additional gestures if they received no reaction from the recipient.

Our results enabled us to draw comparisons with the study by Tanner and Byrne (Tanner, 1998; Tanner & Byrne, 1999). Unlike those researchers, we did not observe the tactile gesture *mouth/lips* and the visual gestures *arm cross, arm swing under, beat sides of head, down, extended palm, face wipe, finger down lips, foot back, hands behind back, hands between legs, hide play face, teeth* and *wrist glance*. The gestures *arm cross, arm swing under*, and *extended palm* were observed in two or three individuals, but the others were idiosyncratic gestures, mainly exclusive to one female, Zura. The auditory gestures *chest beat* and *chest knock* were lumped together in our study into *chest beat*, and the gestures *backhand pound, knock*, and *slap surface* were combined into *slap ground*. The tactile gesture *hands on shoulders* (Tanner, 1998; Tanner & Byrne, 1999) is similar to *hand on* in our study, the gesture *tap other* resembles our description of *punch*, and the gesture *pat off* resembles our description of *touch*. The visual gestures *circle hands* and *go* are elements of our description of the gesture *arm shake*; and the gestures *head nod, head shake, head turn*, and *head twirl* are elements of our description of the gesture *bow*. The gesture *bite* resembles our description of *formal bite*, and the gestures *away* and *up* are elements of our description of *reach*.

Contrary to Tanner and Byrne, we observed the gestures *body slap, chuck up, gallop, ice skating, jump, move, peer, shake, somersault, straw wave, stiff stance, stomp*, and *throw*, and the idiosyncratic gestures *object drum, object on somebody*, and *break wood*. In addition, we differentiated among tactile gestures that were not differentiated by Tanner and Byrne but that were described by them as one gesture type; *tactile-close gestures*. Some of the differences between the two studies are therefore due to the fact that Tanner and Byrne (Tanner, 1998; Tanner & Byrne, 1999) focused in detail on the shape and form of the gesturing hand (e.g., *backhand pound, knock*) and of head movements (*head shake, head turn*), whereas we differentiated between directions of movements (e.g., *push, pull*) and used all means of gestural expressions such as body postures and leg movements.

In addition, we observed no instances of iconic use of gestures. These results might be explained as follows: (1) It could be that our analysis did not focus in sufficient detail on the receivers' responses to detect them; (2) Gesturing of an iconic nature could be a developmental phenomenon, appearing only at adolescence and promoted by special social and physical conditions (Tanner, 1998); (3) Finally, the iconicity of the gestures might exist in the eyes of the human observer (Tomasello & Zuberbühler, 2002).

Contrary to research with chimpanzees and siamangs (Liebal, Pika, & Tomasello, 2004; Tomasello et al., 1997), we found no significant difference in the number of gestures across age classes, which can be explained by the fact that gorillas have the shortest infancy and juvenile stages of all apes (Bogin, 1999). They therefore develop certain aspects of physical maturity and intellectual development at a younger age (e.g., Antinucci, 1990; Parker, Mitchell, & Lyn Miles, 1999; Redshaw, 1978; Spinozzi & Natale, 1989).

In addition, the majority of tactile and visual gestures were already fully developed in gorilla infants aged 1–2 years. This result contradicts the findings of Tanner (1998) and Redshaw and Locke (1976), who did not observe these kinds of gestures in gorillas this young.

With regard to the learning of gestures, we found high levels of agreement concerning the performance of gestures between groups, individual variability concerning the performance of 25 gestures, and three idiosyncratic gestures. These results strongly confirm the hypothesis of Tomasello and Call (1997), who claimed that apes acquire their gestures via an individual learning process called *ontogenetic ritualization*. However, we also found high overlap of gestural repertoires among individuals within groups, as well as group-specific gestures. Because the degree of concordance of gestural repertoires within and between groups is highly similar, these results might be explained by commonly available individual learning conditions. Both groups seem to live in environments that provide similar learning conditions, triggering the acquisition of similar gestural repertoires. However, two distinct gestures were specific to the gorillas in the Apenheul group, and these could not be easily explained by different physical conditions or by different social settings. They therefore provide evidence that social learning might play an important role in the acquisition of some gestures.

Interestingly, Redshaw and Locke (1976), who investigated the development of behavior in two hand-reared lowland gorilla infants living together without any other conspecifics, reported auditory gestures such as *chest beat, clap*, and *slap*. Although both gorillas had never seen another gorilla performing these gestures, they used *clap* and *slap ground* to solicit play, and the gesture *chest beat* was performed in the context of uncertainty and possibly anxiety. In addition, the gesture *slap* was always followed by an approach of the recipient. Our results show that the gestures *chest beat* and *slap ground* were used in more diverse ways: The gesture *chest beat* was used mainly in play situations and the agonistic context. The gesture *slap ground* received in most cases a response in the form of a response gesture (13%) or an action (57%). These findings therefore imply that the production of species-typical gestures might be due to a genetic predisposition, whereas their use of gestures and response toward gestures has to be learned and depends on exchange with group members.

Concerning audience effects, we found that one of the major factors affecting the choice of communicative means in a particular situation was the attentional state of the recipient. All gorillas adjusted their use of gestures to the attentional state of the recipient, using visual gestures mainly when the recipient was looking. The attention of the recipient did not play an important role in the use of tactile and auditory gestures. Our findings are therefore consistent with the results of Tanner and Byrne (Tanner, 1998; Tanner & Byrne, 1999), who observed that silent gestures were mainly performed when the gesturing gorillas already had the attention of the receiver.

With regard to the use of gestures, we observed that gorillas have flexible connections between signal and function, which means that dissociation of means and ends can be found. In addition, tactile gestures represented the most flexible gestures, showing the highest variety of functional categories, whereas auditory and visual gestures were linked to special social contexts such as play, agonistic, and food. In contrast to the nurse and ride contexts in which the variety of gestures was quite low, all gestural signals occurred during play encounters. These findings are consistent with the observations of Tanner (1998), who reported that gesturing was context specific, occurring mainly in play as well as in sexual play.

5. CONCLUSION

In conclusion, the gestural communication of subadult gorillas can be characterized by a great deal of flexibility, with accommodations to the attentional state of the receiver and to various communicative circumstances such as a nonresponding recipient. Future research is needed to shed light on the meaning and function of gestures in adult gorillas, including wild populations living under active selection pressures and in environments with lower visibility.

ACKNOWLEDGMENTS

I am grateful to all the keepers and collaborators of Howletts Wild Animal Park, United Kingdom and Diereupark Apenheul, the Netherlands for their friendliness and helpfulness. The advice on statistics given by Daniel Stahl is gratefully acknowledged. For comments on an earlier draft, I thank Brenda Bradley.

NOTES

1. Difference in structure or function between males and females.
2. Folivorous: Diet consists mainly of plants.
3. Herbivorous: Diet consists mainly of plants and no meat.
4. Frugivorous: Diet consists mainly of fruits.
5. In this theory the basic categories of knowledge that are cognitively constructed during sensorimotor development are space, time, causality, and objects. Although almost nothing is known about primates' understanding of time, many studies have focused on their understanding of objects and their spatial and causal interrelations.

REFERENCES

Altmann, D. (1991). *Practical statistics for medical research.* CRC: Chapman & Hall.

Altmann, J. (1974). Observational study of behaviour: Sampling methods. *Behaviour, 49,* 227–267.

Antinucci, F. (1990). The comparative study of cognitive ontogeny in four primate species. In K. R. Gibson & S. T. Parker (Eds.), *"Language" and intelligence in monkeys and apes: Comparative developmental perspectives* (pp. 157–171).

Bates, E. (1976). *Language and context: The acquisition of pragmatics.* New York: Academic Press.

Bogin, B. (1999). Evolutionary perspectives on human growth. *Annual Review of Anthropology, 28*(10953), 17–25.

Boysen, S. T., Kuhlmeier, V. A., Halliday, P., & Halliday, Y. M. (1999). Tool use in captive gorillas. In S. T. Parker, R. W. Mitchell, & H. L. Miles (Eds.), *The mentalities of gorillas and orangutans: Comparative perspectives* (pp. 179–187). Cambridge, England: Cambridge University Press.

Bradley, B., Doran-Sheehy, D. M., Lukas, D., Boesch, C., & Vigilant, L. (2004). Dispersed male networks in western gorillas. *Current Biology, 14,* 510–513.

Bräuer, J., Call, J., & Tomasello, M. (2005). All Great Ape species follow gaze to distant locations and around barriers. *Journal of Comparative Psychology, 119*(2), 145–154.

Bruner, J. (1981). Intention in the structure of action and interaction. In L. Lipsitt (Ed.), *Advances in infancy research* (Vol. 1, pp. 41–56). Norwood, NJ: Ablex.

Butynski, T. M. (2001). Africa's great apes. In B. B. Beck, T. Stoinski, & M. Hutchins (Eds.), *Great apes and humans* (pp. 3–56). Washington DC: Smithsonian Institution Press.

Byrne, R. W. (1996). The misunderstood ape: Cognitive skills of the gorilla. In A. E. Russon, K. A. Bard, & S. T. Parker (Eds.), *Reaching into thought: The minds of the great apes* (pp. 111–130). Cambridge, England: Cambridge University Press.

Byrne, R. W. (1999). Object manipulation and skill organization in the complex food preparation of mountain gorillas. In H. Lyn Miles (Ed.), *The mentalities of gorillas and orangutans* (pp. 147–159). Cambridge, England: Cambridge University Press.

Byrne, R. W., & Byrne, J. M. E. (1993). Complex leaf-gathering skills of mountain gorillas (*Gorilla g. beringei*): Variability and standardization. *American Journal of Primatology, 31,* 241–261.

Call, J., & Tomasello, M. (1996). The effects of humans on the cognitive development of apes. In A. E. Russon, K. A. Bard, & S. T. Parker (Eds.), *Reaching into thought: The minds of the great apes* (pp. 371–403). Cambridge, England: Cambridge University Press.

Casimir, M. J. (1975). Feeding ecology and nutrition of an eastern gorilla group in Mt. Kahuzi region (Republic of Zaire). *Folia Primatologica, 24,* 81–136.

Cipoletta, C. (2003). Ranging patterns of a western gorilla group during habituation to humans in the Dzanga-Ndoki National Park, Central African Republic. *American Journal of Primatology, 24,* 1207–1226.

Doran, D. M., Greer, D., Mongo, P., & Schwindt, D. (2004). Impact of ecological and social factors on ranging in western gorillas. *American Journal of Primatology, 64*(2), 207–222.

Doran, D. M., & McNeilage, A. (1998). Gorilla ecology and behaviour. *Evolutionary Anthropology, 6*(4), 120–131.

Doran, D., & McNeilage, A. (2001). Subspecific variation in gorilla behavior: The influence of ecological and social factors. In K. J. Stewart (Ed.), *Mountain gorillas: Three decades of research* (pp. 123–149). Cambridge, England: Cambridge University Press.

Doran, D., McNeilage, A., Greer, D., Bocian, C., Mehlman, P., & Shah, N. (2002). Western lowland gorilla diet and resource availability: New evidence, cross-site comparisons, and reflections on indirect sampling methods. *American Journal of Primatology, 58*(3), 91–116.

Dunbar, R. (1996). *Grooming, gossip and the evolution of Language.* London: Faber & Faber Ltd.

Estes, R. D. (1992). *The behavior guide to African mammals.* Berkeley, CA: University of California Press.

Fay, J. M. (1989). Hand-clapping in western lowland gorillas. *Mammalia, 53*(3), 457–458.

Fontaine, B., Moisson, P., & Wickings, E. (1995). Observations of spontaneous tool making and tool use in a captive group of western lowland gorillas (*Gorilla gorilla gorilla*). *Folia Primatologica, 65*(4), 219–223.

Fossey, D. (1972). Vocalizations of the mountain gorilla. *Animal Behaviour, 20,* 36–53.

Fossey, D. (1974). Observations on the home range of one group of mountain gorillas (*Gorilla g. beringei*). *Animal Behaviour, 22,* 568–581.

Fossey, D. (1983). *Gorillas in the mist.* London: Hodder & Stoughton.

Fossey, D., & Harcourt, A. H. (1977). Feeding ecology of free-ranging mountain gorillas (*Gorilla gorilla beringei*). In T. H. Clutton-Brock (Ed.), *Primate ecology* (pp. 415–447). London: Academic Press.

Fruth, B., & Hohmann, G. (1996). Nest building behavior in the great apes: The great leap forward? In W. C. McGrew, L. F. Marchandt, & T. Nishida (Eds.), *Great ape societies* (pp. 225–240). Cambridge, England: Cambridge University Press.

Gallup, G. G. (1970). Chimpanzees: Self-recognition. *Science, 167*, 86–87.

Goldsmith, M. L. (1996). *Ecological influences on the ranging and grouping behavior of western lowland gorillas at Bai Hokou in the Central African Republic*. Stony Brook, NY: State University of New York.

Goldsmith, M. L. (1999). Ecological constraints on the foraging effort of western gorillas (*Gorilla gorilla gorilla*) at Bai Hoekou, Central African Republic. *International Journal of Primatology, 20*(1), 1–23.

Goldsmith, M. L. (2003). *Comparative behavior and ecology of a lowland and highland gorilla population: Where do Bwindi gorillas fit?* Cambridge: Cambridge University Press.

Gomez, J. C. (1990). The emergence of intentional communication as a problem-solving strategy in gorilla. In S. T. G. Parker & K. R. (Ed.), *'Language' and intelligence in monkeys and apes* (pp. 333–355). Cambridge, England: Cambridge University Press.

Gomez, J. C. (1991). Visual behaviour as a window for reading the mind of others in primates. In A. Whiten (Ed.), *Natural theories of mind: Evolution, development and simulation of everyday mindreading* (pp. 195–207). Oxford, England: Basil Blackwell.

Gomez, J. C. (1999). Development of sensorimotor intelligence in infant gorillas: The manipulation of objects in problem-solving and exploration tasks. In S. T. Parker, W. Mitchell, & H. L. Miles (Eds.), *The mentalities of gorillas and orangutans* (pp. 160–178). Cambridge, England: Cambridge University Press.

Gregory, W. K. (1950). *The anatomy of the gorilla*. New York: Columbia University Press.

Groves, C. P. (2001). *Primate taxonomy*. Washington, DC: Smithsonian Institution Press.

Harcourt, A. H. (1979a). Social relationships among adult female mountain gorillas. *Animal Behaviour, 27*, 251–264.

Harcourt, A. H. (1979b). The social relationships and group structure of wild mountain gorillas. In A. Hamburg & E. R. McCown (Eds.), *The great apes* (pp. 187–192). Menlo Park, CA: Benjamin/Cummings.

Harcourt, A. H. (1979c). Social relationships between adult male and female mountain gorillas in the wild. *Animal Behaviour, 27*, 325–342.

Harcourt, A. H. (1981). Intermale competition and the reproductive behavior of the great apes. In C. E. Graham (Ed.), *Reproductive biology of the great apes* (pp. 301–318). New York: Academic Press.

Harcourt, A. H. (1985). Gorilla. In D. Macdonald (Ed.), *Primates* (pp. 136–143). New York: Torstar Books.

Harcourt, A. H., & De Waal, F. B. M. (1992). *Coalitions and alliances in humans and other animals*. Oxford, England: Oxford University Press.

Harcourt, A. H., & Stewart, K. J. (1986). Vocalizations and social relationships of wild gorillas: A preliminary analysis. In D. M. Taub & F. A. King (Eds.), *Current perspectives in primates social dynamics* (pp. 346–356). New York: Van Nostrand Reinhold.

Harcourt, A. H., & Stewart, K. J. (1994). Gorillas' vocalizations during rest periods: Signals of impending departure? *Behaviour, 130*(1–2), 29–40.

Harcourt, A. H., & Stewart, K. J. (1996). Function and meaning of wild gorilla 'close' calls 2. Correlations with rank and relatedness. *Behaviour, 133*(11–12), 827–845.

Harcourt, A. H., & Stewart, K. J. (2001). Vocal relationships of wild mountain gorillas. In M. M. Robbins, P. Sicotte, & K. J. Stewart (Eds.), *Mountain gorillas: Three decades of research* (pp. 241–262). Cambridge, England: Cambridge University Press.

Harcourt, A. H., Stewart, K. J., & Fossey, D. (1976). Male emigration and female transfer in wild mountain gorilla. *Nature, 263*, 226–227.

Harcourt, A. H., Stewart, K. J., & Hauser, M. D. (1993). Function and meaning of wild gorilla 'close' calls 1. Repertoire, context, and interspecific comparison. *Behaviour, 124*(1–2), 89–122.

Heyes, C. (1994). Reflections on self-recognition in primates. *Animal Behaviour, 46*, 177–188.

Heyes, C. M. (1998). Theory of mind in nonhuman primates. *Behavioral and Brain Science, 21*, 101–148.

Humphrey, N. K. (1976). The social function of intellect. In P. P. G. Bateson & R. A. Hinde (Eds.), *Growing points in ethology* (pp. 303–317). Cambridge, England: Cambridge University Press.

Jolly, A. (1966). Lemur social behaviour and primate intelligence. *Science, 153*, 501–506.

Kaessmann, H., Wiebe, V., Weiss, G., & Pääbo, S. (2001). Great ape DNA sequences reveal a reduced diversity and an expansion in humans. *Nature Genetics, 27*, 155–156.

Kawai, M. (1965). Newly acquired pre-cultural behaviour of the natural troop of Japanese monkeys on Koshima Islet. *Primates, 6*(1), 1–30.

Kuroda, S. J. (1996). Sympatric chimpanzees and gorillas in the Ndoki Forest, Congo. In C. McGrew, L. F. Marchandt, & T. Nishida (Eds.), *Great ape societies* (pp. 71–81). Cambridge, England: Cambridge University Press.

Liebal, K., Pika, S., Call, J., & Tomasello, M. (2004). Great ape communicators move in front of recipients before producing visual gestures. *Interaction studies, 5*(2), 199–219.

Liebal, K., Pika, S., & Tomasello, M. (2004). Social communication in siamangs (*Symphalangus Syndactulus*): Use of gestures and facial expression. *Primates, 45*(2), 41–57.

MacDonald, S. E. (1994). Gorillas' (*Gorilla gorilla gorilla*) spatial memory in a foraging task. *Journal of Comparative Psychology, 108*, 107–113.

Meder, A. (1993). *Gorillas*. Berlin: Springer Verlag.

Mitani, M., Moutsambote, J., & Oko, R. (1992). Preliminary results of the studies of wild western lowland gorillas and other diurnal primates in the Ndoki forest, Northern Congo. In N. Itoigawa, Sugiyama, P. Sackett, & R. K. R. Thompson (Eds.), *Topics in primatology* (Vol. 2, pp. 215–224). Tokyo: University of Tokyo Press.

Mitchell, R. W. (1999). Deception and hiding in captive lowland gorillas. *Primates,* (32), 523–527.

Nakamichi, M. (1999). Spontaneous use of sticks as tools by captive gorillas (*Gorilla gorilla gorilla*). *Primates, 40*(3), 487–498.

Natale, F., Antinucci, F., Spinozzi, G., & Poti, P. (1986). Stage 6 object concept in nonhuman primate cognition: A comparison between gorilla (*Gorilla gorilla gorilla*) and Japanese macaque (*Macaca fuscata*). *Journal of Comparative Psychology, 100*(4), 335–339.

Nishihara, T. (1995). Feeding ecology of western lowland gorillas in the Nouabale-Ndoki National Park, northern Congo. *Primates, 36*, 151–168.

Ogden, J., & Schildkraut, D. (1991). *Compilation of gorilla ethograms*. Atlanta, GA: Gorilla Behavior Advisory Group.

Parker, S. T., Kerr, M., Markowitz, H., & Gould, J. (1999). A survey of tool use in zoo gorillas. In S. T. Parker & R. W. Mitchell & H. L. Miles (Eds.), *The mentalities of gorillas and orangutans: Comparative perspectives* (pp. 188–193). Cambridge: Cambridge University Press.

Parker, S. T., Mitchell, R. W., & Boccia, M. L. (1994). *Self-awareness in animals and humans*. Cambridge, England: Cambridge University Press.

Parker, S. T., Mitchell, R. W., & Lyn Miles, H. (1999). *The mentalities of gorillas and orangutans*. Cambridge, England: University Press.

Parnell, R. J. (2002). Group size and structure in western lowland gorillas (*Gorilla gorilla gorilla*) at Mbeli Bai, Republic of Congo. *American Journal of Primatology, 56*, 193–206.

Parnell, R. J., & Buchanan-Smith, H. M. (2001). Animal behaviour: An unusual social display by gorillas. *Nature, 412*, 294.

Patterson, F. (1978). Conversations with a gorilla. *National Geographic, 134*(4), 438–465.

Patterson, F. (1979). Linguistic capabilities of a lowland gorilla. In R. L. Shiefbusch & J. H. Hollis (Eds.), *Language intervention from ape to child* (pp. 327–356). Baltimore: University Park Press.

Patterson, F., & Linden, E. (1981). *The education of Koko*. New York: Owl Books.

Patterson, F., & Tanner, J. (1988). Gorilla gestural communication. *Gorilla: Journal of the Gorilla Foundation, 12*(1), 2–5.

Patterson, F. G., & Cohn, R. (1994). Self-recognition and self-awareness in lowland gorillas. In S. T. Parker, M. L. Boccia, & R. Mitchell (Ed.), *Self-awareness in animals and humans* (pp. 273–290). Cambridge, England: Cambridge University Press.

Peignot, P., & Anderson, J. R. (1999). Use of experimenter-given manual and facial cues by gorillas (*Gorilla gorilla*) in an object-choice task. *Journal of Comparative Psychology, 113*(3), 253–260.

Piaget, J. (1954). *The construction of reality in a child*. New York: Norton.

Pika, S., Liebal, K., & Tomasello, M. (2003). Gestural communication in young gorillas (*Gorilla gorilla*): Repertoire, learning and use. *American Journal of Primatology, 60*(3), 95–111.

Pika, S., & Tomasello, M. (2001). 'Separating the wheat from the chaff': A novel food processing technique in captive gorillas (*Gorilla g. gorilla*). *Primates, 42*(2), 167–170.

Redshaw, M. (1978). Cognitive development in human and gorilla infants. *Journal of Human Evolution, 7*, 133–141.

Redshaw, M., & Locke, K. (1976). The development of play and social behaviour in two lowland gorilla infants. *The Journal of the Jersey Wildlife Preservation Trust, 13th Annual Report*, 71–86.

Remis, M. J. (1997). Gorillas as seasonal frugivores: Use of variable resources. *American Journal of Primatology, 43*, 87–109.

Remis, M. J. (2003). Are gorillas vacuum cleaner of the forest floor? The roles of body size, habitat, and food preferences on dietary flexibility and nutrition. In A. Taylor & M. L. Goldsmith (Eds.), *Gorilla biology: A multidisciplinary perspective* (pp. 385–404). Cambridge, England: Cambridge University Press.

Robbins, M. M. (1995). A demographic analysis of male life history and social structure of mountain gorillas. *Behaviour, 132*, 21–47.

Robbins, M. M. (2001). Variation in the social system of mountain gorillas: The male perspective. In M. M. Robbins, P. Sicotte, & K. J. Stewart (Eds.), *Mountain gorillas: Three decades of research at Karisoke* (pp. 30–58). Cambridge, England: Cambridge University Press.

Rogers, M. E., Williamson, E. A., Tutin, C. E. G., & Fernandez, M. (1990). Gorilla diet in the Lope Reserve, Gabon: A nutritional analysis. *Oecologia, 84*, 326–339.

Schaller, G. B. (1963). *The mountain gorilla, ecology and behavior.* Chicago: University of Chicago Press.

Schaller, G. B. (1964a). The behavior of the mountain gorilla. In I. DeVore (Ed.), *Primate behavior field studies of monkeys and apes* (pp. 324–367). New York: Holt, Rinehart & Winston.

Schaller, G. B. (1964b). Behavioral comparisons of the apes. In I. DeVore (Ed.), *Primate behavior field studies of monkeys and apes* (pp. 474–481). New York: Holt, Rinehart & Winston.

Schaller, G. (1965). The behaviour of the mountain gorilla. In I. de Vore (Ed.), *Primate behaviour* (pp. 324–367). New York: Holt, Rinehart & Winston.

Sicotte, P. (1995). Interpositions in conflicts between males in bimale groups of mountain gorillas. *Folia Primatologica, 65*(1), 14–24.

Spinozzi, G., & Natale, F. (1989). Early sensorimotor development in gorilla. In F. Antinucci (Ed.), *Comparative cognition and neuroscience: Cognitive structure and development in nonhuman primates* (pp. 21–38).

Stoinski, T. S., Wrate, J. L., Ure, N., & Whiten, A. (2001). Imitative learning by captive western lowland gorillas (Gorilla gorilla gorilla) in a simulated food-processing task. *Journal of Comparative Psychology, 115*(3), 272–281.

Swartz, K. B., & Evans, S. (1994). Social and cognitive factors in chimpanzee and gorilla mirror behaviour and self-recognition. In S. T. Parker, R. Mitchellm & M. L. Boccia (Eds.), *Self-awareness in animals and humans* (pp. 189–206). Cambridge, England: Cambridge University Press.

Tanner, J. E. (1998). *Gestural communication in a group of zoo-living lowland gorillas.* Unpublished doctoral dissertation, University of St. Andrews, St. Andrews.

Tanner, J. E. (2004). Gestural phrases and gestural exchanges by a pair of zoo-living lowland gorillas. *Gesture, 4*(1), 25–42.

Tanner, J. E., & Byrne, R. (1996). Representation of action through iconic gesture in a captive lowland gorilla. *Current Anthropology, 37*(1), 162–173.

Tanner, J. E., & Byrne, W. B. (1993). Concealing facial evidence of mood: Perspective-taking in a captive Gorilla. *Primates, 34*(4), 451–457.

Tanner, J. E., & Byrne, R. (1999). The development of spontaneous gestural communication in a group of zoo-living lowland gorillas. In S. T. Parker, R. W. Mitchell, & H. L. Miles (Eds.), *The mentalities of gorillas and orangutans: Comparative perspectives* (pp. 211–239). Cambridge, England: Cambridge University Press.

Taylor, A., & Goldsmith, M. L. (2003). *Gorilla biology: A multidisciplinary perspective.* Cambridge, England: Cambridge University Press.

Tomasello, M. (1996). Do apes ape? In C. M. G. Heyes & B. G. Jr. (Ed.), *Social learning in animals: The roots of culture* (pp. 319–346). San Diego: Academic Press.

Tomasello, M. (1999). Emulation learning and cultural learning. *Behavioral and Brain Sciences, 21,* 703–704.

Tomasello, M., & Call, J. (1997). *Primate cognition.* New York: Oxford University Press.

Tomasello, M., Call, J., Warren, J., Frost, T., Carpenter, M., & Nagell, K. (1997). The ontogeny of chimpanzee gestural signals. In S. Wilcox, B. King, & L Steels (Ed.), *Evolution of communication* (pp. 224–259). Philadelphia, PA: John Benjamins Publishing Company.

Tomasello, M., Gust, D., & Frost, G. T. (1989). A longitudinal investigation of gestural communication in young chimpanzees. *Primates, 30*(1), 35–50.

Tomasello, M., & Zuberbühler, K. (2002). Primate vocal and gestural communication. In M. Bekoff, C. S. Allen, & G. Burghardt (Eds.), *The cognitive animal: Empirical and theoretical perspectives on animal cognition* (pp. 293–299). Cambridge, MA: MIT Press.

Tutin, C. E. G. (2003). *An introductory perspective: Behavioral ecology of gorillas.* Cambridge, England: Cambridge University Press.

Tutin, C. E. G., & Fernandez, M. (1993). Composition of the diet of chimpanzees and comparisons with that of sympatric lowland gorillas in the Lope Reserve, Gabon. *American Journal of Primatology, 30*(3), 195–211.

Tutin, C. E. G., Fernandez, M., Rogers, M. E., Williamson, E. A., & McGrew, W. C. (1991). Foraging profiles of sympatric lowland gorillas and chimpanzees in the Lope Reserve, Gabon. *Philosophical Transactions of the Royal Society, Series B, 334,* 179–186.

Tutin, C. E. S. (1996). Ranging and social structure of lowland gorillas in the Lope Reserve, Gabon. In C. McGrew, L. F. Marchandt, & T. Nishida (Eds.), *Great ape societies* (pp. 58–70). Cambridge, England: Cambridge University Press.

Watts, D. P. (1996). Comparative socio-ecology of gorillas. In T. Nishida (Ed.), *Great ape societies* (pp. 16–28). Cambridge, England: Cambridge University Press.

Watts, D. P. (1997). Agonistic interventions in wild mountain gorilla groups. *Behaviour, 134*(1–2), 23–57.

Watts, D. P. (1998a). Long-term habitat use by mountain gorillas (*Gorilla gorilla beringei*). 2. Reuse of foraging areas in relation to resource abundance, quality, and depletion. *International Journal of Primatology, 19*(4), 681–702.

Watts, D. P. (1998b). Seasonality in the ecology and life histories of mountain gorillas (*Gorilla gorilla beringei*). *International Journal of Primatology, 19,* 929–948.

Whiten, A., & Byrne, R. W. (1988). Tactical deception in primates. *Behavioral and Brain Sciences,* (11), 233–244.

Wrangham, R. (1980). An ecological model of female-bonded primate groups. *Behaviour, 75,* 262–300.

Yamagiwa, J. (1983). Diachronic changes in two eastern lowland gorilla groups (*Gorilla gorilla graueri*) in the Mt. Kahuzi Region, Zaire. *Primates, 24,* 174–183.

Yamagiwa, J., Basabose, K., Kaleme, K., & Yumoto, T. (2003). Within-group feeding competition and socioecological factors influencing social organization of gorillas in the Kahuzu-Biega National Park, Democratic Republic of Congo. In A. Taylor & M. L. Goldsmith (Eds.), *Gorilla biology: A multidisciplinary perspective* (pp. 328–356). Cambridge, England: Cambridge University Press.

Yamagiwa, J., & Kahekwa, J. (2001). Dispersal patterns, group structure, and reproductive parameters of eastern lowland gorillas at Kahuzi in the absence of infanticide. In M. M. Robbins, P. Sicotte, & K. J. Stewart (Eds.), *Mountain gorillas: Three decades of research* (pp. 89–122). Cambridge, England: Cambridge University Press.

CHAPTER 6

Gestures in Siamangs (Symphalangus syndactylus)

Katja Liebal
University of Portsmouth

Figure 6.1. Siamang.

1. INTRODUCTION TO THE SPECIES

1.1. Taxonomy

Siamangs (*Symphalangus syndactylus*) belong to the family of gibbons or small apes (*Hylobatidae*) and are one out of four genera within this group (Roos & Geissmann, 2001). Gibbons represent the most ancient branch within the Hominoidae, because they split approximately 18 million years ago from the line leading to the great apes (Waddell & Penny, 1996). They are therefore characterized by a number of primitive features. For example, they have sitting pads of cornified, hairless skin (ischial callosities), and unlike the great apes, they do not build sleeping nests (Bartlett, 1999).

The division and phylogeny of the different species of small apes is still disputed. According to Groves (2001) there are at least 10 different species (but see also Geissmann, 2002), all restricted to the tropical rainforest of Southeast Asia. They represent a unique and highly specialized group of nonhuman primates characterized by a highly arboreal lifestyle, brachiating locomotion, and a monogamous social structure associated with the occupation of a territory and a complex singing behavior (Rowe, Goodall, & Mittermeier, 1996).

1.2 Morphology

Gibbons are the smallest of the apes and show only very minimal expression of sexual dimorphism, particularly in body size, cranial features, and canine tooth dimensions (Frisch, 1963, 1973; Gaulin & Sailer, 1984; Schultz, 1956, 1962, 1973). Siamangs are the largest species of small apes and are the only representatives of this group that live sympatrically with other gibbon species (*Hylobates agilis, Hylobates lar*) throughout their whole range of distribution (Geissmann, 2003a). With an approximate weight between 9–12 kg they are twice as heavy as other gibbon species (Geissmann, 1993; Schultz, 1933). Their long arms and fingers represent adaptations for brachiating locomotion, allowing siamangs to move rapidly and leap across large gaps between trees (Preuschoft, 1988). Both sexes are black and have a laryngeal air sac that is inflated during the production of their species-specific complex duet songs.

1.3. Distribution and Ecology

Siamangs are restricted to the montane rain forest on the island of Sumatra and the peninsular Malaysia. They live preferentially in altitudes between 700–900 m (Chivers, 1974; Chivers & Davis, 1979), where they inhabit the canopy between 20–40 m. Being an exclusively arboreal species, they almost never enter the ground (Gittens & Raemaekers, 1980).

Siamangs spend 55% of their daily activity foraging, 29% resting, and 16% traveling (Raemaekers & Chivers, 1980). They are often considered to be a folivorous species because their diet consists of a higher proportion of leaves in comparison to that of other gibbon species (Chivers, 1972, 1973, 1974; Gittens & Raemaekers, 1980). Because siamangs also feed on a variety of fruits, supplemented by small proportions of animal protein (Chivers & Raemaekers, 1986), their food preferences and diet composition may vary between populations depending on food abundance in their habitat (Chivers, 1977; MacKinnon, 1977).

Although many gibbon species are close to extinction (Geissmann, 2003b), siamangs seem to represent a stable population, with an estimate of approximately 360,000 individuals (MacKinnon, 1987). However, there are no recent surveys on the siamang population, with the exception of some studies restricted to certain areas such as the Bukit Barisan Selatan National Park (O'Brian, Kinnaird, Nurcahyo, Iqbal, & Rusmanto, 2004).

1.4. Social Structure and Behavior

Siamangs are one of the 14% of primate species that live in a monogamous social structure (Rutberg, 1983). There is virtually no sexual dimorphism and no differentiated role behavior between the adult male and female within one group. Group life is characterized by strong bonding between family members, which spend most of their time in close proximity and are only rarely separated by more than 10 m (Chivers, 1974). However, grooming and sexual interactions between the adults become rare once the strong bonding between the pair partners is established (Kleiman, 1977).

Each siamang family inhabits a particular home range with a size between 15 and 35 ha. Seventy-five percent of the home ranges are defended as territory against other siamang groups (Chivers, 1976). Some researchers believe such territorial defense to be one probable function of siamangs' complex duet songs (Haimoff, 1986; Marler & Tenaza, 1977; Marshall & Marshall, 1976). Colishaw (1992) also discussed the attraction of mates and the bonding of pair partners as possible functions of gibbon songs.

In addition to the adult male and female, a siamang family can consist of one to four offspring, which are born with an interbirth interval of approximately 2 to 3 years (Chivers, 1974; Palombit, 1992; Rijksen, 1978).

Until the infant is 8 months old, the mother carries it in a ventral clinging position. After the offspring is weaned (at an age of approximately 1 year), or when a new infant is born, paternal care becomes increasingly important (Chivers, 1974, 1976). Thus, the adult male may carry the juvenile offspring, although this is a variable behavior and is not observed in all pairs (Chivers, 1974).

Play behavior in siamangs is not as important as in other primate species, accounting for only 1% of siamangs' daily activity (Gittins & Raemaekers, 1980). Because there are no peers within a siamang family, play bouts mostly occur between offspring of different ages and involve the adult male as an important partner (Liebal, 2001). As the offspring matures, it becomes increasingly isolated from the social interactions within its group, a process called *peripheralization* (Fox, 1977). This finally leads to emigration of the maturing individual from its natal group and the formation of a new group.

1.5. Cognition

Very little is known about the cognitive skills of gibbons in both the physical and social domains, and most of the few studies that exist refer to other gibbon species such as the white-handed gibbon (*Hylobates lar*) rather than to siamangs (Tomasello & Call, 1997). Since the review on the learning skills of gibbons by Abordo (1976) was published, the state of the art in the field has basically not changed. Possible reasons for the lack of studies on gibbons, as well as for their poor performance in most of the experiments that have been done, are that (1) gibbons in general show a very low motivation level (Thompson, Kirk, Koestler & Bourgeois, 1965), and (2) the designs of the experiments have not considered the morphological features of gibbons' hands (Abordo, 1976). Beck (1967) found that once the experimental set up was adapted to the fact that gibbons are not able to grasp small objects from flat surfaces with their fingers, most individuals solved a problem in which they had to pull a string under different conditions to obtain food.

1.5.1. Physical Cognition

Tool use is reported for wild white-handed gibbons, which have been observed to drop branches onto human intruders (Carpenter, 1940). The only observation referring to siamangs in this regard is from an anonymous report cited in McGrew (1992) about a siamang that made a swing out of a rope. Within a comparative study investigating the manipulatory skills of 74 different nonhuman primate species when presented with nylon rope and wooden cube, Torigoe (1985) included five gibbons, two of which were siamangs. Considering the manipulatory patterns on these objects, gibbons were classified together with great apes and *Cebus* in one group characterized by the high variety of body parts involved when performing different physical actions on the objects. However, when analyzing the number of kinds of manipulation patterns, the gibbons were more similar to macaques, mangabeys, and baboons. Furthermore, gibbons did not perform secondary manipulation patterns, which involve relating objects to other environmental objects as opposed to great apes, *Cebus*, and Old World monkeys (Torigoe, 1985). Parker (1973) investigated the manipulatory behavior and responsiveness of white-handed gibbons. The gibbons were more similar to one species of terrestrial monkey than to the two species of arboreal brachiating monkeys on all measurements of responsiveness and manipulation. Furthermore, they did not use the manipulandum in a tool-like fashion, as great apes do.

In terms of problem solving, there is one report about a single white-cheeked gibbon that gradually solved how to open a puzzle box by generalizing the solution from simpler opening mechanisms to the more complex box (Boutan, 1914). However, Drescher and Trendelenburg (1927) concluded from similar experiments that gibbons' performance when opening a box was inferior to that of gorillas and chimpanzees. They also found that gibbons, like monkeys, were only able to obtain a piece of food using a hoe when the hoe was placed behind, but not in front of, the food reward.

In regard to learning skills, Abordo (1971) found that gibbons performed similar to rhesus macaques, whereas Rumbaugh and McCormack (1967) concluded from a series of different learning tasks that gibbons generally performed poorly and were more similar to squirrel monkeys than to Old World monkeys. They were also characterized by a very low transfer index in a reversal learning task, in which their performance was grouped along with that of several monkey species in between prosimians and the great apes (Rumbaugh, 1970). However, Rumbaugh and McCormack (1967) hypothesized that gibbons' likely predisposition to attend to visual stimuli that are close to their eyes in the immediate foreground is related to their arboreal lifestyle. Therefore, their tendency to look at, rather than through, the transparent experimental apparatus may have influenced their performance (Rumbaugh & McCormack, 1967).

The overall conclusion from those studies is that the cognitive skills of gibbons may resemble those of monkeys (see also Harlow, Uehling, & Maslow, 1932; Thompson et al., 1965), although their low level of motivation, their problems concentrating on tasks, and inappropriate designs in the experimental set ups may influence their performance. However, virtually nothing is known about the physical–cognitive skills of siamangs, because most of the few existing studies consider other gibbon species.

1.5.2. Social Cognition

Studies on the social cognitive skills of siamangs are virtually nonexistent. In terms of tactical deception in gibbons, there is only one report of concealment and one of the creation of an image to misinterpret the agent's behavior (Byrne & Whiten, 1992). Chivers (as cited in Byrne & Whiten, 1990) described that on several occasions, siamang infants may create an affiliative image by producing distress calls in case the adult males traveled without them. However, those instances are rare compared to reports of deception in great apes, and in chimpanzees in particular (Byrne & Whiten, 1990). The general impression is that tactical deception does not play a role in the social interactions of siamangs or gibbons in general because of their isolated, tightly knit nuclear families with individuals that know each other very well (Raemaekers, as cited in Byrne & Whiten, 1990).

In regard to studies on self-recognition, white-handed gibbons and one siamang hybrid were tested for their responses to mirrors (Hyatt, 1998). They showed mirror-mediated and self-directed behavior, for example, the exploration of different body parts. As with monkeys (see Anderson, 1984), they did not pass the mark test because they did not show any reactions to some dye put on their foreheads when looking at the mirror afterward (Lethmate & Dücker, 1973; Ujhelyi, Merker, Buk, & Geissmann, 2000).

1.6. Communication: State of the Art

Most of the little that is known about social communication in small apes comes from research concerning their complex singing behavior (e.g., Geissmann, 1993; Haimoff, 1986). The songs are species specific and sexual dimorphic. They serve to defend resources, such as territory and mates, or to attract new partners (Colishaw, 1992). Siamangs produce complex duets that seem to strengthen the existing bonds between adult pair partners (Geissmann, 1999; Geissmann & Orgeldinger, 2000). However, the structural features of these species-typical vocalizations is inherited (Geissmann, 1984), resulting in stereotyped songs with a very restricted flexibility of vocal production. Almost nothing is known about vocal utterances used for intragroup communication. Chivers (1976) mentioned *squeals, bleating distress calls, gurgles, soft grunts*, and *glunks*, and Fox (1977) distinguished at least five different vocalizations that "seemed to be primarily an expression of the emotional state."

In regard to facial expressions, Chivers (1976) reported for wild siamangs a graduated variation of facial expressions ranging from a *relaxed open-mouth face* to a *staring*, which have also been described for captive individuals (Orgeldinger, 1999). However, Fox (1977) concluded that the number of facial displays in siamangs is less significant in comparison to their gestural repertoire.

There are very few studies investigating siamangs' gestural communication, as well as that of gibbons in general. As for other ape species, existing studies describe some gestures and the contexts in which they are used (e.g., Fox, 1977; Orgeldinger, 1999), but they do not focus on individual differences or on the flexible use of the gestural repertoire. Chivers (1974) conducted his pioneering study on the behavior of wild siamangs on the peninsula of Malaysia and found that siamangs use only very few communicative behaviors in comparison to white-handed gibbons, apparently because of siamangs' strong bonding between pair partners (Chivers, 1976). Ellefson (1974) and Palombit (1992) compared the behavior of wild siamangs and white-handed gibbons and found no striking differences concerning the use of gestures between the two gibbon species. Ellefson (1967) remarked that white-handed gibbons sometimes lower their head to invite another individual for grooming, in contrast to siamangs, in which this behavior is not observed. On the other hand, the *upward thrust* gesture observed in siamangs was not found in white-handed gibbons (Palombit, 1992).

More systematic investigations of siamang communication have been conducted with captive animals. Fox (1977) and Orgeldinger (1999) report a number of different tactile and visual gestures but conclude that the siamang's repertoire is generally limited in comparison to that of great apes (Orgeldinger, 1999). Both of these studies, however, only documented gestures as produced by members of the species in general as opposed to a description of the individual gestures used by each siamang.

Therefore, this chapter focuses on gestures in captive siamangs, with the goals of systematically documenting their repertoire and examining individual variability and flexibility of gesture use. The results are interpreted with regard to the ecology, social organization, and cognitive skills of siamangs. It was expected that the arboreal lifestyle of siamangs, and the consequent low visibility within their habitat, should lead to a preponderance of vocal signals rather than to a wide repertoire of visual–gestural signals (Maestripieri, 1999; Marler, 1965). In other words, if siamangs use any gestures at all, they should particularly perform tactile gestures rather than visual gestures. With respect to their social structure, it is proposed that siamangs living in small family groups need very few communicative signals because they are characterized by a high degree of synchrony (Chivers, 1974) and because most social interactions take fairly predictable forms (Maestripieri, 1999). In terms of cognition, the skills of gibbons seem to be relatively modest and more similar to that of monkeys than to great apes. Therefore, siamangs' communication is expected to be more like that of monkeys, consisting of more tactile gestures, fewer manual gestures, and perhaps less flexible use of gestures in different functional contexts (Grigor'eva & Deriagina, 1987; Tomasello & Zuberbühler, 2002).

The goals of this chapter are (1) to document the gestures produced by siamangs (*Symphalangus syndactylus*) from several captive groups, including adults and their offspring, (2) to describe the functional context of each gesture, (3) to establish individual differences in gestural repertoires with respect to group, age, and sex, and (4) to provide some account of the cognitive processes involved, focusing on flexible use and combination of gestures as well as on their adaptability for specific communicative circumstances.

2. METHODS

2.1. Individuals

In the present study, 14 individuals from 4 different groups were observed (as shown later in Table 6.2). Two groups (Krefeld 1 and 2) were housed at the Krefeld Zoo (Germany) and two groups (Howletts A and B) at Howletts Wild Animal Park (UK). Krefeld 1 consisted of one adult male and female, respectively, one subadult male and a juvenile female. Similarly, Krefeld 2 was comprised of one pair of adult siamangs, a subadult female and a juvenile male. From Howletts A, only the infant was observed. The composition of Howletts B was atypical because in addition to one adult female, one adult male, and its offspring (one juvenile and one infantile female), the group also comprised an additional adult male.

The classification of the different age classes is based on Geissmann (1991, 1993) because the siamangs of the present study were all captive individuals. Thus, individuals younger than 2 years of age are considered infants, juveniles are between 2 and 4 years old, subadults are between 4 and 6 years old, and adults are older than 6 years. According to this classification, there were two infants, three juveniles, two subadults, and seven adults, representing six males and eight females. All adult individuals except two (Kuku-Gog and Jogog) were wild born; all offspring were born in captivity.

2.2. Data Collection

Focal-animal sampling (Altmann, 1974) was applied to calculate the total frequencies of particular gestures and to therefore enable the comparisons across individuals, groups, age classes, and sex. A digital video camera (SONY DCR-TRV900E) was used to record a total of 10 hours per individual, resulting in a total of 140 hours of observation on tape. Every focal animal was selected in a random order and was videotaped in 15-min bouts.

The methods of data analysis and the corresponding statistical tests are reported in Liebal, Pika, & Tomasello (2004); therefore, detailed information is not reported in this chapter. The results described in the following sections refer only to significant differences.

2.3. Description of the Gestural Repertoire

Following, the observed gestures are described according to their sensory modality together with their total frequency (in brackets). A total of 20 different gestures were observed, consisting of 12 tactile and 8 visual gestures. No auditory gestures were observed.

2.3.1. *Visual Gestures*

- *Direct positioning*–Approach the recipient without touching, and follow the recipient slowly but closely ('on his trail') in case the recipient moves away (26).
- *Jerking body movements*–Hang in front of the recipient and move the body up and down by angling the arms repeatedly. This may also be performed in a sitting position with the sender supporting its body by putting its arms on the ground in front of it and producing the same jerking body movements by bending its arms (31).
- *Offer body part*–Lie down on the belly in front of the recipient or present another body part for grooming. A less common version of this gesture consists of sitting with the body oriented toward the recipient and lowering the head as an invitation for grooming (210).
- *Present genitals*–Sit or hang in front of the recipient and raise the posterior to present the genital region (44).

- *Extend arm*–Direct an arm toward the recipient (3).
- *Shake object*–Push an object rapidly back and forth (58).
- *Throw back head*–Move the head repeatedly back and forth with a short movement (63).
- *Wrist offer*–Approach the recipient with extended arm and offer a bent wrist to the recipient by holding it in front of the recipient's face (7).

2.3.2. Tactile Gestures

- *Embrace*–Approach the recipient frontally or laterally and put one or two arms around the other's body (32).
- *Embrace with feet*–Seize the recipient ventrally or dorsally with both legs (12).
- *Formal bite*–Touch the recipient with the open mouth on any body part and bite it with a low intensity (78).
- *Gentle touch*–Put the hand or foot on any body part of the recipient (253).
- *Hold tight*–Seize the hand or foot of the recipient (23).
- *Nudge*–Touch the recipient by a fast movement of hand or foot; unlike *slap*, in which a flat hand is used, *nudge* involves the use of single fingers or a fist (297).
- *Pull*–Grasp any body part of the recipient by hand or foot and yank it with a short and forceful movement (322).
- *Push*–Apply pressure against some recipient's body part with a short and vigorous movement (44).
- *Rub under arms*–Move the hands up and down along the other's back (4).
- *Rub with feet*–Touch the bottom or back of the other with the feet and move them gently to and fro (6).
- *Shake body part*–Seize an arm or leg of the recipient and move it to and fro with short, vigorous movements (3).
- *Slap*–Hit the recipient with a flat hand (rarely with a foot) on any body part (239).

3. GESTURAL REPERTOIRE

3.1. Overview

A total of 1,755 gestures were observed, representing a median number of 0.9 gestures per individual and per hour. Tactile gestures were used significantly more often than visual gestures (73% vs. 27%, respectively).

The most frequent tactile gestures were *pull* (322 instances), followed by *nudge* (297 instances), and *gentle touch* (253 instances; see section 2.3). *Offer body part* was the most frequent visual gesture (210 instances).

Because the names of gestures may differ between the studies mentioned in section 1.6, Table 6.1 provides a summary of the terms used in the current chapter in comparison to other studies of both wild and captive siamangs as well as other gibbon species. This is supplemented by the functional contexts in which the gestures were used.

3.2. Context of Use

In terms of frequency distribution across the different functional contexts, siamangs used the majority of their gestures in the context of play (37.4%), followed by grooming (23.2%), and agonistic behavior (11.7%). All other functional contexts (sexual behavior, affiliation, nursing, singing, ingestion, submissive behavior) represented less than 10% of the contexts in which gestures occurred (Fig. 6.2).

When comparing the use of tactile and visual gestures in the different functional contexts (Fig. 6.2), only tactile gestures were used in the contexts of singing and ingestion. This gesture modality also represented the majority of gestures observed in the nursing (90%), play (88%), affiliation (86%), and agonistic (75%) contexts, whereas visual gestures dominated in the contexts of sexual and submissive behavior (73% and 86%, respectively).

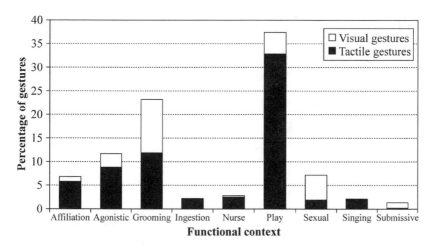

Figure 6.2. Median percentages of different gesture modalities used across functional contexts.

TABLE 6.1

Terms Used in the Current Chapter in Comparison to Other Studies in Both Wild and Captive Siamangs as well as to Other Gibbon Species Supplemented by the Functional Context

	Siamang (Symphalangus syndactylus)				White-handed gibbon (Hylobates lar)		Agile gibbon (Hylobates agilis)	
Liebal, Pika and Tomasello			Other authors					
Tactile gesture	Functional context	Gesture [Translation] (Author, year)	Functional context	Gesture (Author, year)	Functional context	Gesture (Author, year)	Functional context
Tactile gestures							
Embrace	affiliative, grooming	Frontal embrace (Fox, 1977)	nursing/carrying infant	Embrace (Carpenter, 1940)	greeting		
		Embrace (Palombit, 1992)	affiliative	Embrace (Ellefson, 1967)	submissive		
		Umarmen [Embrace] (Orgeldinger, 1999)	reassurance, greeting	Embrace (Baldwin & Teleki,1976)	vocalizing, arousal		
				Embrace (Palombit, 1992)	affiliative		
Formal bite	agonistic, grooming	Gehemmt Beißen [Inhibited bite] (Orgeldinger, 1999)	play, nursing, sexual				
Gentle touch	play, affiliative	Kurzzeitig berühren [Short touch] (Orgeldinger, 1999)	play, aggressive, affiliative	Touch (Baldwin & Teleki, 1976)	play		
Hold tight	play, agonisti	Festhalten [Hold] (Orgeldinger, 1999)	play	Holding (Ellefson, 1967)	play		
Nudge	play	Grab (Fox, 1977)	play				
Pull	play, grooming	Heranziehen [Pull] (Orgeldinger, 1999)	play				
Push	grooming, agonistic	Wegstoßen [Push] (Orgeldinger, 1999)	play	Push (Elllefson, 1967)	play		
Shake body part	play	Shaking (Fox, 1977)	play				

Behavior	Function	Comparative term (source)	Function
Slap	play, agonistic	Slap, kick, jerk, hit (Fox, 1977)	play, agonistic
		Schlagen [Slap] (Orgeldinger, 1999)	play, aggressive
		Slap, Cuff (Baldwin & Teleki, 1976)	play
		Hit, Kick, Jerk (Ellefson, 1974)	play
		Strike (Baldwin & Teleki, 1976)	agonistic, play
Visual gestures			
Jerking body movements	sexual, play	Upward thrusts (Palombit, 1992)	sexual
		Ruckartiges Körperbewegen [Jerking body movements] (Orgeldinger, 1999)	play, sexual, follow
Offer body part	grooming	Anbieten des Körperteiles [Offer body part] (Orgeldinger, 1999)	grooming
		Present (Palombit, 1992)	grooming
		Lowering head (Ellefson, 1967)	grooming
		Body present (Baldwin & Teleki, 1976)	grooming
		Present (Palombit, 1992)	grooming
		Present (Gittins, 1979)	grooming
Present genitals	sexual, submissive	Genitales präsentieren [Present genitals] (Orgeldinger, 1999)	sexual, reassurance
		Present genitals (Fox, 1977)	aggressive
		Posterior present (Baldwin & Teleki, 1976)	reassurance
		Genital present (Baldwin & Teleki, 1976)	sexual
		Sexual crouch (Baldwin & Teleki, 1976)	sexual, submissive
		Sexual crouch (Ellefson, 1967)	sexual
Throwback head	play	Kopf hochreißen [Throwback head] (Orgeldinger, 1999)	follow, sexual
		Head tilt (Baldwin & Teleki, 1976)	play, travel
		Throwing back head (Carpenter, 1940)	antagonistic

3.3. Variability

3.3.1. Individual Differences

Table 6.2 gives an overview of the individual use of the different gestures, along with corresponding information regarding the age class and sex of the siamangs, as well as their group affiliation. None of the individuals used all of the gestures observed. The individual repertoires ranged from 8 to 13 different gestures, with a median of 10 gestures, representing 50% of the total gestural repertoire (Table 6.2). Furthermore, individuals used a higher variety of tactile gestures ($Mdn = 7.5$) as compared to visual gestures ($Mdn = 3$).

Table 6.2 also shows the proportion of individuals using each gesture. There were four gestures that were each observed in single individuals only (*wrist offer, direct positioning, rub under arms, rub with feet*), whereas four tactile gestures (*slap, nudge, pull, gentle touch*) were produced by all individuals.

3.3.2. Age Differences

In terms of age differences, there were some signals performed only by adults, for example the tactile gestures *embrace with feet, rub under arms*, and *rub with feet*, which were all gestures used in the sexual context (see Table 6.2). Furthermore, only adults performed the visual gestures *direct positioning* and *extend arm. Shake body part* was observed only in subadults and juveniles but not in adults and infants. Infants did not perform the gestures *formal bite* and *hold tight*.

Figure 6.3 shows the median number of tactile and visual gestures used depending on age. Infants utilized a median number of 8.5 different gestures, juveniles performed 9, subadults 11, and adults 10.5 gestures. No significant differences were found when comparing the total numbers of gestures used, nor with regard to the varieties of tactile and visual gestures performed by young siamangs in comparison to adults. In terms of frequency, both young and adult siamangs used tactile gestures significantly more often than visual gestures (79% and 70%, respectively).

Focusing on the number of gestures used in particular functional contexts, both young and adult siamangs performed their highest number of gestures within the play context ($Mdn = 7$). The same number of gestures was produced by adults engaged in agonistic behavior, whereas young siamangs used their lowest variety of gestures in this context ($Mdn = 2$).

TABLE 6.2

Distribution of Gestures Among Individuals Arranged According to Their Age Class

	Xhali	Demagogue	Guildo	Agog	Alice	Helge	Karen	Ringo	Elvis	Jogog	Gog	Kathrin	Ellen	Kuku-Gog	Percent of individuals using it
Age and sex	if	if	jm	jf	jf	sm	sf	am	am	am	am	af	af	af	
Group	A	B	2	B	1	1	2	1	1	B	B	2	1	B	
Tactile gestures															
Embrace		x	x	x	x			x	x	x		x	x	x	70
Embrace with feet								x		x					14
Formal bite			x	x	x	x	x	x	x	x	x	x	x	x	86
Gentle touch	x	x	x	x	x	x	x	x	x	x	x	x	x	x	100
Hold tight					x	x		x	x	x	x			x	50
Nudge	x	x	x	x	x	x	x	x	x	x	x	x	x	x	100
Pull	x	x	x	x	x	x	x	x	x	x	x	x	x	x	100
Push		x	x	x	x					x	x		x	x	57
Rub under arms										x					7
Rub with feet										x					7
Shake body part			x		x										14
Slap	x	x	x	x	x	x	x	x	x	x	x	x	x	x	100
Visual gestures															
Direct positioning										x					7
Jerking body movements	x			x		x						x		x	36
Offer body part	x	x	x	x	x	x	x		x	x	x	x	x	x	93
Present genitals		x	x			x						x		x	36
Extend arm								x						x	36
Shake object	x	x		x	x	x	x	x				x	x	x	70
Throw back head	x	x	x	x										x	36
Wrist offer								x							7
Total of gestures	8	9	12	9	9	11	10	10	9	12	10	10	9	13	

Note. (i = infant; j = juvenile; s = subadult; a = adult), sex (f = female; m = male).
Group affiliation refers to Howletts (A, B) and Krefeld (1, 2)

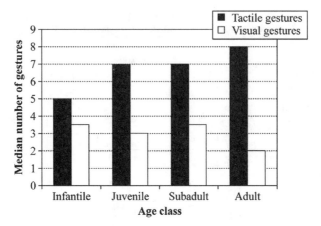

Figure 6.3. Median numbers of tactile and visual gestures used depending on age.

3.3.3. Group Differences

The gestures *rub under arms, rub with feet,* and *direct positioning* were performed in only one group by a single adult male. It seems that this can be traced back to two social factors of this particular group. First, the group was special because it contained two adult males competing for sexual access to one adult female, resulting in a higher level of agonistic interactions compared to the other groups (Liebal, 2001). *Direct positioning* was one gesture used in the agonistic context. *Rub under arms* and *rub with feet* were both gestures observed in the sexual context. Because the adult females of the other groups were pregnant, almost no sexual interactions with their mates were observed, which may explain why the gestures named earlier were not present in those two groups. Another gesture observed in only one group was *wrist offer* performed by one maturing subadult individual, within agonistic interactions with her parents or when she was approaching them. There was no particular gesture that was restricted to all members of just one group.

To determine whether the gestural repertoire was more uniform within a group than between groups, Cohen's kappas were calculated (Bakeman & Gottman, 1986). Kappas within groups (Krefeld 1 = .65; Krefeld 2 = .65; Howletts B = .66) were basically the same as those between groups (.65 and .66) and represented a general "good" level of agreement (Altman, 1991). These results indicate that the same degree of individual variability of gestural repertoires existed both within and between groups.

3.3.4.Sex Differences

Sex differences were obvious in the higher number of tactile gestures used by males. For example, *embrace with feet, rub with feet,* and *rub under arms* were tactile signals used exclusively by males in the sexual context, whereas females initiated a copulation through visual gestures, for example *jerking body movements* and *throw back head.* However, *throw back head* was also displayed by young siamangs of both sexes. Therefore, it is conceivable that the function of this gesture depended on age, with young siamangs using it to initiate play or to get the attention of their parents, and adult females using it as a sexual solicitation.

3.4. Flexibility

3.4.1. Combinations

There were 184 successive combinations of gestures (i.e., sequences) recorded. Figure 6.4 shows that most often, two gestures were combined (72.8%), followed by three-gesture sequences (17.9%), and then four-gesture sequences (5.4%). Combinations of five or more gestures represented mostly single instances. The highest number of gestures combined was nine.

3.4.2. Audience Effects

Figure 6.5 shows the percentage of gestures that the sender performed when the recipient was either attending or not attending, de-

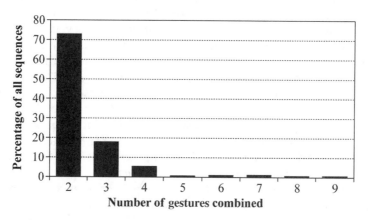

Figure 6.4. Gesture sequences as a function of the number of gestures combined.

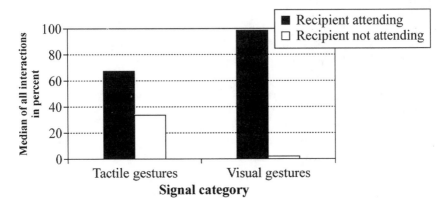

Figure 6.5. Median proportions of tactile and visual gestures used depending on the attentional state of the recipient.

pending on gesture modality. Individuals used visual gestures almost exclusively toward an attending recipient (98.2%), whereas tactile gestures were performed 66.9% of the time toward an attending recipient. Both tactile and visual gestures were performed more often toward an attending recipient, although visual gestures were directed more often toward an attending recipient than tactile gestures.

3.4.3. Means–Ends Dissociation

3.4.3.1. One Gesture for Multiple Contexts.   For every gesture, its proportional distribution across the functional contexts was calculated (Table 6.3). Five gestures (29.0%) were observed in only one context, whereas all other gestures were used in at least three or more functional contexts. Two gestures (10%) were performed in three and four different contexts, respectively, and three gestures (15%) were used in five functional contexts. One gesture (5%) was observed in six different contexts, two gestures (10%) in seven contexts, and one gesture (5%) in eight functional contexts. Two gestures occurred in all functional contexts. More specifically, *embrace with feet, rub under arms,* and *rub with feet* were only observed within sexual behavior, whereas *shake body part* was exclusively used in a play context. *Direct positioning* was related to agonistic interactions and *wrist offer* occurred only in the submissive context. In contrast, *gentle touch* and *nudge* were observed in all functional contexts.

Overall, tactile gestures were used for five different ends, whereas visual gestures were performed in four different contexts. Individuals

TABLE 6.3
Median Proportion of Gestures Used Across the Different Functional Contexts and the Total Number of Contexts a Certain Gesture Was Used For

Gesture	Affiliative	Agonistic	Grooming	Ingestion	Parental Care	Play	Sexual	Singing	Submissive	Total Number of Contexts
Embrace	x	x	x			x	x		x	6
Embrace with feet							x			1
Formal bite	x	x	x	x	x	x	x			7
Gentle touch	x	x	x	x	x	x	x	x	x	9
Hold tight	x	x				x				3
Nudge	x	x	x	x	x	x	x	x	x	9
Pull	x	x	x	x	x	x	x	x		8
Push	x	x	x	x	x	x	x			7
Rub under arms							x			1
Rub with feet							x			1
Shake body part						x				1
Slap	x	x	x	x		x	x	x		7
Direct positioning		x								1
Jerking body movements		x			x	x	x			4
Offer body part	x		x			x	x		x	5
Present genitals		x				x	x		x	4
Extend arm	x				x		x			3
Shake object	x	x		x		x		x		5
Throw back head	x		x			x	x	x		5
Wrist offer									x	1
Total number of gestures	12	12	9	7	8	15	15	5	5	

used a higher number of tactile gestures in the different contexts compared to visual gestures.

3.4.3.2. One Context With Multiple Gestures.
Overall, most (N = 15, 75%) of the 20 gestures were observed within the context of play

and sexual behavior, respectively, followed by agonistic and affiliation behavior ($N = 12$, 60%). Nine gestures (45%) were used in the context of grooming, 8 gestures (40%) in the context of nursing, and 7 gestures (35%) in the context of ingestion. The fewest number of gestures was used within the submissive and singing contexts, respectively ($N = 5$, 25%).

Individuals performed 3.5 different gestures within one functional context, and for 84% of all contexts, more than one gesture was used. In terms of gesture modality, 2.8 different tactile gestures were produced per context compared to 0.7 visual gestures.

3.5. Function of gestures

The median proportion of the time that recipients responded to gestures was 65.5%. Thus, 43.1% of the time, the recipient changed its attentional state from not attending to attending, whereas 36.5% of the time, the recipient reacted with an action, for example play (21.9%), grooming (6.2%), or agonistic behavior (4.0%). The recipient responded by producing a gesture 20.4% of the time.

3.6. Handedness

The median proportion for the use of the left hand was 49%; correspondingly, the right hand was used 51% of the time. Therefore, no hand preference was found for the performance of manual gestures.

4. DISCUSSION

The siamangs in the present study displayed a multifaceted and variable gesture repertoire, which was most often used in the contexts of play, grooming, and agonistic behavior. The majority of gestures were tactile, and these were also used more frequently than were visual gestures, regardless of age. No auditory gestures were observed. Tactile gestures also dominated in most of the functional contexts, with the exception of the sexual and submissive contexts.

Many of the gestures of siamangs described in this chapter are also reported for other gibbon species, in particular the white-handed gibbon (Baldwin & Teleki, 1976; Ellefson, 1974). However, very little is known in this regard about other gibbon species.

Fox (1977) observed *slaps, kicks,* and *jerks* in the agonistic and play behavior of captive siamangs. For white-handed gibbons (*Hylobates lar*), a number of tactile gestures has been described, for example *touch, strike, slap,* and *cuff* (Baldwin & Teleki, 1976). *Embrace* was also observed in several other studies on siamangs and white-handed gibbons (e.g., Ellefson, 1974; Fox, 1977; Orgeldinger, 1999; Palombit, 1992) where it occurred in the contexts of nursing or carrying, or served as a reassurance or greeting gesture.

A very noticeable visual gesture was the *wrist offer*. This gesture, not previously described for siamangs, is an important gesture in the communicative repertoire of chimpanzees. Approaching a dominant individual with an extended arm and offering the back of the flexed hand is an expression of submissiveness and serves as a reassurance gesture in conflict situations (Goodall, 1986). In the present study, the *wrist offer* of the subadult siamang was observed in the same context in which it was performed by the maturing subadult individual toward her parents during agonistic interactions (Liebal et al., 2004). To date, no similar behavior has been described for orangutans, bonobos, or gorillas (Liebal, Pika, & Tomasello, 2006; Pika, Liebal, & Tomasello, 2003, 2005).

In siamangs, the *offer body part* was the most frequent visual gesture, and it was primarily used in the context of grooming. Most often the sender would lie down on its belly in front of the recipient and offer its back for grooming. In contrast, white-handed gibbons initiate grooming by taking up a sitting position and then lowering the head (Ellefson, 1967). Young siamangs used the *jerking body movement* and *throw back head* to initiate play or to get the attention of their parents, in contrast to adults, who performed this gesture in the sexual context. Orgeldinger (1999) referred to the use of *present genitals* in conflict situations. For white-handed gibbons, Ellefson (1974) and Baldwin and Teleki (1976) described a *sexual crouch* gesture as an invitation for mating; this gesture was also used as a submissive gesture between young and adult siamangs, or between subordinate and dominant individuals. They also mentioned a *head tilt* used in the play context that resembles the *throw back head* described in this chapter.

Each individual used approximately 50% of the total gestural repertoire, but the kind of gestures performed varied depending on group, age, and sex. In terms of group, all differences could be traced back to either housing conditions (e.g., using the ground in play activities), special social situations (e.g., the process of peripheralizing subadults), atypical group composition causing agonistic interactions, or the pregnancy of the adult females and the consequent low number of sexual interactions. However, the comparison of the gestural repertoires revealed a very similar degree of concordance both within and between groups. These results suggest that most of the gestures are used by the majority of individuals and that the different individual repertoires are very uniform, similar to groups of captive gorillas also living in small and stable groups (Pika et al., 2003).

In terms of age, there were no significant differences regarding the total number of gestures used by young siamangs in comparison to adults. However, there was an increase until 6 years of age, whereas the total number of gestures decreased slightly in adults. Differences between age classes were more striking in the number of gestures used in the different functional contexts. Although both young and adult siamangs performed the highest variety of gestures in the play context, adults also used a wide range of gestures within the agonistic context as opposed to young siamangs. Similar findings were yielded in a long-term study investigating the development of gestural communication in young chimpanzees (Tomasello et al., 1997). The increase in gestures up until the age of 6 years was explained by the frequent play behavior of young chimpanzees. Consistent with the present results for siamangs, adult chimpanzees in that study used some gestures in the context of agonistic and sexual behavior that were not part of the gestural repertoire of younger chimpanzees, but overall they performed a lower number of gestures compared to the youngsters. In contrast, Pika et al. (2003) found that young gorillas peaked in the number of gestures performed at the age of 2–3 years, which was explained by their rather short maturation period compared to other great ape species. Differences in the gestural repertoire of siamang males and females were not very distinct except for the use of different gestures during sexual behavior.

In terms of flexibility, siamangs performed the majority of gestures in at least three or more different functional contexts. Tactile gestures were used in a greater number of different contexts than were visual gestures. Furthermore, for the majority of contexts, siamangs performed more than one gesture. Particularly within the play, sexual, and agonistic contexts, a variety of different gestures were observed. Siamangs adjusted the gestures they used depending on the attentional state of the recipient, and they performed visual gestures only if the recipient was visually attending. Finally, the combination of gestures observed in the present study might present a possibility to increase the flexibility of a relatively limited gesture repertoire by combining single gestures into complex gesture sequences (Liebal, Call, & Tomasello, 2004). Summarizing the results of the different measurements, the findings indicate that the gestures were used in a flexible way and do not represent stereotyped behavior linked to a particular social context.

Both the special ecology of siamangs and their monogamous social structure may have contributed to this unique profile of gesture use. As opposed to ground-dwelling species, which perform a variety of visual postures (Hinde & Rowell, 1962; Kummer & Kurt, 1965; van Hooff, 1962, 1967), the majority of gestures used by siamangs were tactile. This result supports the hypothesis proposed by Marler (1965) and Maestripieri (1999) that the siamang's arboreal habitat, with its restricted range of vision, should be more conducive to vocal and tactile signals than to the visual–gestural mode. Thus, if gestures play any role at all, tactile gestures should be more prominent than visual gestures, as was found in siamangs.

In terms of social structure, Chivers (1976) suggested that the small social groups, lacking a dominance hierarchy and containing only highly familiar individuals that engage in most activities together, may reduce the need for a wide and highly variable gestural repertoire. Moreover, the social life of siamangs is characterized by a high degree of synchrony in the activities of the different individuals for about 60–75% of their waking time; but the coordination of the individual behaviors seems to be achieved by mutual observation rather than by communication (Chivers, 1974). The results showed that siamangs use fewer gestures than great apes living in more complex social societies. This seems to support the hypothesis of Maestripieri (1999) that primate species in which most social interactions take fairly predictable forms need very few communicative signals. However, it was not the case that the repertoire of siamangs was as limited as suggested by Chivers (1974, 1976), because young individuals in particular used a variety of both tactile and visual gestures.

Due to the lack of studies addressing the cognitive skills of siamangs, it is difficult to interpret the results presented here regarding possible influences on the characteristics of the observed repertoire and its use. The gestural communication of siamangs shows some similarities to that of monkeys and other similarities to that of great apes. For example, great apes use a variety of manual gestures (including visually based ones) to solicit play and other activities from groupmates, and on occasion, they even incorporate objects into their gestures (Tomasello, Call, Nagell, Olguin, & Carpenter, 1994). In this respect, siamangs appear more like monkeys, as they performed only one object-based gesture. Also like monkeys but not great apes, siamangs performed more tactile and fewer visual gestures in general. On the other hand, siamangs used most of their gestures very flexibly in terms of both adjustments to the state of the recipient and means–ends dissociation, as described for chimpanzees (Tomasello et al., 1994, 1997).

5. CONCLUSION

The siamangs used a gestural repertoire consisting of 20 tactile and visual gestures. Tactile gestures represented the most dominant gesture modality, used in particular in the affiliative and agonistic contexts, whereas visual gestures dominated the contexts of sexual and submissive behaviors. No auditory gestures were observed. The majority of gestures were performed in the play context and during grooming.

In terms of variability, there were some gestures observed only in adults, mostly those used in the sexual or agonistic contexts. The number of gestures initially increased with age, but dropped after the individuals reached adulthood. Group differences were mainly traced back to social circumstances or housing conditions. Overall, the individual repertoires showed a very similar degree of concordance both within and between groups. Most gestures were used flexibly, with the majority performed in three or more functional contexts, and almost a third of gestures being used in combination with other gestures. Siamangs also adjusted their signals appropriately for the recipient and used visual gestures only when the recipient was already attending.

REFERENCES

Abordo, E. J. (1971). *Reversal shift, nonreversal shift, and discrimination reversal learning in gibbons and vervets.* Unpublished doctoral dissertation, University of California Riverside.

Abordo, E. J. (1976). The learning skills of gibbons. In D. M. Rumbaugh (Ed.), *Gibbon and siamang* (Vol. 4, pp. 106–134). Basel: Karger.

Altmann, D. (1991). *Practical statistics for medical research.* London: Chapman & Hall.

Altmann, J. (1974). Observational study of behavior: Sampling methods. *Behaviour, 49,* 227–267.

Anderson, J. (1984). Monkeys with mirrors: Some questions for primate psychology. *International Journal of Primatology, 5*(1), 81–98.

Bakeman, R., & Gottman, J. (1986). *Observing interaction: An introduction to sequential analysis.* Cambridge, England: Cambridge University Press.

Baldwin, L. A., & Teleki, G. (1976). Patterns of gibbon behavior on Hall's Island, Bermuda: A preliminary ethogram for *Hylobates lar.* In D. Rumbaugh (Ed.), *Gibbon and siamang* (Vol. 4, pp. 21–105). Basel: Karger.

Bartlett, T. (1999). The gibbons. In P. F. Dolhinow & A. Fuentes (Eds.), *The nonhuman primates* (pp. 44–49). Mountain View, CA: Mayfield.

Beck, B. B. (1967). A study of problem solving by gibbons. *Behaviour, 28,* 95–109.

Boutan, L. (1914). Les deux méthodes l'enfant [The two methods of the child]. *Actes Social Linn. Bordeaux, 68,* 3–146.

Byrne, R. W., & Whiten, A. (1990). Tactical deception in primates: The 1990 database. *Primate Report, 27,* 1–101.

Byrne, R. W., & Whiten, A. (1992). Cognitive evolution in primates: Evidence from tactical deception. *MAN, 27*(3), 609–627.

Carpenter, C. R. (1940). A field study in Siam of the behavior and social relations of the gibbon (*Hylobates lar*). *Comparative Psychology Monographs, 16,* 1–212.

Chivers, D. J. (1972). The siamang and the gibbon in the Malay Peninsula. In D. M. Rumbaugh (Ed.), *Gibbon and siamang* (Vol. 1, pp. 103–135). Basel: Karger.

Chivers, D. J. (1973). Introduction to the socio-ecology of Malayan forest primates. In R. P. Michael & H. H. Crook (Eds.), *Comparative ecology and behaviour of primates* (pp. 101–146). London: Academic Press.

Chivers, D. J. (1974). The siamang in Malaya: A field study of a primate in tropical rain forest. *Contributions to primatology* (Vol. 4, pp. 1–335). Basel: Karger.

Chivers, D. J. (1976). Communication within and between family groups of siamang (*Symphalangus syndactylus*). *Behaviour, 57,* 116–135.

Chivers, D. J. (1977). The feeding behaviour of siamang (*Symphalangus syndactylus*). In T. H. Clutton-Brock (Ed.), *Primate ecology: Studies of feeding and ranging behaviour in lemurs, monkeys and apes* (pp. 355–382). London: Academic Press.

Chivers, D. J., & Davis, G. (1979). Abundance of primates in the Krau Game Reserve Peninsula Malaysia. *Miscellaneous Series* (Department of Geography, University of Hull), 22, 9–36.

Chivers, D. J., & Raemaekers, J. J. (1980). Long-term changes in behaviour. In D. J. Chivers (Ed.), *Malayan forest primates. Ten years' study in tropical rain forest* (pp. 209–260). New York: Plenum Press.

Colishaw, G. (1992). Song function in gibbons. *Behaviour, 121*(1–2), 131–153.

Drescher, K., & Trendelenburg, W. (1927). Weiterer Beitrag zur Intelligenzprüfung an Affen (einschliesslich Antropoiden) [Further report on the investigation of intelligence in monkeys and great apes]. *Journal of Comparative Physiology A: Neuroethology, Sensory, Neural, and Behavioral Physiology, 5,* 613–642.

Ellefson, J. O. (1967). *A natural history of gibbons in the Malay Peninsula.* Unpublished doctoral dissertation, University of California, Berkeley.

Ellefson, J. O. (1974). A natural history of white-handed gibbons in the Malayan peninsula. In D. M. Rumbaugh (Ed.), *Gibbon and siamang* (Vol. 3, pp 1–136), Basel: Karger.

Frisch, J. E. (1963). Dental variability in a population of gibbons (*Hylobates lar*). In D. Brothwell (Ed.), *Dental anthropology* (pp. 15–28). Oxford, England: Pergamon.

Frisch, J. E. (1973). The hylobatid dentition. In D. Rumbaugh (Ed.), *Gibbon and siamang* (Vol. 2, pp. 55–95), Basel: Karger.

Fox, G. J. (1977). *Social dynamics in siamang.* Unpublished doctoral dissertation, University of Wisconsin, Milwaukee.

Gaulin, S. J. C., & Sailer, L. D. (1984). Sexual dimorphism in weight among the primates: The relative impact of allometry and sexual selection. *International Journal of Primatology, 5*(6), 515–535.

Geissmann, T. (1984). Inheritance of song parameters in the gibbon song analysed in two hybrid gibbons (*Hylobates pileatus* × *Hylobates lar*). Folia Primatologica, 42, 216–235.

Geissmann, T. (1991). Reassessment of age of sexual maturity in gibbons (*Hylobates spp*). *American Journal of Primatology, 23,* 11–22.

Geissmann, T. (1993). *Evolution of communication in gibbons (Hylobates spp).* Unpublished doctoral Dissertation, University of Zürich.

Geissmann, T. (1999). Duetting songs of the siamang, *Hylobates syndactylus*: II. Testing the pair-bonding hypothesis during a partner exchange.

Geissmann, T. (2002). Taxonomy and evolution of gibbons. In C. Soligo, G. Anzenberger, & R. D. Martin (Eds.), Anthropology and primatology into the third millennium: The Centenary Congress of the Zürich Anthropological Institute. *Evolutionary Anthropology, 11*(1), pp. 28–31. New York: Wiley-Liss.

Geissmann, T. (2003a). *Vergleichende Primatologie* [Comparative Primatology]. Berlin, Heidelberg, New York: Springer.

Geissmann, T. (2003b). Symposium on gibbon diversity and conservation: Concluding resolution. *Asian Primates, 8*(3), 28–29.

Geissmann, T., & Orgeldinger, M. (2000). The relationship between duet songs and pair bonds in siamangs, *Hylobates syndactylus*. *Animal Behaviour, 60*, 805–809.

Gittens, S. P., & Raemaekers, J. J. (1980). Siamang, lar and agile gibbons. In J. D. Chivers (Ed.), *Malayan forest primates. Ten years' study in tropical rain forest* (pp. 63–105). New York: Plenum Press.

Goodall, J. (1986). *The chimpanzees of Gombe: Patterns of behavior.* Cambridge, MA: Harvard University Press,

Grigor'eva, O. M., & Deriagina, M. A. (1987). Gestural forms of communication in primates. I. Development of gestural communication in ontogenesis and phylogenesis. *Biologicheskie Nauki, 1*, 45–50.

Groves, C. P. (2001). *Primate taxonomy.* Washington, DC: Smithsonian Institution Press.

Haimoff, E. H. (1986). Acoustic and organizational features of gibbons songs. In H. C. Preuschoft, D. J. Chivers, W. Y. Brockelmann, & N. Creel (Eds), *The lesser apes: Evolutionary and behavioural biology* (pp. 333–353). Edinburgh, Scotland: Edinburgh University Press.

Harlow, H. F., Uehling, H., & Maslow, A. H. (1932). Comparative behavior of primates. I. Delayed reaction tests on primates from the lemur to the orangutan. *Journal of Comparative Psychology, 13*, 313–343.

Hinde, R. A., & Rowell, T. E. (1962). Communication by postures and facial expressions in the rhesus monkey, *Macaca mulatta*. *Proceedings of the Zoological Society of London, 138*, 1–21

Hyatt, C. W. (1998). Responses of gibbons (*Hylobates lar*) to their mirror images. *American Journal of Primatology, 45*, 307–311.

Kleiman, D. G. (1977). Monogamy in mammals. *Quarterly Review of Biology, 52*, 39–69.

Kummer, H., & Kurt, F. (1965). A comparison of social behavior in captive and wild hamadryas baboons. In H. Vagtborg (Ed), *The baboon in medical research* (pp. 65–80). University of Texas, Austin.

Lethmate, J., & Dücker, G. (1973). Experiments on self-recognition in a mirror in orangutans, chimpanzees, gibbons and several monkey species. *Zeitschrift für Tierpsychologie, 33*, 248–269.

Liebal, K. (2001). *Soziale Kommunikation in Siamang-Familien (Hylobates syndactylus) in Zoologischen Gärten* [Social communication in captive siamang families (*Hylobates syndactylus*)]. Unpublished diploma thesis, University of Leipzig.

Liebal, K., Call, J., & Tomasello, M. (2004). Use of gesture sequences in chimpanzees (*Pan troglodytes*). *American Journal of Primatology, 64*, 377–396.

Liebal, K., Pika, S. & Tomasello, M. (2004). Social communication in siamangs (*Symphalangus syndactylus*): Use of gestures and facial expressions. *Primates, 45*(1), 41–57.

Liebal, K., Pika, S., & Tomasello, M. (2006). Gestural communication of orangutans (*Pongo pygmaeus*). *Gesture, 6*, 1–38.

MacKinnon, J. R. (1977). A comparative ecology of Asian apes. *Primates, 18*, 747–772.

MacKinnon, K. (1987). Conservation status of primates in Malesia, with special reference to Indonesia. *Primate Conservation, 8,* 175–183

Maestripieri, D. (1999). Primate social organization, gestural repertoire size, and communication dynamics: a comparative study of macaques. In B. J. King (Ed.), *The evolution of language: Assessing the evidence from nonhuman primates* (pp. 55–77). Santa Fe, NM: School of American Research.

Marler, P. (1965). Communication in monkeys and apes. In I. DeVore (Ed.), *Primate behaviour: Field studies of monkeys and apes* (pp. 544–584). New York: Holt, Rinehart & Winston.

Marler, P., & Tenaza, R. (1977). Signaling behavior of apes with special reference to vocalizations. In T. A. Sebeok (Ed.), *How animals communicate* (Vol. II, pp. 965–1033). London: Indiana University Press.

Marshall, J. T., & Marshall, E. R. (1976). Gibbons and their territorial songs. *Science, 193,* 235–237.

McGrew, W. C. (1992). *Chimpanzee material culture: Implications for human evolution.* Cambridge, England: Cambridge University Press.

O'Brien, T.G., Kinnaird, M.F., Nurcahyo, A., Iqbal, M., & Rusmanto, M. (2004). Abundance and distribution of sympatric gibbons in a threatened Sumatran rain forest. *International Journal of Primatology, 25,* 267–284.

Orgeldinger, M. (1999). *Paarbeziehungen beim Siamang-Gibbon (Hylobates syndactylus) im Zoo: Untersuchungen über den Einfluß von Jungtieren auf die Paarbindung* [Relationships in siamang pairs: Influence of offspring on adult pair bonding]. Münster: Schüling Verlag.

Palombit, R. A. (1992). Pair bonds and monogamy in wild siamang (*Hylobates syndactylus*) and white-handed gibbon (*Hylobates lar*). Unpublished doctoral dissertation, University of California, Davis.

Parker, C. E. (1973). Manipulatory behavior and responsiveness. In D. M. Rumbaugh (Ed.), *Gibbon and siamang,* (Vol. 2, pp. 185–207). Basel: Karger.

Pika, S., Liebal, K., & Tomasello, M. (2003). Gestural communication in young gorillas (*Gorilla gorilla*): Gestural repertoire, learning and use. *American Journal of Primatology, 60,* 95–111.

Pika, S., Liebal, K., & Tomasello, M. (2005). Gestural communication in subadult bonobos (*Pan paniscus*): Repertoire and use. *American Journal of Primatology, 65,* 39–61.

Preuschoft, H. (1988). Kleine Menschenaffen oder Gibbons [Small apes or gibbons]. In B. Grzimek (Ed.), *Grzimeks Enzyklopädie* (Vol. 2, pp. 326–356). München: Kindler.

Raemaekers, J. J., & Chivers, D. J., (1980). Socio-ecology of Malayan forest primates. In D. J. Chivers (Ed.), *Malayan forest primates: Ten years' study in tropical rain forest* (pp. 279–316). New York: Plenum Press.

Rijksen, H. D. (1978). *A field study on Sumatran orang utans (Pongo pygmaeus abelli Lesson 1827): Ecology, behaviour and conservation.* Wageningen, The Netherlands: H. Veenman and Zonen.

Roos, C., & Geissmann, T. (2001). Molecular phylogeny of the major Hylobatid divisions. *Molecular Phylogenetics and Evolution, 19,* 486–494.

Rowe, N., Goodall, J., & Mittermeier, R. A. (1996). *The pictorial guide to the living primates.* East Hampton, NY: Pogonias Press.

Rumbaugh, D. M. (1970). Learning skills of anthropoids. In L. A. Rosenblum (Ed.), *Primate behavior: Developments in field and laboratory research,* (Vol. 1, pp. 1–70). New York: Academic Press.

Rumbaugh, D. M., & McCormack, C. (1967). The learning skills of primates: A comparative study of apes and monkeys. In D. Starck, R. Schneider, & H.-J. Kuhn (Eds.), *Neue Ergebnisse der Primatologie* (pp. 289–306). Stuttgart: Gustav Fischer Verlag.

Rutberg, A. T. (1983). The evolution of monogamy in primates. *Journal of Theoretical Biology, 104,* 93–112.

Schultz, A. H. (1933). Observations on growth, classification and evolutionary specialization of gibbons and siamangs. *Human Biology, 5,* 212–255, 385–428.

Schultz, A. H. (1956). Postembryonic age changes. In H. Hofer, A. H. Schultz, & D. Starck (Eds.), *Primatologica: Handbuch der Primatenkunde* (Vol. 1, pp. 887–964). Basel: Karger.

Schultz, A. H. (1962). Metric changes and sex differences in primate skulls. *Zeitschrift für Morphologie und Anthropologie, 52,* 239–255.

Schultz, A. H. (1973). The skeleton of the Hylobatidae and other observations on their morphology. In D. M. Rumbaugh (Ed.), *Gibbon and siamang* (Vol. 2, pp. 1–54). Basel: Karger.

Thompson, W. D., Kirk, R. E., Koestler, A. G., & Bourgeois, A. E. (1965). A comparison of operant conditioning responses in the baboon, gibbon, and chimpanzee. In H. Vagtborg, (Ed.), *The baboon in medical research: Proceedings of the first international symposium on the baboon and its use as an experimental animal* (pp. 81–93). Austin: University of Texas Press.

Tomasello, M., & Call., J. (1997). *Primate cognition.* New York, Oxford: University Press.

Tomasello, M., Call, J., Nagell, K., Olguin, R., & Carpenter, M. (1994). The learning and the use of gestural signals by young chimpanzees: A trans-generational study. *Primates, 35,* 137–154.

Tomasello, M., & Zuberbühler, K. (2002). Primate vocal and gestural communication. In M. Bekoff, C. S. Allen, & G. Burghardt (Eds.), *The cognitive animal: Empirical and theoretical perspectives on animal cognition* (pp. 293–299). Cambridge: The MIT Press.

Torigoe, T. (1985). Comparison of object manipulation among 74 species of honhuman primates. *Primates, 26*(2), 182–194.

Ujhelyi, M., Merker, B., Buk, P., & Geissmann, T. (2000). Observations on the behavior of Gibbons (*Hylobates leucogenys, H. gabriellae, and H. lar*) in the presence of mirrors. *Journal of Comparative Psychology, 114*(3), 253–262.

van Hooff, J. A. R. A. M. (1962). Facial expressions in higher primates. *Symposia of the Zoological Society of London, 8,* 97–125.

van Hooff, J. A. R. A. M. (1967). The facial displays of the catarrhine monkeys and apes. In D. Morris (Ed.), *Primate ethology* (pp. 7–68). London: Weidenfels and Nicolson.

Waddell, P. J., & Penney, D. (1996). Evolutionary trees of apes and humans from DNA sequences. In A. Lock & C. R. Peters (Eds.), *Handbook of human symbolic evolution* (pp. 53–73). Oxford: Clarendon Press.

CHAPTER 7

Gestural Communication in Barbary Macaques (Macaca sylvanus): An Overview

Nana Hesler
Julia Fischer
German Primate Center

Figure 7.1.   Barbary macaques.

1. INTRODUCTION

*T*he desire to understand the roots of human language is a major force driving the study of nonhuman primate communication. Although a number of authors see the precursor to human speech in the vocalizations of monkeys and apes (Fischer, 2002; Fitch, 2000; Hauser, 1996; Seyfarth, Cheney, & Marler, 1980a), more recent contributions highlight the importance of gestural signals (Arbib, 2005; King, 1999). One main argument is that nonhuman primates have excellent voluntary control over their hands (Corballis, 2002; Rizzolatti & Arbib, 1998), whereas they lack voluntary control over the laryngeal muscles that are involved in controlling the structure of vocal patterns (Jürgens, 2002). Moreover, area F5 in the monkey brain that controls manual movements appears to be homologous to the human Broca area that is involved in human speech production (Arbib, 2005).These findings support the hypothesis that human language evolved via gestural signs (Arbib, 2005; Corballis, 2002). Unfortunately, few studies have so far examined the gestural communication of monkeys in detail. Although it is clear that monkeys can perform a precision grip, for instance, evidence suggests that they use manual gestures much less frequently than do apes (Maestripieri, 1998). Moreover, it remains unclear whether nonhuman primate gestural communication is really more elaborate than their vocal communication.

A sound comparison of monkeys' and apes' abilities in the different signaling modalities has so far been hampered by an imbalance in knowledge (Tomasello & Zuberbühler, 2002): whereas most studies on vocal communication have been conducted on monkeys (for a review, see Ghazanfar & Santos, 2004), the vast majority of studies on the use of gestural signals have been done on apes (Bard, 1992; DeWaal, 1988; Liebal, Call, & Tomasello, 2004b; Liebal, Pika, & Tomasello, 2004a; Nishida, Kano, Goodall, McGrew, & Nakamura, 1999; Pika, 2003; Savage-Rumbaugh, Wilkerson, & Bakemann, 1977; Tanner & Byrne, 1996; Tomasello, Call, Nagell, Olguin, & Carpenter, 1994; Tomasello et al., 1997; Tomasello et al., 1985; Van Lawick-Goodall, 1972). However, some recent studies have helped to fill our gap in knowledge about the structure, use, and function of vocal signals in apes and gestural signals in monkeys (ape vocal communication: Arcadi, 1996; Crockford & Boesch, 2003; Crockford, Herbinger, Vigilant, & Boesch, 2004; Marshall, Wrangham, & Arcadi, 1999; Mitani, Hasegawa, Gros-Louis, Marler, & Byrne, 1992; monkey gestural communication: Deag, 1974; Dube & Tomasello, 2003; Maestripieri, 1997; Preuschoft, 1992; Preuschoft, Paul, & Küester, 1998).

An important research question regarding the cognitive processes underlying communicative acts is whether signals are used flexibly and can be adjusted to different situations or if they are produced in a rather fixed way according to internal variables such as the motivational state or according to a fixed response to certain stimuli (Tomasello & Call, 1997). Flexibility can be characterized by a so-called 'means–end dissociation' (Bruner, 1981), that is, different signals are used in order to achieve the same goal whereas the same signal may be used to accomplish different goals (see other chapters this volume). Another possible indication for flexible signal use is the number of different ways in which signals are combined (Dube & Tomasello, 2003). Moreover, signalers could show flexibility by using signals in an appropriate modality according to the attentional state of the recipient. For instance, signalers should not use a visual signal when the intended recipient is not looking, but rather use a tactile or auditory one.

The range of studies on apes presented in this book demonstrates that the gestural communication of great apes as well as small apes shows flexibility according to the characteristics outlined earlier. Monkeys also appear to communicate in a flexible way when using gestures and postures (Dube & Tomasello, 2003; Maestripieri, 1997; Parr & Maestripieri, 2003;). However, a broader range of species studied is desirable to fully understand to which degree the criteria for flexible signaling applies in monkeys as well. Moreover, for the species studied here—the Barbary macaques (*Macaca sylvanus*)—detailed knowledge of their vocal communication is available (for example, Fischer & Hammerschmidt, 2002; Fischer & Hammerschmidt, 2004; Hammerschmidt & Fischer, 1998a). This allows us to directly compare their vocal and nonvocal communication.

In this study, we describe the nonvocal communication of Barbary macaques. We provide a detailed description of the gestural repertoire of this species. Earlier studies have already published some information on Barbary macaque gestures (Deag, 1974; Preuschoft, 1992; Preuschoft et al., 1998; Preuschoft & Van Schaik, 2000; Roshani, Todt, & Janik, 1994; Zeller, 1980). We relate our definitions to those established in these studies and in studies on other macaque species (Maestripieri, 1997; Van Hooff, 1962, 1967). We analyze age- and sex-related differences in gesture usage. We also categorize the signals according to the perceptual modalities of potential recipients. To examine the flexibility of signal usage, we investigate context-related differences in gesture usage, and signal combinations. Third, we compare their nonvocal to their vocal communication. Finally, we aim to identify some of the differences between monkeys and apes.

We define gestures as all visual, tactile, and auditory signals that are expressed through movements of the body or face, except for vocalizations. For this, behavior patterns that seem to serve no other function than a communicative one are considered as signals.

2. INTRODUCTION TO THE SPECIES

2.1. Taxonomy

The genus *Macaca* represents the most widely distributed nonhuman primate genus. Depending on which authors are followed, it contains up to 20 species (Fa, 1989; Morales & Melnick, 1998; Tosi, Morales, & Melnick, 2000). Macaques, together with the genera *Papio* (baboons), *Mandrillus* (mandrills and drills), *Theropithecus* (Gelada monkeys), and *Cercocebus* (mangabeys) comprise the tribe *Papionini* (Fa, 1989). *Papionini* belong to the old world monkeys (*Cercopithecoidea*), which are the sister group to the superfamily *Hominoidea* comprising small and great apes and humans (Smuts, Cheney, Seyfarth, Wrangham, & Struhsaker, 1987).

The fossil record indicates that macaques diverged from other *Papionini* in northern Africa in the late Miocene 7–8 million years ago. They invaded Eurasia about 5.5 million years ago, then split into several phyletic lineages. Whereas all other species dispersed in Asia, the Barbary macaque is the last African representative. Based on fossil and morphological (Delson, 1980) as well as molecular studies (Hayasaka, Fujii, & Horai, 1996; Morales & Melnick, 1998), Barbary macaques are located at the base of the phylogenetic tribe of *Macaca* being the sister group to all other macaque species.

2.2. Morphology

Macaques in general are medium sized monkeys with stout bodies and hairless faces (Falk, 2000; Nowak, 1999). The best known species probably is the rhesus macaque (*Macaca mulatta*), who is a sacred animal in the Hindu religion. In the western world, rhesus macaques have been used extensively for scientific experiments, giving name to the Rh factor of the blood (Nowak, 1999). The smallest macaque species, the toque macaque (*Macaca sinica*), weighs about 2.5–6.1 kg (Nowak, 1999), whereas the Barbary macaque with an average body weight of 15.3–17 kg (males) or 10.2–11 kg (females), represents one of the heaviest species with stout physics and, exceptional within the genus, no tail (Fa, 1989). Adult Barbary macaques reach a shoulder height of about 40 cm and a head-to-tail length of about 60 cm (Paul, 1984). As many macaques and other primates, they show sexual dimorphism not only in body size, but also in dentation in that adult males in contrast to females grow long canines (Fa, 1984; Plavcan, 2001). Females in estrous show anogenital swellings

(Fa, 1989). Barbary macaques have a yellowish brown fur that becomes very thick in winter. Infants are born in a short, almost dark fur, that is gradually replaced by a very fleecy one in bright beige at the age of about 5 months (Fa, 1989).

2.3. Distribution and Ecology

Owing to their variable diet that consists of leaves and barks of the evergreen cedar (*Cedrus sp.*) and other trees, different parts of grasses and herbs, and also invertebrate animals as insects, Barbary macaques can live in a variety of habitats (Drucker, 1984). Currently, their presence is restricted to mountainous regions of Morocco and Algeria (Von Segesser, Ménard, Gaci, & Martin, 1999) where they live in 2,000+m altitude (Ménard & Vallet, 1993). There is also a small population on the Rock of Gibraltar. The wild population is currently estimated at a maximum of 15,000 and the species is listed as vulnerable in the 'IUCN *Red List*' (Von Segesser et al., 1999). Barbary macaques are mainly terrestrial during the day but climb on trees or rocks in order to sleep at night (Ansorge, Hammerschmidt, & Todt, 1992). Possibly as an adaptation to the rather harsh conditions of their habitat, Barbary macaques are seasonal breeders with a mating season in autumn and a birth season in spring (Küster & Paul, 1996).

2.4. Social Structure and Behavior

In general, the social system is organized as in most macaque species. Barbary macaques live in large multimale-multifemale groups with a mean size of about 30 individuals and a more or less balanced sex ratio (Von Segesser et al., 1999). In contrast to most other macaques, Barbary macaques have a highly promiscuous mating system (Von Segesser et al., 1999). Females stay in their natal groups whereas adolescent males migrate to other groups. Within the social group, females form matrilinear subgroups where kin-related females maintain preferential bonds and support each other during conflicts. Compared to other macaque species, the social system of Barbary macaques is rather tolerant, that is, the influence of dominance status and kinship on intraspecific social dynamics is not as extreme as in other species, such as in rhesus macaques (Flack & De Waal, 2004; Preuschoft, Paul, & Küester, 1998; Preuschoft & Van Schaik, 2000; Thierry, 2000). Among females, there is a quite stable linear dominance hierarchy (Chapais, 2004; Gachot-Neveu & Ménard, 2004) that depends on matrilines (Thierry, 2000). Among males, the structure of dominance relations is less clear (Preuschoft & Van Schaik, 2000). Generally, adult males dominate over females. A characteristic of the social behavior of Barbary macaques is intense alloparental care by males (Deag & Crook, 1971; Taub, 1980) and infants play a highly important role in social behavior of both sexes.

2.5. Cognition

Few studies have been conducted on the cognitive abilities of this species. Most of these addressed the issue of kin recognition. Hammerschmidt and Fischer (1998a) showed that mothers preferentially turn to their own infant's calls, both after playback and in response to natural calling. Fischer (2004) used playback experiments to examine the developmental trajectory of infant responses to their own mother's calls versus another female's calls of the same social group. Although infants of other species spend most of their time with the mothers, it was possible to exploit the extensive alloparental care system that provided a natural separation of the infant from the mother. Although infants at about one month of age showed no responses to the playback of either their mother's or another female's calls, they looked significantly longer toward the (hidden) speaker at an age of 10 weeks (Fischer, 2004). Both studies suggest that individual recognition by voice occurs regularly—at least among kin. There are anecdotal observations (C. Teufel, personal communication) that suggest that Barbary macaques have an understanding of third-party relationships within their group, but this has not yet been successfully tested. We know of no study that has looked at the cognitive abilities in the physical domain in this species.

2.6. Communication: State of the Art

Concerning the communication system of Barbary macaques, only few studies have addressed the gestural communication of this species. For example, Zeller (1980) considered the single facial components of the threat display and found that the mouth is the most variable component and that variation can mainly be related to kinship, and to a lesser degree to sex and age. Preuschoft (1992) examined the behavioral context of the facial expressions "bared teeth display" and "relaxed open mouth display." She found indications that the bared teeth display is a homologue of the human smile, and the relaxed open mouth display a homologue of the human laughter, supporting the hypothesis of different origins of these two human facial expressions. In later works, she investigated the use of gestural signals in competitive situations and found differences between the sexes (Preuschoft et al., 1998; Preuschoft & Van Schaik, 2000). Roshani et al. (1994) investigated the occurrence of yawning in male Barbary macaques. The study revealed a correlation to particular social contexts, suggesting that yawning is an expression of the internal variables tension and conflict, but also for a certain voluntary control of its performance. Mehlman (1996) examined the branch shaking behavior in Barbary macaques with respect to the common interpretation that it is an aggressive or defensive signal used to maintain or increase the distance between different social groups. He found no support of this hypothesis, as branch shaking is mainly an intragroup display with heterogeneous signal functions, and without a correlation to agonistic contexts.

Compared to the gestural communication in Barbary macaques, their vocal behavior has been studied extensively (Fischer, Hammerschmidt, & Todt, 1995; Kipper & Todt, 2002; Todt, Hammerschmidt, Ansorge, & Fischer, 1995; Todt, Hammerschmidt, & Hultsch, 1992). The vocal repertoire of this species can be characterized as variations on a few themes, namely screams, shrill barks, geckers, and low frequency pants (Fischer & Hammerschmidt, 2002; Hammerschmidt & Fischer, 1998b). Occasionally, Barbary macaques produce tonal 'coolike' calls, and nasally sounding girneys. Intergradations occur frequently, and in a quantitative analysis, no unique cluster solution emerged (Hammerschmidt & Fischer, 1998b). According to this analysis, the authors defined as 'call types' those call exemplars that represented cluster centers. However, the delineations between clusters were not always obvious. There was also no clear-cut relationship between call types and the situations in which they occurred. For instance, pant calls were given in agonistic encounters when one animal was threatening another, but also when a subject observed an interaction between group members and an infant, clearly an affiliative situation. Likewise, tonal calls were recorded from females that were threatened as well as from females who were in search of their infant. Although noisy and complex screams were most often observed in highly charged contexts such as contact aggression, it is important to keep in mind that this context category encompasses a wide variety of situations. Some call types, for instance noisy screams, were given by members of all age and sex classes. The same is true for shrill barks, with the exception that infants did not produce them. Highly undulated screams, in contrast, were most frequently given by infant and juvenile macaques, and only rarely by members of older age classes (Fischer & Hammerschmidt, 2002). Whereas it was difficult to identify clear-cut rules to explain the overall structure of the repertoire, studies that examined the acoustic variation within call types found systematic variation with context or the physiological state of the caller. For instance, Semple (1998) showed that the mating calls of Barbary macaque females varied with reproductive state. Using playback experiments, he also demonstrated that males respond differentially to these variants. In a similar fashion, Fischer and colleagues (Fischer et al., 1995) found that the shrill barks—which function as alarm calls in this species—revealed subtle but consistent differences in relation to the context in which they were given. Playback experiments adopting the habituation-recovery paradigm revealed that Barbary macaques categorized the calls according to the context in which they were given, and not solely based on acoustic similarity (Fischer, 1998), in a fashion very similar to the phenomenon of categorical perception found in human speech (Fischer, 2006). This study showed that a functionally referential call system does not necessarily need to be based on acoustically distinct alarm calls, like the alarm calls of vervet monkeys, *Chlorocebus aethiops* (Seyfarth et al., 1980a; Seyfarth, Cheney, & Marler, 1980b) or Diana monkeys, *Cercopithecus diana diana* (Zuberbühler, 2000).

3. METHODS

3.1. Study Site

The study was carried out in the monkey park 'La Forêt des Singes' in Rocamadour, France. The park is open to visitors and extends on 20 ha of oak forest, *Quercus spp.*, juniper scrub, *Juniperius spp.* and open meadow. About 130 Barbary macaques live here under semifree conditions in three social groups. They are fed several times a day with cereals, monkey chow, fruits, and vegetables; water is provided *ad libitum*. In addition, the animals forage on naturally growing vegetation such as leaves and bark of trees, herbs, leaves, seeds, and invertebrate animals, and they spend much time searching for food. They can range freely in the park whereas the visitors are restricted to pathways but are allowed to feed the monkeys with special food. The animals are fully habituated to human observers. All of them are individually recognizable and tattooed with a number at the inner thigh. For this study, the largest group was chosen, which during the time of the study consisted of 52 animals. Table 7.1 shows the group composition. One of the adult males died during the observation period. Several studies have already been conducted in this population, in particular a series of studies on their vocal behavior (overview in Fischer & Hammerschmidt, 2002) so that a comparison of the vocal and gestural behavior is not affected by confounding factors such as a different habitat or other ecological variables. For

Table 7.1
Composition of the Study Group

Age class	Sex	Age (years)	N
infants	females males	< 1	1 4
young juveniles	females males	1 to < 2	1 1
older juveniles	females males	2 to < 4	- 2
subadults	females males	4 to < 5 4 to < 7	1 3
adults	females males	5 7	24 15

further information on park management and size, see Turckheim and Merz (1984).

3.2. Data Collection

In order to compile the gestural repertoire of Barbary macaques, focal and *ad libitum* observations and 10 h film recordings (Sony DCR-PC100E) of the animals' behaviors were carried out during 3.5 months between July, 2003 and July, 2004. Here, we provide a qualitative analysis of our observations. We describe the typical variants of given behavior patterns and also provide a list of terms used by other authors (see Appendix). Based on our observations and film material, we assigned each signal to the context in which it occurred. We established the following contexts: play, affiliative interaction that lead to friendly interactions like huddling or grooming, and three variants of agonistic interactions: submissive, undecided, and dominant.

4. GESTURAL REPERTOIRE

4.1. Ethogram

We observed and described 37 different gestures in Barbary macaques; 13 facial expressions and movements, 13 manual gestures, and 11 postures.

Facial Expressions and Movements

Because some of the facial displays are usually combined with certain body movements, these are described here as well.

- Relaxed open mouth face
  The mouth is half to wide open and the teeth are covered by the lips, at least the upper incisors. The lower incisors are often visible (Figs. 7.2–7.4). Frequently, the signaler approaches its mouth toward the recipient as if to bite him ("mock bite"). As vocalizations, pants may be uttered (Fischer & Hammerschmidt, 2002; Kipper & Todt, 2002). *Relaxed open mouth face* is performed during play. It seems to initiate play, but occurs also during ongoing play.
- Chatter
  The next four expressions, *chew-smack, lip-smack, teeth-chatter* and *chatter at body parts* have a repeated opening and closing of the mouth in common and have often been seen to grade into one another (*chew-smack* into *lip-smack, lip-smack* into *teeth-chatter* and vice versa). *Teeth chatter* also grades into *bared teeth display*. The mouth is not opened very wide, so the movement can be performed very fast. In the following the term, 'chatter' will be used to refer to all variants. In general, *chatter* is performed during diverse friendly interactions, but *teeth-chatter* in particular also occurs as a reaction to threats or to approaches of dominant animals.

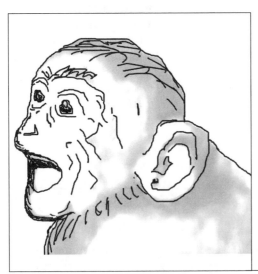

Figure 7.2. Relaxed open mouth face of an infant during play.

Figure 7.3. Relaxed open mouth face of a juvenile during rough-and-tumble play.

Figure 7.4. Rough-and-tumble play between two juveniles: mock bite, relaxed open mouth face, and grab.

1. *Chew-smack:* The lips are closed and somewhat protruded while the jaw opens and closes. The movement may begin slowly and then accelerate.
2. *Lip-smack:* Again the lips are a little protruded, but open and close with the opening and closing of the mouth. A smacking sound may be produced.
3. *Teeth-chatter:* The lips and corners of the mouth are retracted backward and upward, exposing teeth and sometimes gums

(Fig. 7.5). Except for the movement of the jaw, *teeth-chatter* resembles the *bared teeth display*. The teeth may produce a clicking sound. The movement of the lower jaw can be very small and fast. Additionally, the tongue may be protruded when the mouth is open and retracted quickly before the mouth is shut again ("tongue protrusion," Maestripieri, 1997; "tongue smacking," Deag, 1974; Van Hooff, 1967). *Teeth-chatter* may be accompanied by *head-flag*. Additionally soft vocalizations may occur.

4. *Chatter at body parts:* While *chattering* in close body contact, such as during triadic interactions (see later) or handling with infants, the signaler may approach its mouth toward body parts of the receiver, until he almost or really touches it. Often this behavior is directed toward genitalia. When the signaler *chatters at* an infant, he often lifts it and holds it closer to his mouth or touches the genitalia with his fingers (*touch genitalia*). The signaler may also stop to *chatter* for a moment and touch the genitalia of the baby with his lips.

Chatter, above all *lip-smack, teeth-chatter,* and *chatter at body parts*, are part of a typical behavioral pattern called triadic interaction or agonistic buffering (Deag & Crook, 1971; Taub, 1980) where usually two adults sit in body contact, hold one infant or little juvenile, and *chatter* (Fig. 7.6). The adults approach their heads normally to the child while *chattering*, often lifting and lowering the head or turning the head from side to side (*head-flag*). Frequently the animals *hug* and *knead* each other. Often they

Figure 7.5. Teeth-chatter with the tongue protruded by an adult female. This display is mainly used in friendly interactions.

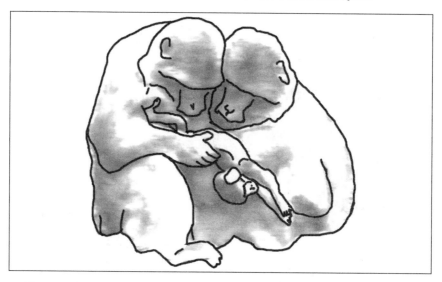

Figure 7.6.   Triadic interaction between two adult males and an infant.

chatter at the genitalia of the child and touch the genitalia of the infant with lips or hands (*touch genitalia*). One or both of the adults may hold the infant at its thighs and lift it over their head, *chattering at* its genitalia. The body positions are variable; often the adults sit next to each other, opposite each other or, more rarely, behind each other. There are also other interactions similar to triadic interactions but with different constellations of participants: For example, only one adult holds an infant or young juvenile and *chatters at* it or at its genitalia. Or, with no infant involved, two or more animals sit, stand, or lie in body contact and *chatter* at each other or at genitalia or other body parts of the other. So often two females stand or lie in antiparallel position and each one *chatters at* the genitalia of the other one (Fig. 7.15).

- Bared teeth display
  The jaws are closed or opened very little. The lips and the corner of the lips are retracted backward and upward so that the teeth are clearly visible. Often, this display grades into *teeth chatter* (Figs. 7.7 and 7.8). We labeled this facial expression only as *bared teeth display* when there is no *chattering*, otherwise it is referred to as *teeth-chatter*.
- Bared teeth gecker face
  The mouth is little to half opened, the lips and corners of the mouth are somewhat retracted revealing the teeth. This expres-

Figure 7.7. Teeth-chatter grading into the bared teeth display by a subadult female. This expression is used in a friendly and submissive context.

Figure 7.8. Bared teeth display of a subadult male. The teeth are clenched and the corners of the lips are retracted backwards.

sion grades often into the *(unvocalized) scream face*. In contrast to the *(unvocalized) scream face*, in the *bared teeth gecker face,* the mouth is opened less wide. The *bared teeth gecker face* occurs in association with gecker calls (Deag, 1974; Fischer & Hammerschmidt, 2002), but also without vocalizations. The *bared teeth gecker face* with and without vocalization is often shown as a protest reaction to threats or other agonistic behavior and frequently it grades into the *(unvocalized) scream face* and vice versa.

- (Unvocalized) scream face
  The mouth is wide open. The lips are retracted and the teeth are exposed. Sometimes the gums are visible (Fig. 7.9). The *scream face* ("scream threat," Shirek-Ellefson, 1972) accompanies screaming (Fischer & Hammerschmidt, 2002; Shirek-Ellefson, 1972) but there is also a silent *scream face* without vocalization. Both occur during conflicts; often a conflict consists of several animals who look at the others and scream ("scream fight"). The *unvocalized scream face* was often seen in animals observing distant conflicts. It may grade into the *bared teeth gecker face.*
- Stare
  The signaler *stares* at the recipient with wide-open eyes and raised eyebrows, showing the paler skin above the eyelids. The mouth is shut or opened only slightly. Often the *stare* is accompanied by a short movement of the head and sometimes the shoulders toward the receiver (*head bob*), and eventually by *slap ground*. The *stare* seems to be a low-intensity form of the *rounded mouth threat* and grades often into it.
- Rounded mouth threat face
  Like in the *stare*, the signaler stares at the recipient and raises the eyebrows, but the mouth is opened without showing the teeth. The corners of the mouth and the lips are moved forward and downward. The opening of the mouth varies from a narrow gap ("staring open-mouthed face," Deag, 1974) to an almost round hole ("staring open-mouthed pout face," Deag, 1974). The *rounded mouth threat face* is usually accompanied by *head bobs*, and eventually by *slap ground* or a quick approach toward the re-

Figure 7.9. (Unvocalized) scream face of an adult female uttered during agonistic encounters.

cipient (see Figs. 7.10 and 7.11). The whole threat pattern is carried out synchronously in a short movement toward the receiver and may be performed repeatedly in bouts. As vocalization, *pants* may be uttered (Fischer & Hammerschmidt, 2002). Grading into the *staring open mouth pant face* is possible. For more details, see Zeller (1980).

• Staring open mouth pant face
  The signaler stares at the recipient and raises its eyebrows. The mouth is half to wide open. The corners of the mouth are retracted somewhat downward and the canines may be visible.

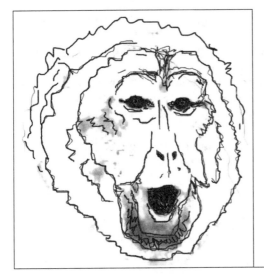

Figure 7.10. Rounded mouth threat face by an adult female subject.

Figure 7.11. Signal combination typically used during threats: stare, rounded mouth threat face, head bob and slap ground, here depicted for a male subject.

Pants may be uttered as vocalizations. It occurs during conflicts; frequently when the signaler is opposing an opponent and often it is accompanied by a short movement of the signaler toward the recipient (*lunges*).

* Bite
  Real biting and pretending to bite ("formal bite," Liebal, Pika et al., 2004) are difficult to distinguish. In both cases, the signaler opens its mouth wide, approaches it to the body of the receiver, and places the mouth on it. Often, especially during play, the signaler first *pulls* and then *bites* a certain part of the body. *Bite* also occurs in agonistic situations, in attacks, or during mountings.
* Yawn
  When the signaler *yawns*, the lips fully retract showing teeth and gums or only half retract, so that only the tips of the teeth are visible (Fig. 7.12). *Yawning* occurs often during triadic interactions and was interpreted as a correlate of internal tension and as an agonistic signal (Roshani et al., 1994), but animals *yawn* as well in calm nonsocial situations.

Manual Gestures

* Sweep
  The signaler moves one hand in a sweeping movement in front of its body over the ground. It was observed during play and during conflicts, when the signaler was confronting the opponent.

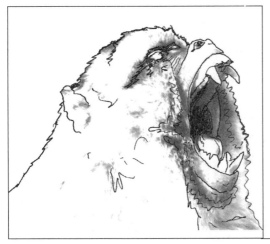

Figure 7.12. Adult male yawning, functioning as a threat gesture.

- Touch

  The signaler touches the recipient with the palm of one hand or with fingers without *slapping, grabbing, pulling,* or *hugging*. It is performed during friendly interactions in close body contact or during play.

- Hug

  One animal puts one or both arms around another animal. Often, animals sit together within body contact and *hug* each other (see Fig. 7.13). It occurs also during other friendly interactions in close body contact such as triadic interactions or play.

- Knead

  While *hugging* another animal, the signaler *kneads* the other's fur by opening and closing the hand, sometimes performing a tapping movement with the hand. It was seen during triadic interactions and, as *hugging*, in other friendly interactions in close body contact. *Kneading* in the tapping variety also occurred when the signaler held a baby and tapped the baby with the hand.

- Touch genitalia

  One animal *touches the genitalia* of another one. There are many different ways of performing it, such as two males sitting in front of each other, one touching the penis of the other; or during *inspecting the anogenital area* or *mountee reaches back*. (See "hand to object's anogenital area," Deag, 1974 and "genital manipulation," Maestripieri, 1997).

- Touch own genitalia

  The signaler *touches its own genitalia* with a hand. This gesture was seen in different situations: during triadic interactions,

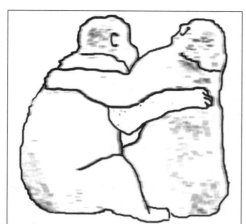

Figure 7.13. Hug. Two adult females sitting in close contact, embracing each other and often kneading each other's fur.

during *mountings* when the mountee reaches back, and accompanying *teeth-chatter* as a reaction to a threat.

- Hip-touch
  The signaler touches the receiver from behind with one or both hands on its waist ("hands on waist," Deag, 1974) or at the sides of her swelling ("hand to object's anogenital area," Deag, 1974), sometimes holding it like this for a while (Fig. 7.14). Rarely the feet are put in this way as well. It occurs usually as a reaction to *presenting* and before *mounting*.
- Mountee reaches back
  During *mountings*, the mountee often *reaches back* beside his body in order to grab the hind leg of the mounter and pull him toward himself. In male–male *mountings*, the mountee often *reaches back* in this way or under its body to touch its own or the mounter's genitalia (*touch genitalia, touch own genitalia*).
- Slap at hands
  During conflicts, when the signaler is opposing the recipient, he *slaps* the receiver *at his/her hands* or at the ground close to the receiver's hands. The hand movement is directed in front of the sender's own body. *Slap at hands* often accompanies *lunges*.
- Slap
  The signaler *slaps* another animal briefly with its hand. This occurs often during play, but also in agonistic situations, such as accompanying threats.
- Slap ground
  The animal stomps with one hand in a vertical movement at the ground without locomotion (see Fig. 7.11). This signal usually

Figure 7.14. Hip touch. The female presents her behind to a male who touches her hips and inspects her anogenital area.

accompanies threats, but was also seen during play sessions.
- Pull
  To grab another animal, like *grab*, but pulling longer. As in *grab*, the signaler often *pulls* at the ear or top of the head. Again, the typical situations in which it was seen are play and agonistic situations like threats or struggles.
- Grab
  The signaler *grabs* another animal, often at the ear or at the top of the head, and pulls shortly. Like *slap*, it occurs during play and in agonistic situations like struggles.

Postures

- Headstand
  The animal is somehow touching the ground with its head. Sometimes it looks to the recipient between its hind legs. Such *headstands* are regularly performed during social play, but occur also as a reaction to threats.
- Head-flag
  The signaler turns the head from side to side or lifts and lowers the head (Fischer & Hammerschmidt, 2002). It was seen only during intense *teeth-chatter* as in triadic interactions.
- Expose belly
  Lying on its back or on its side, the signaler stretches out its limbs in the air or on the ground so that its belly is exposed. Often it occurs during grooming sessions and it appears to be a request for grooming.
- Invitation to ride
  The signaler directs its behind toward an infant or young juvenile, lowers the hindquarters or the whole body and looks at the infant. The signaler may *chatter*. There are reduced forms in which the signaler only directs his behind toward the infant and looks at it. Usually the infant reacts by climbing on the back of the signaler. A similar pattern is shown by estrus females inviting mates to mate, although here the behind is not lowered but rather *presented* to the male (see later).
- Present
  The signaler presents its hindquarters toward the recipient. The animal may bend the front legs and bring the hindquarters in a higher position than the rest of the body. *Present* occurs also in a lying position, with the body pressed on the ground, but the signaler may also just stand still in front of the receiver and direct its hindquarters toward it (see Fig. 7.14). The signaler

may look at the receiver, the head turned back, and sometimes *teeth-chatter*. *Present* is usually performed by subdominants toward dominants, such as when a dominant animal approaches. Frequently, females are also presenting to each other in the "antiparallel" position, lip smacking and chattering at each others' behinds (Fig. 7.15).

- Mount
  The mountee stands on its four legs and the mounter approaches it from behind. The mounter climbs on the mountee, clings his hands to the waist or sides of the mountee's body (*hip-touch*) and puts his feet on the hind legs of the mountee above his ankle. Often the mounter performs pelvic thrusts; rhythmic dorso-ventral movements of the pelvis (Deag, 1974). Frequently the mounter *bites* the mountee during mountings in the back (Preuschoft & Van Schaik, 2000). Male–female *mounting* normally is preceded by *presenting* and often by inspecting the anogenital region. During *mountings,* the mountee often looks back to the mounter and/or *reaches back*; he may also scream. Often both animals *teeth-chatter*. Male–female mounting occurs regularly when a male comes into proximity of a female; male–male mounting was often seen during conflicts.
- Lunge
  The signaler is lunging toward the receiver briefly. In contrast to *head bob* (and to "lunges" in Deag, 1974), the animal walks or runs some steps. Animals perform *lunges* during conflicts, when signaler and recipient oppose each other, and frequently *lunges* are accompanied by *threats, staring open mouth pant face,*

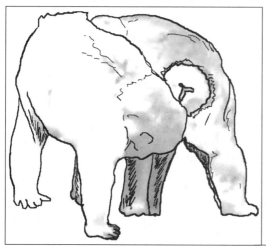

Figure 7.15. Two females in the antiparallel position, inspecting and lip-smacking at each other's behinds.

and screaming or pants as vocalizations.

- Show–look
  During conflicts with screaming or *unvocalized scream face*, one animal stands still and looks first to the opponent, then turns its head to one or both sides, looking in these directions. Apparently this behavior pattern serves to recruit allies in conflict situations, because often another animal then arrives and supports the signaler (Fischer & Hammerschmidt, 2002; Maestripieri, 1997).

- Head bob
  A short movement of the head or head and shoulders toward the recipient, which usually accompanies *rounded mouth threat* and sometimes *stare* (see also "lunges," Deag, 1974).

- Drag a hind leg
  The performer stretches one hind leg back in a manner that the back of the foot touches the ground and the palm of the foot is directed upward. In this position, the animal may walk or run some steps, intensely limping. Or the foot is kept in the same position and raised above the ground. *Drag a hind leg* was seen most often during conflicts, either when signaler and recipient opposed each other or when the signaler was fleeing from the recipient. But it occurred also in other situations, such as. accompanying *present*.

- Shake branch
  The signaler clings on an exposed object like a tree or fence and shakes it to and fro producing a sound. Sometimes it was observed after a resting animal heard vocalizations from conflicts nearby, but also in a variety of different situations, which are difficult to assign to a specific social context (Mehlman, 1985).

4.2. Variability: Age and Sex Differences

Table 7.2 shows in which age and sex classes the gestures were seen. Animals belonging to distinct age classes use different numbers of gestures. Subadults and adults showed the highest number with almost 30 different signals. Rarely or never seen in adults are the relaxed open mouth face and handstand. Both are typical play signals. In infants, we observed five different gestures, among these teeth-chatter, relaxed open mouth face, and other signals belonging to the affiliative and play contexts. Juveniles range in number of signals used. As to the sex classes, one gesture, mounting, was only performed by males. Male–female mounting as well as male–male mounting was observed.

TABLE 7.2
Age, Sex, and Classes in Which the Signals Were Seen
'+': frequently, 'o': rarely, '?': unsure.[1]

	Signal	Infant	Young Juvenile	Older Juvenile	Subadult Female	Subadult Male	Adult Female	Adult Male
Facial Expressions and Movements	relaxed open mouth face	+	+	+	+	+	o	o
	lip-smack		+	+	+	+	+	+
	teeth-chatter	+	+	+	+	+	+	+
	bared teeth display			o	o	o	o	o
	unvocalized scream face				+	+	+	+
	stare					+	+	+
	rounded mouth threat face		+	+	+	+	+	+
	staring open m. pant face				+	+	+	+
	bite			+	+	+	+	+
	yawn			+	+	+	+	+
Manual	touch	+	+	+	+	+	+	+
	hug			+	+	+	+	+
	knead				+	?	+	+
	touch genitalia	+	+	+	+	+	+	+
	hip-touch				+	+	+	+
	slap at hands				+	+	+	+
	slap			+	+	+	+	+
	slap ground				+	+	+	+
	pull			+	+	+	+	+
	grab		+	+	+	+	+	+
Headstand	postures				+	+	+	
	head-flag	+				+	+	+
	expose belly				+	+	+	+
	invitation to ride				+	+	+	+
	present			+	+	+	+	+
	mount					+	+	
	lunge				+	+	+	+
	show-look				+	+	+	+
	head bob			+	+	+	+	+
	drag a hind leg		o		o	o	o	
	shake branch				+	+	+	

[1] Some signals described in the gestural repertoire occurred so rarely or were distinguished from other signals only late into the study. Therefore the following signals are not dealt with: chew-smack, chatter at body parts, bared teeth gecker face, sweep, touch own genitalia, mountee reaches back.

4.3. Perceptual Modality

In Table 7.3, the main perceptual modalities of the gestures are given. With 26 signals, the majority of observed gestures are transmitted visually, followed by the tactile modality with 13 signals. Seven signals are transmitted auditorily, but all of these are visible as well and except for one, these signals do not necessarily produce sound.

TABLE 7.3
Main Perceptual Modalities (visual, auditory, tactile[1]) of the Observed Signals. '(x)' Indicates That the Corresponding Channel is Not Necessarily Involved.

		Signal	Perceptual Modality		
			Visual	*Auditory*	*Tactile*
Facial Expressions and Movements		relaxed open mouth face	x		
		chew-smack	x		
		lip-smack	x	(x)	
		teeth-chatter	x	(x)	
		chatter at body parts	(x)	(x)	(x)
		bared teeth display	x		
		bared teeth gecker face	x		
		unvocalized scream face	x		
		stare	x		
		rounded mouth threat face	x		
		staring open mouth pant face	x		
		bite			x
		yawn	x		
Manual		sweep	x	(x)	
		touch			x
		hug			x
		knead			x
		touch genitalia			x
		touch own genitalia	x		
		hip-touch			x
		mountee reaches back			x
		slap at hands	x	(x)	(x)
		slap			x
		slap ground	x	(x)	
		pull			x
		grab			x

	Signal	Perceptual Modality		
		Visual	*Auditory*	*Tactile*
	headstand	x		
	head-flag	x		
	expose belly	x		
	invitation to ride	x		
	present	x		
Postures	mount			x
	lunge	x		
	show-look	x		
	head bob	x		
	drag a hind leg			
	shake branch	x	x	

¹Note. Although almost all tactile signals can be visible as well, specifically to third parties, we did not mark them as such because this is presumably not the main modality for the recipient.

4.4. Flexibility

4.4.1. Combinations

The Barbary macaques used most of the gestures in simultaneous combinations (Fig. 7.16) They combined the majority of the gestures with not only one but several different gestures. Especially some facial expressions, for example lip-smack and teeth-chatter, are combined with diverse other gestures, including manual gestures and postures.

4.4.2. Context of Use

Table 7.4 shows the contexts in which we observed the gestures. Most signals were shown in the affiliative context, for example hug, lip-smack, teeth-chatter, and the accompanying head-flag, but also pull. In the play context, almost as many signals have been observed, like the typical relaxed open-mouth face and many different manual gestures like slap, touch, hug, and pull. Some gestures occurred less frequently in the agonistic contexts of submissive, undecided, and dominant. For the submissive context, present and the bared teeth display should be mentioned. An important dominant signal is the rounded mouth threat face,

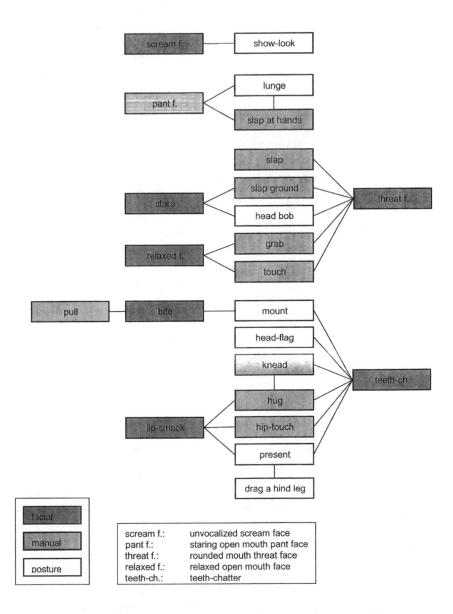

Figure 7.16. Simultaneous combinations of two signals. Signals that have been observed in combinations are connected. The different shadings refer to the signal categories facial expressions and movements, manual gestures and postures. For the same reasons as mentioned earlier, the following signals are not dealt with; chew-smack, chatter at body parts, bared teeth gecker face, sweep, touch own genitalia, mountee reaches back.

Number of Assumed Contexts	Signal	Play	Affiliative	Submissive	Undecided	Dominant
	relaxed open mouth face	x				
	chatter at body parts		x			
	knead		x			
	head-flag		x			
	invitation to ride		x			
	bared teeth display			x		
	present			x		
	bared teeth gecker face				X	
	unvocalized scream face				x	
1 Context	staring open mouth pant face				x	
	hip-touch				x	
	mountee reaches back				x	
	slap at hands				x	
	mount				x	
	lunge				x	
	show-look				x	
	stare					x
	rounded mouth threat face					x
	head bob					x
	touch	x	x			
	hug	x	x			
	pull	x	x			
	expose belly	x	x			
	slap	x			x	
2 Contexts	sweep	x				x
	slap ground	x				x
	chew-smack		x	x		
	lip-smack		x	x		
	teeth-chatter		x	x		
	touch own genitalia		x	x		

(continued)

TABLE 7.4   (continued)

Number of Assumed Contexts	Signal	Context				
		Play	*Affiliative*	*Submissive*	*Undecided*	*Dominant*
3 Contexts	headstand	x	x	x		
	bite	x	x			x
	touch genitalia	x	x			x
	grab	x	x			x
Context Unclear	yawn				?	?
	drag a hind leg			?		
	shake branch					

Note. 'Number of Contexts' indicates in how many contexts the signals were used. '?' Marks unclear cases.

often accompanied by head bobs and slap ground. Typical gestures within the context undecided are the unvocalized scream face, show–look, and lunge. Three signals, yawn, drag a hind leg, and shake branch could not be related to a specific context.

The number of contexts in which gestures have been observed ranges from one to three (out of five defined contexts). About half of the gestures occurred in only one context, most often in the context undecided. The other half of the gestures occurred in more than one contexts, most often in two. Here, the contexts play and affiliative were typical, and also affiliative and submissive. In all of the contexts, several gestures were shown, ranging from seven different gestures in the undecided agonistic context to over a dozen gestures in the affiliative context.

5. DISCUSSION

5.1. Gestural Repertoire

Overall, our study shows good agreement with the ethograms of other authors (Deag, 1974; Maestripieri, 1997; Van Hooff, 1962, 1967), indicating a good observer reliability across study cites and generations. Variations are mostly caused by a slightly different categorization of behavior patterns. The number of gestures used by Barbary macaques seems to range in the same order of magnitude as in the ape species, namely gorillas, *Gorilla gorilla* (Pika et al., 2003), chimpanzees, *Pan troglodytes* (Tomasello et al., 1985, 1994, 1997), bonobos, *Pan paniscus* (Pika, 2003), and siamangs, *Symphalangus syndactylus* (Liebal et al., 2004a). In Barbary macaques, facial expressions make up a considerable part of gestural signals and play a major role in their nonvocal communication system, which is quite usual in old world monkeys and apes (Maestripieri, 1997, 1998; Shirek-Ellefson, 1972; Van Hooff, 1962, 1967). Pika et al. (2003), Pika (2003), and Tomasello et al. (1985, 1994, 1997) did not analyze facial expressions, rendering a full comparison impossible. Interestingly, siamangs apparently have only four facial expressions (Liebal et al., 2004a). This may be due to their arboreal habitat with poor visibility.

Concerning manual gestures and postures, a comparison of the gestural repertoires presented in studies on gorillas, chimpanzees, bonobos, and siamangs (see other chapters this volume) reveals concordances as well as some differences: Several gestures like touch, slap, grab, pull, embrace, or bite are described in several species. Also, the description of signals used in the play context seems to be similar across different species. A number of gestures also occur in different species, but differ in some aspects. For instance, in contrast to the great and small ape species, Barbary macaques never use the fist or knuckles when they perform manual gestures like slap. Slap ground occurred in all species except for siamangs; but in the bonobos, it was shown only by one individual and only in the play context, whereas in Barbary macaques, all age and sex classes except for infants and young juveniles performed slap ground and usually it accompanied threats, but also occurred during play. The actual function of slap ground within both the contexts play and during threats (dominant context) may be the same though, namely getting attention from the receiver (Tomasello et al., 1997). There are also gestures restricted to one or two species, like body beat or chest beat, which was only observed in gorillas or show look, head-flag, or knead in Barbary macaques.

5.2. Age and Sex Classes

With increasing age, the number of performed gestures increased in Barbary macaques. Other species show the same pattern. However, in apes, the number of gestures decreases again before the animals enter adulthood (Liebal et al., 2004a; Pika, 2003; Pika et al., 2003; Tomasello et al.,

1997;). This might be due to the fact that the vast majority of gestures is used in the play context, frequently restricted to juvenile animals. In Barbary macaques, younger animals use fewer of the gestures that are typically used in agonistic encounters, and adult animals do not use play signals anymore (see Table 7.1 and 7.2). Subadults, however, use signals that are used both in the contexts undecided and play. In siamangs, signals used in agonistic contexts also increase up to the age class of subadults and signals used in the play context are used less frequently in adults. The only signal that is exclusive to a certain sex class in Barbary macaques is mounting, which is performed only by males. Mounting occurs between males and females, but also between males. Interestingly, dominant males also allow subordinate males to mount them so that it cannot be used to construct dominance hierarchies. In siamangs as well, certain signals in the sexual context are used exclusively by males (Liebal et al., 2004a).

5.3. Perceptual Modality

In Barbary macaques, most signals are visual, about half as many are tactile signals and the remaining can be assigned to the auditory modality. Siamangs in contrast use a slightly higher number of different tactile signals than visual ones. This difference may be due to their arboreal habitat (Liebal et al., 2004a). In gorillas (Pika et al., 2003), chimpanzees (Tomasello et al., 1997), and bonobos (DeWaal, 1988; Pika, 2003), there is more or less the same number of visual and tactile gestures and much less auditory ones. The share of manual gestures compared to other tactile or visual gestures except for facial expressions is higher in the great apes (Pika, 2003; Pika et al., 2003; Tomasello et al., 1997) than in Barbary macaques and Siamangs (Liebal et al., 2004a).

5.4. Flexibility

5.4.1. Combinations

Most of the described signals occurred in simultaneous combinations as well, and most signals can be combined with different other signals. This again indicates some flexibility in signal use (Dube & Tomasello, 2003). Like in siamangs, most combinations exist of one facial expression and another signal (Liebal et al., 2004a).

5.4.2. Context- Related Usage

Almost half of the signals are used in at least two contexts, and in all contexts, the animals performed several different gestures, suggesting that Barbary macaques use gestures flexibly. In this respect, there seems to be no fundamental difference between the gestural communication in Barbary macaques and apes (Liebal et al., 2004a; Pika, 2003; Pika et al., 2003; Tomasello et al., 1994, 1997). Among all signals that occur in more than two contexts, most occur in the play context and in affiliative situations. Because a remarkable diversity of behavioral patterns from a variety of contexts is a characteristic of play (Kipper & Todt, 2002; Smith, 1978), this is not surprising. In spite of the variety of patterns used during play, many affiliative signals are used to initiate play. We also found that the same signal was used in affiliative interactions as well as to indicate submission. Firstly, in both cases, the function is to establish and deepen social bonding (Preuschoft, 1992). Also, a similar pattern was also observed in stump-tailed macaques and pigtail macaques (Maestripieri, 1996a, 1996b).

It is important to note, however, that there are problems when one wishes to relate signal use to the context in which the signal is given. Often, social contexts are defined by the behavior the animals are showing. This clearly constitutes a source for circular arguing. One striking example is the play context that is solely defined by specific forms of behavior. Therefore, situations in which the behavior can be related to external variables such as the appearance of predators or the occurrence of food lend themselves more easily to analyses of context-related differences in signal use (Crockford & Boesch, 2003; Fischer et al., 1995; Seyfarth & Cheney, 1980; Tomasello & Zuberbühler, 2002). One possible solution is to relate the occurrence of the signal to its assumed function. The function, in turn, is established by observing the responses of the recipients (Bauers & DeWaal, 1991; Tomasello et al., 1997). However, it is not always possible to break up the link between the actual behavior and the description of the context. Again, the most striking example is a play context, because play typically leads to play. In spite of these limitations, we are currently preparing a study in which we analyze which signals elicit which types of responses. Thereby, we aim to identify the function of the various signals (Hesler & Fischer, unpublished).

5.5. Comparison to Vocal Communication

Barbary macaques reveal a highly graded vocal repertoire with some prototypical call variants and frequent examples of intergraded versions occurring. With the aid of a multivariate analysis, however, we were able to identify seven major call types (Hammerschmidt & Fischer, 1998a). We found most call types occur in several contexts whereas in one context, several call types may be used. Whereas some contexts are more specific (e.g., mating), others reveal a higher diversity of calls used (e.g., agonistic interactions). This also holds when single bouts of calls are analyzed (Hammerschmidt & Fischer, 1998a). To some degree, therefore, their vocal communication also fulfills the criteria for flexible signal use. Nevertheless, there is good reason to believe that their vocal communication can be viewed predominantly as an expression of their emotions rather than a voluntary signal use. Controlled analyses will be needed to check whether additional criteria like "response waiting" accompany gesture use only, or also the use of vocal signals. In the long run, however, it is essential to study both the vocal and gestural communication in concert. This present overview also demonstrated that certain gestures typically may occur in combination with calls, and certainly, calls are excellent attention getters.

6. CONCLUSION

Overall, we found that Barbary macaques show flexibility using one gesture in different contexts. They also combine numerous signals with different other signals, suggesting that they do use gestures flexibly according to the criteria developed previously. In this respect, there seems to be no fundamental differences to apes. Future studies should address the vocal and gestural domain to develop a full understanding of multimodal signal use (Partan & Marler, 1999) and its underlying cognitive processes.

ACKNOWLEDGMENTS

We thank Ellen Merz very much for the permission to work at "La Forêt des Singes" at Rocamadour and the staff on site for their support and hospitality. Many thanks also to the Department of Developmental and Comparative Psychology at the Max Planck Institute for Evolutionary Anthropology in Leipzig for its financial support during the stay at Rocamadour. We are very grateful that Mike Tomasello and Josep Call offered for us to contribute to this book. Thanks also to Christoph Teufel for discussion, support, and company.

REFERENCES

Ansorge, V., Hammerschmidt, K., & Todt, D. (1992). Communal roosting and formation of sleeping clusters in Barbary macaques (*Macaca sylvanus*). *American Journal of Primatology, 28*, 271–280.

Arbib, M. (2005). From monkey-like action recognition to human language: An evolutionary framework for neurolinguistics. *Behavioral and Brain Sciences, 28*, 105–167.

Arcadi, A. C. (1996). Phrase structure of wild chimpanzee pant hoots: Patterns of production and interpopulation variability. *American Journal of Primatology, 39*, 159–178.

Bard, K. A. (1992). Intentional behavior and intentional communication in young free-ranging orangutans. *Child Development, 63*, 1186–1197.

Bauers, K. A., & DeWaal, F. B. M. (1991). "Coo" vocalizations in stumptailed macaques: A controlled functional analysis. *Behaviour, 119*, 143–160.

Bruner, J. S. (1981). Intention in the structure of action and interaction. *Advances in Infancy Research, 1*, 41–56.

Chapais, B. (2004). How kinship generates dominance structures: A comparative perspective. In B. Thierry, M. Singh, & W. Kaumanns (Eds.), *Macaque societies—A model for the study of social organization* (pp. 186–208). Cambridge, England: Cambridge University Press.

Corballis, M. C. (2002). *From hand to mouth.* Princeton, NJ: Princeton University Press.

Crockford, C., & Boesch, C. (2003). Context-specific calls in wild chimpanzees, *Pan troglodytes verus*: Analysis of barks. *Animal Behaviour, 66*, 115–125.

Crockford, C., Herbinger, I., Vigilant, L., & Boesch, C. (2004). Wild chimpanzees produce group-specific calls: A case for vocal learning? *Ethology, 110*, 221–243.

Deag, J. M. (1974). *A study of the social behavior and ecology of the wild Barbary macaque, Macaca Sylvanus L. 1758.* Unpublished doctoral Dissertation, University of Bristol.

Deag, J. M., & Crook, J. H. (1971). Social behaviour and agonistic buffering in the wild Barbary macaque, *Macaca sylvanus. Folia Primatologica, 15*, 183–200.

Delson, E. (1980). Fossil macaques, phyletic relationships and a scenario of deployment. In D. M. Taub (Ed.), *The macaques: Studies in ecology, behaviour and evolution* (pp. 10–30). New York: Van Nostrand Reinhold.

DeWaal, F. B. M. (1988). The communicative repertoire of captive bonobos (*Pan paniscus*), compared to that of chimpanzees. *Behaviour, 106*, 183–251.

Dube, A., & Tomasello, M. (2003). Signal combinations in Hamadryas Baboons (*Papio hamadryas hamadryas*). *Folia Primatologica, 74*, 179–230.

Drucker, G. R. (1984). The feeding ecology of the Barbary macaque and Cedar forest conservation in the Morroccan Moyen Atlas. In J. F. Fa (Ed.), *The Barbary macaque: A case study in conservation* (pp. 79–111). New York: Plenum Press.

Fa, J. E. (1984). *The Barbary macaque: A case study in conservation.* New York: Plenum Press.

Fa, J. E. (1989). The genus *Macaca*: A review of taxonomy and evolution. *Mammal Reviews, 19*, 45–81.

Falk, D. (2000). *Primate diversity.* New York: Norton.

Fischer, J. (1998). Barbary macaques categorize shrill barks into two call types. *Animal Behaviour, 55,* 799–807.

Fischer, J. (2002). Developmental modifications in the vocal behaviour of nonhuman primates. In A. A. Ghazanfar (Ed.), *Primate audition* (pp. 109–125). Boca Raton, FL: CRC Press.

Fischer, J. (2004). Emergence of individual recognition in young macaques. *Animal Behaviour, 67,* 655–661.

Fischer, J. (2006). Categorical perception. In K. Brown (Ed.), *Encyclopedia of language & linguistics* (Vol. 2, pp. 248–251). Oxford, England: Elsevier.

Fischer, J., & Hammerschmidt, K. (2001). Functional referents and acoustic similarity revisited: The case of Barbary macaque alarm calls. *Animal Cognition, 4,* 29–35.

Fischer, J., & Hammerschmidt, K. (2002). An overview of the Barbary macaque, *Macaca sylvanus,* vocal repertoire. *Folia Primatologica, 73,* 32–45.

Fischer, J., Hammerschmidt, K., & Todt, D. (1995). Factors affecting acoustic variation in Barbary macaque (*Macaca sylvanus*) disturbance calls. *Ethology, 101,* 51–66.

Fitch, W. T. (2000). The evolution of speech: A comparative review. *Trends in Cognitive Sciences, 4,* 258–266.

Flack, J. C., & De Waal, F. B. M. (2004). Dominance style, social power, and conflict management: A conceptual framework. In B. Thierry, M. Singh, & W. Kaumanns (Eds.), *Macaque societies—A model for the study of social organization* (pp. 157–185). Cambridge, England: Cambridge University Press.

Gachot-Neveu, H., & Ménard, N. (2004). Gene flow, dispersal patterns, and social organization. In B. Thierry, M. Singh, & W. Kaumanns (Eds.), *Macaque societies—A model for the study of social organization* (pp. 117–134). Cambridge, England: Cambridge University Press.

Ghazanfar, A. A., & Santos, L. R. (2004). Primate brains in the wild: The sensory bases for social interactions. *Nature Reviews Neuroscience, 5,* 603–616.

Hammerschmidt, K., & Fischer, J. (1998a). Maternal discrimination of offspring vocalizations in Barbary macaques (*Macaca sylvanus*). *Primates, 39,* 231–236.

Hammerschmidt, K., & Fischer, J. (1998b). The vocal repertoire of Barbary macaques: A quantitative analysis of a graded signal system. *Ethology, 104,* 203–216.

Hauser, M. D. (1996). *The evolution of communication.* Cambridge, MA: MIT Press.

Hayasaka, K., Fujii, K., & Horai, S. (1996). Molecular phylogeny of macaques: Implications of nucleotide sequences from an 896–base pair region of mitochondrial DNA. *Molecular Biology and Evolution, 13,* 1044–1053.

Jürgens, U. (2002). Neural pathways underlying vocal control. *Neuroscience and Biobehavioral Reviews, 26,* 235–258.

King, B. J. (1999). *The origins of language: What nonhuman primates can tell us.* Santa Fe, NM: School of American Research Press.

Kipper, S., & Todt, D. (2002). The use of vocal signals in the social play of Barbary macaques. *Primates, 43,* 3–17.

Küster, J., & Paul, A. (1996). Female–female competition and male mate choice in Barbary macaques (*Macaca sylvanus*). *Behaviour, 133,* 763–790.

Liebal, K., Pika, S., & Tomasello, M. (2004). Social communication in siamangs (*Symphalangus syndactylus*): Use of gestures and facial expressions. *Primates, 45,* 41–57.

Liebal, K., Call, J., & Tomasello, M. (2004). Use of gesture sequences in chimpanzees. *American Journal of Primatology, 64,* 377–396.

Maestripieri, D. (1996a). Gestural communication and its cognitive implications in pigtail macaques (*Macaca nemestrina*). *Behaviour, 133*, 997–1022.

Maestripieri, D. (1996b). Social communication among captive stump-tailed macaques (*Macaca arctoides*). *International Journal of Primatology, 17*, 785–802.

Maestripieri, D. (1997). Gestural communication in macaques: Usage and meaning of nonvocal signals. *Evolution of Communication, 1*, 193–222.

Maestripieri, D. (1998). Primate social organization, gestural repertoire size, and communication dynamics—A comparative study of macaques. In B. King (Ed.), *The evolution of language: Assessing the evidence from nonhuman primates* (pp. 55–77). Santa Fe, NM: School of American Research.

Marshall, A. J., Wrangham, R. T., & Arcadi, A. C. (1999). Does learning affect the structure of vocalizations in chimpanzees? *Animal Behaviour, 58*, 825–830.

Mehlman, P. (1985). Heterogeneous form and signal function in branch shaking behaviour of the Barbary macaque (*Macaca sylvanus L.*). *American Journal of Primatology, 8*, 351.

Mehlman, P. (1996). Branch shaking and related displays in wild Barbary macaques. In J. E. Fa & D. G. Lindburg (Eds.), *Evolution and ecology of macaque societies* (pp. 503–526). Cambridge, England: Cambridge University Press.

Ménard, N., & Vallet, D. (1993). Population dynamics of *Macaca sylvanus* in Algeria: An 8-year study. *American Journal of Primatology, 30*, 101–118.

Mitani, J. C., Hasegawa, T., Gros-Louis, J., Marler, P., & Byrne, R. W. (1992). Dialects in wild chimpanzees? *American Journal of Primatology, 27*, 233–243.

Morales, J. C., & Melnick, D. J. (1998). Phylogenetic relationships of the macaques (Cercopithecidae: Macaca), as revealed by high resolution restriction site mapping of mitochondrial ribosomal genes. *Journal of Human Evolution, 34*, 1–23.

Nishida, T., Kano, T., Goodall, J., McGrew, W. C., & Nakamura, M. (1999). Ethogram and ethnography of mahale chimpanzees. *Anthropological Science, 107*, 141–188.

Nowak, R. M. (1999). *Walker's primates of the world*. Baltimore, MD: Johns Hopkins University Press.

Parr, L. A., & Maestripieri, D. (2003). Nonvocal communication. In D. Maestripieri (Ed.), *Primate psychology* (pp. 324–358). Cambridge, MA: Harvard University Press.

Partan, S., & Marler, P. (1999). Behavior: Communication goes multimodal. *Science, 283*, 1272–1273.

Paul, A. (1984). *Zur sozialstruktur und sozialisation semi-freilebender Berberaffen (Macaca sylvanus) L. 1758* [On the social structure and socialization of semi free living Barbary macaques]. Unpublished doctoral dissertation, Universität Göttingen.

Pika, S. (2003). *Gestural communication in subadult bonobos (Pan Paniscus): Gestural repertoire and use*. Unpublished doctoral dissertation, Westfälische Wilhelmsuniversität Münster, Abteilung für Entwicklungsphysiologie und Verhaltensforschung.

Pika, S., Liebal, K., & Tomasello, M. (2003). Gestural communication in subadult gorillas (*Gorilla gorilla*): Gestural repertoire, learning, and use. *American Journal of Primatology, 60*, 95–111.

Plavcan, J. (2001). Sexual dimorphism in primate evolution. *Yearbook of Physical Anthropology, 44*, 25–53.

Preuschoft, S. (1992). "Laughter" and "smile" in Barbary macaques (*Macaca sylvanus*). *Zeitschrift für Tierpsychologie, 91*, 220–236.

Preuschoft, S., Paul, A., & Küester, J. (1998). Dominance styles of female and male Barbary macaques. *Behaviour, 135*, 731–755.

Preuschoft, S., & Van Schaik, C. P. (2000). Dominance and communication. In F. Aureli & F. B. M. DeWaal (Eds.), *Natural conflict resolution* (pp. 77–105). Berkeley, CA: University of California Press.

Rizzolatti, G., & Arbib, M. A. (1998). Language within our grasp. *Trends in Neurosciences, 21*, 188–194.

Roshani, A., Todt, D., & Janik, V. M. (1994). Yawning in male Barbary macaques. In J. J. Roeder, B. Thierry, J. R. Anderson, & N. Herrenschmidt (Eds.), *Current primatology: Vol 2. Social development, learning and behaviour* (pp. 81–85). Strasbourg, Germany: Université Louis Pasteur.

Savage-Rumbaugh, E. S., Wilkerson, B. J., & Bakeman, R. (1977). Spontaneous gestural communication among conspecifics in the pygmy chimpanzee (*Pan paniscus*). In G. H. Bourne (Ed.), *Progress in ape research* (pp. 97–116). New York: Academic Press.

Semple, S. (1998). The function of Barbary macaque copulation calls. *Proceedings of the Royal Society of London Series B-Biological Sciences, 265*, 287–291.

Seyfarth, R. M., & Cheney, D. L. (1980). The ontogeny of vervet monkey alarm calling behavior: A preliminary report. *Zeitschrift für Tierpsychologie, 54*, 37–56.

Seyfarth, R. M., Cheney, D. L., & Marler, P. (1980a). Vervet monkey alarm calls: semantic communication in a free-ranging primate. *Animal Behaviour, 28*, 1070–1094.

Seyfarth, R. M., Cheney, D. L., & Marler, P. (1980b). Monkey responses to three different alarm calls: Evidence of predator classification and semantic communication. *Science, 210*, 801–803.

Shirek-Ellefson, J. (1972). Social communication in some old world monkeys and gibbons. In P. Dolhinow (Ed.), *Primate patterns* (pp. 297–311). New York: Holt, Rinehart & Winston.

Smith, E. O. (1978). A historical view on the study of play—Statement of the problem. In E. O. Smith (Ed.), *Social play in primates* (pp. 1–32). New York: Academic Press.

Smuts, B. B., Cheney, D. L., Seyfarth, R. M., Wrangham, R. W., & Struhsaker, T. T. (1987). *Primate societies.* Chicago, IL: University of Chicago Press.

Tanner, J. E., & Byrne, R. W. (1996). Representation of action through iconic gesture in a captive lowland gorilla. *Current Anthropology, 37*, 162–173.

Taub, D. M. (1980). Testing the 'agonistic buffering' hypothesis: The dynamics of participation in the triadic interaction. *Behavioral Ecology and Sociobiology, 6*, 187–197.

Thierry, B. (2000). Covariation of conflict management patterns across macaque species. In F. Aureli & F. B. M. DeWaal (Eds.), *Natural conflict resolution* (pp. 106–128). Berkeley, CA: University of California Press.

Todt, D., Hammerschmidt, K., Ansorge, V., & Fischer, J. (1995). The vocal behaviour of Barbary macaques: Call features and their performance in infants and adults. In E. Zimmermann, J. D. Newman, & U. Jürgens (Eds.), *Current topics in primate vocal communication* (pp. 141–160). New York: Plenum Press.

Todt, D., Hammerschmidt, K., & Hultsch, H. (1992). The behaviour of Barbary macaques (*Macaca sylvanus*) L. 1758: Perspective and projects of a long-term study. *Primate Report, 32*, 19–30.

Tomasello, M., & Call, J. (1997). *Primate cognition.* New York: Oxford University Press.

Tomasello, M., Call, J., Nagell, K., Olguin, R., & Carpenter, M. (1994). The learning and use of gestural signals by young chimpanzees—A trans-generational study. *Primates, 35,* 137–154.

Tomasello, M., Call, J., Warren, J., Frost, G. T., Carpenter, M., & Nagell, K. (1997). The ontogeny of chimpanzee gestural signals: A comparison across groups and generations. *Evolution of Communication, 1,* 223–259.

Tomasello, M., George, B. L., Kruger, A. C., Jeffrey, M., Farrar, M. J., & Evans, A. (1985). The development of gestural communication in young chimpanzees. *Journal of Human Evolution, 14,* 175–186.

Tomasello, M., & Zuberbühler, K. (2002). Primate vocal and gestural communication. In C. Allen, M. Bekoff, & G. M. Burghardt (Eds.), *The cognitive animal* (pp. 293–299). Cambridge, MA: MIT Press.

Tosi, A. J., Morales, J. C., & Melnick, D. J. (2000). Comparison of Y chromosome and mtDNA phylogenies leads to unique inferences of macaque evolutionary history. *Molecular Phylogenetics and Evolution, 17,* 133–144.

Turckheim, G. D., & Merz, E. (1984). Breeding Barbary macaques in outdoor open enclosures. In J. F. Fa (Ed.), *The Barbary macaque: A case study in conservation* (pp. 241–261). New York: Plenum Press.

van Hooff, J. A. R. A. M. (1962). Facial expressions in higher primates. *Symp Zoological Society of London, 8,* 97–125.

van Hooff, J. A. R. A. M. (1967). The facial displays of the catarrhine monkeys and apes. In D. Morris (Ed.), *Primate ethology* (pp. 7–68). London: Weidenfeld & Nicolson.

Van Lawick-Goodall, J. (1972). A preliminary report on expressive movements and communication in the Gombe stream chimpanzees. In P. Dolhinow (Ed.), *Primate patterns* (pp. 25–84). New York: Holt, Rinehart and Winston.

Von Segesser, F., Ménard, N., Gaci, B., & Martin, R. D. (1999). Genetic differentiation within and between isolated Algerian subpopulations of Barbary macaques (*Macaca sylvanus*): evidence from microsatellites. *Molecular Ecology, 8,* 433–442.

Zeller, A. C. (1980). Primate facial gestures: A study of communication. *International Journal of Human Communication, 13,* 565–606.

Zuberbühler, K. (2000). Referential labelling in Diana monkeys. *Animal Behaviour, 59,* 917–927.

CHAPTER 8

Comparing the Gestures of Apes and Monkeys

Josep Call
Michael Tomasello
Max Planck Institute for Evolutionary Anthropology

*E*ach of the six species studied has its own repertoire of gestural signals. There are some commonalities across all of these species, other commonalities among only some of the species, and some unique features of particular species. In this chapter, we attempt to explicate these commonalities and differences, first with respect to the repertoires themselves, second with respect to processes of learning and development, and third with respect to flexibility of use, including as a special case adjustments for audience. In many cases we offer possible explanations of species similarities and differences based on similarities and differences of genetic relatedness, ecology, social structure, and cognition. It should be noted at the outset that the comparison focuses mostly on the five ape species, because the one monkey species was observed in a somewhat different manner and direct monkey–ape comparisons were not possible in all areas (e.g., audience effects). Nevertheless, whenever the data on macaques afforded meaningful comparisons with the ape data sets, we included them in this chapter. Differences in how the ape species were observed are also noted where relevant.

Two things should be noted at the outset. First, recall that we are only focused on intentional gestures, that is, those gestures that are used most flexibly in interaction with others; all of the species have many other facial expressions, body postures, and gestures that are used in fairly stereotypic and inflexible ways. Second, for purposes of the current study, all of the individuals of all the different species were observed in humanmade contexts, which (unlike the wild) were all fairly comparable physically in terms of opportunities for seeing one another, traveling, climbing, and so forth.

8.1. GESTURAL REPERTOIRE

The gestural repertoires of the five ape species differed with regard to size, composition, and function. In terms of size, Figure 8.1 presents both (a) the overall number of gestures (types) observed across all the individuals of each species, and (b) the average number of gestures (types) per individual in each species. The gorillas seem to have the largest repertoire—slightly so in terms of overall number (33), much more so in terms of number per individual (20). It is unlikely that this is due to a particular observer because the same observer (Pika) also observed the bonobos, and their repertoire is among the smallest. Also, it is worth noting that the chimpanzees' repertoire is about average in size even though they were observed over more time across several different studies than the other species—and so again observer or sampling biases would not seem to be playing a major role. Overall, there is no clear pattern across the species in terms of repertoire size (except perhaps the three species with the largest bodies—gorillas, orangutans, chimpanzees—have the largest overall repertoire sizes). How-

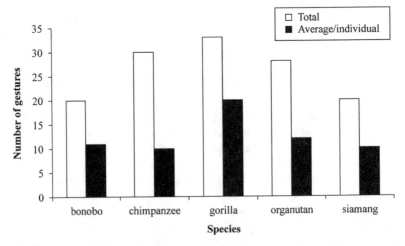

Figure 8.1. Size of gesture repertoires of the five ape species.

ever, Barbary macaques, with a repertoire of 25 gestures (after excluding facial expressions) fall within the range of the great apes. In contrast, Maestripieri (2005) has reported gestural repertoires for rhesus, stumptail, and pigtail macaques below 20 gestures. This discrepancy, however, may have arisen because some behaviors like grabbing or slapping were considered gestures by some authors but not by others.

In terms of gestural modality, independent of repertoire size, we may compute a proportion of visual, tactile, and auditory gestures for each species. Figure 8.2 presents these proportions. The striking pattern observed is that the Asian apes (orangutans, siamangs) have no auditory gestures—such as ground slap, stomp, or clap (drumming on things, including the self)—whereas these constitute from around 5% to 20% of the gestures used by the African apes (chimpanzees, bonobos, gorillas). In complementary fashion, there is a greater number of tactile gestures in the Asian, as compared with the African, apes. (There is little difference in the percentage of visual gestures between these two taxa, although the Asian species use somewhat fewer.) Genetic relatedness is thus an obvious explanatory possibility for the different sensory modalities used for gestural communication among these five ape species. It should also be noted, consistent with this pattern, that the Barbary macaques in the current study also have no auditory attention getters (they sometimes slap the ground toward one another in play or as a threat), and the hamadryas baboons observed using our same methods (Dube, unpublished data) also showed little evidence of any auditory attention-getters. And so a reasonable hypothesis is that the use of auditory attention getters is a specialization of the African apes for gaining the visual attention of others to the self and its current mood state (see following).

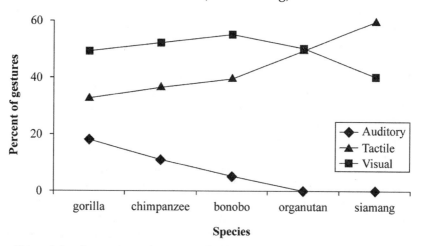

Figure 8.2.   Proportions of gestures of different types for the five ape species.

Another interesting possibility—not independent of genetic relatedness—is arboreality. Not only are the Asian apes in general more arboreal than the African apes, but the bonobos are most arboreal and the gorillas are the least arboreal among the African apes. This orders exactly with the decline in auditory and rise in tactile gestures in Figure 8.2; that is, there is a negative correlation of arboreality and auditory gestures, and a positive correlation of arboreality and tactile gestures. It is thus possible that for some reason—perhaps because the hands are freer on the ground than in the trees—using the body to make noises to attract attention is not a primary strategy of more arboreal species. Also, perhaps arboreal species rely more on tactile gestures because they are so often in close proximity to one another. It is also possible that arboreal species rely more on vocalizations, although this would not seem to be the case with orangutans. Against this pattern is the fact that the two monkey species referred to earlier (Barbary macaques and hamadryas baboons) are fairly terrestrial and have no auditory attention getters.

There could be cognitive factors at work in this pattern of gesture use, in the specific sense that some species might be more attuned to the attentional states of others. We present evidence later—in the section entitled Adjustments for Audience—that the chimpanzees and bonobos, in particular, are especially attentive to the visual perspective of others in many contexts. With auditory gestures, the signaler attempts to get the recipient to attend to her visually—or, if the recipient is already visually oriented in the correct direction, to attend in a more active manner—so as to see the state she is in, as expressed in more involuntary displays such as piloerection and facial expressions. Auditory attention getters, in our hypothesis, are saying "Look at me and you will be able to tell what I want!"; for example, "Look at me and you will be able to tell from my posture and expression that I am in a play mood." We will come back to this hypothesis again after we have presented data for the different species concerning adjustments for audience.

In terms of the specific gestures used, Figure 8.3 lists those gestures in common to each pair of species. The tactile gestures push, pull, and touch are common to all five species, with perhaps some small variations in the different cases. Four of the five species initiate interactions with others by presenting or offering a body part visually (all but gorillas), and four of the five species also initiate interactions with others by a shaking/waving/offering an object visually (all but bonobos). Quantitatively, the most overlap is among the three species of African apes (10–11 gestures in common for all three pairs) and the two species of Asian apes (10 gestures in common). The least overlap is among the bonobos and the two Asian apes (5 gestures in common for each of the

	Chimpanzee	Bonobo	Gorilla	Orangutan	Siamang
Chimpanzee	-	Push **Present** Pull **Reach** Touch **Look** Clap **Swagger** Stomp Ground slap	Embrace *Body slap* Touch *Ground slap* Push *Clap* Pull *Stomp* Bite **Wave object** **Reach**	Embrace **Offer body** Formal bite **Shake object** Pull **Throw** Push Touch	Embrace **Offer body** Pull **Shake object** Push **Wrist offer** Formal bite Gentle touch
Bonobo	-	-	Touch *Clap* Push *Slap ground* Pull *Stomp* Punch **Bow** Slap **Shake** **Somersault**	Pull **Present** Push Slap Touch	Pull **Present** Push Slap Touch
Gorilla	-	-	-	Touch **Bite** Embrace **Shake object** Pull Push	Touch **Shake object** Embrace Pull Push Slap
Orangutan	-	-	-	-	Embrace **Extend arm** Formal bite **Shake object** Gentle touch Hold tight Nudge Pull Push Slap
Siamang	-	-	-	-	-

Figure 8.3. Gestures used in common among the five different species.

two pairs)—that, in this case, argues against arboreality as an explanation because bonobos are the most arboreal of the African apes.

In terms of gestures unique to each species, we must be very careful as many gestures between species are similar yet subtly different. What we can do, however, is to list those gestures that are most distinctive to a particular species, differing most clearly from those of the others. The gestures most distinct to each species (and used by the majority of individuals observed here) are as follows:

- Gorillas: chest beat, arm shake
- Orangutans: lip touch, offer arm with food
- Bonobos: (none)
- Chimpanzees: arm raise, hand beg, rub chin, lip lock, spit at, throw stuff
- Siamangs: throw back head

The source of these distinctive gestures is unknown. In particular, it is unknown the degree to which these might be unlearned. However, they are all used reasonably flexibly, and so at the very least, it would seem that their deployment depends on the way individuals of the different species interact with one another. It should also be noted that the larger number here for the chimpanzees might be due to the fact that they were observed more than were the other species in several different studies.

Also of interest are the functions for which the different species use their gestures. Figure 8.4 presents a proportional breakdown of the gestures of the different species as a function of five very general functional categories. The most general pattern is that play is the primary functional context for the use of gestures for four of the five species (40–50% for all except orangutans) that might be due, at least partially, to the fact that many of the individuals observed were juveniles. Another striking pattern is the infrequent use of gestures in traveling contexts for the two Asian species (around 17% for African apes; around 1% for Asian apes), and the infrequent use of gestures for feeding in the Siamangs. The Asian apes also have proportionally more gestures used in agonistic contexts (about double), as well as in affiliative contexts (about triple). These differences lead, once again, to an overall difference between the African and the Asian apes. Overall, more than 80% of the gestures used by the African apes come in the three categories play, travel, feeding, whereas over 80% of the gestures used by the Asian apes come in the three categories play, affiliation, agonism. Again, arboreality would not seem to be a good explanation for these findings, as the bonobos clearly pattern with the other African apes (including the very terrestrial gorillas).

	Function				
	Play	Ride/Travel Locomotion	Agonism	Nurse/Feed	Sex/Affiliation /Grooming
Chimpanzees	45	15	10	20	10
Bonobos	55	15	3	19	8
Gorillas	40	20	5	25	10
Orangutans	22	2	16	28	20
Siamangs	40	-	12	2	42
Barbary macaques	48	-	39	-	52

Figure 8.4. Proportion of gestures used in different contexts by the different species.

In terms of the body part used, the majority of gestures were performed with the limbs (including hands and feet) as opposed to the head or the body (Fig. 8.5)—something that was also true of Barbary macaques and other macaque species (Maestripieri, 2005). Focusing on gestures performed with the limbs showed that upper as opposed to lower limbs accounted for more than 90% of the gestures in Barbary macaques, gorillas, chimpanzees, and orangutans whereas the upper limb predominance dropped to about 70% in siamangs and bonobos.

Another aspect that differentiated the repertoire of the various species was the incorporation of objects as part of the gestures. Chimpanzees and orangutans used objects in this fashion in more than 15% of their gestures, gorillas in 12% whereas bonobos, siamangs, and Barbary macaques did so in 5% or less of their gestures. Moreover, most of the gestures in great apes, but not in siamangs and Barbary macaques, involved detached objects that individuals manipulated freely. These data fit nicely with the propensity to use tools observed in this species both in the wild (McGrew, 1992; van Schaik, Fox, & Fechtman, 2003) and in the laboratory (Tomasello & Call, 1997).

We clearly cannot present any definitive explanations for the gestural repertoires used by the different ape species. Genetic relatedness, ecology, cognition, and to some degree social structure, are all correlated with one another in complex ways. And we have not taken into account here in any systematic way the communicative alternatives, in terms of vocalizations or facial expressions, available to each species. Nevertheless, there does seem to be a fairly consistent difference in the nature of

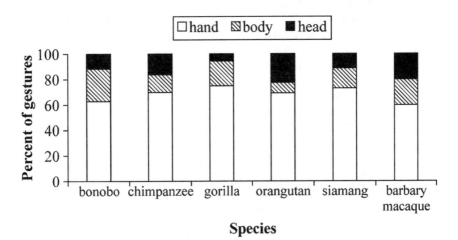

Figure 8.5. Proportion of gestures executed with limbs, body, and head for all species.

the gestural repertoires between the African apes and the Asian apes—most especially with regard to the use (or nonuse) of auditory gestures and the functions for which gestures are used. Additionally, great apes appear more likely to incorporate detached objects into their gestures, with orangutans and chimpanzees being the species most inclined to do so. This at least suggests some possible species differences that may constrain theories of the evolution of primate gestural communication.

8.2. LEARNING

There are three basic possibilities for how apes acquire their gestures. First, ape gestures may be species-typical behaviors shaped by evolution and not by learning. In this case, we would expect relatively high uniformity in gestures across all individuals within a species—and inflexible use across contexts. Those are not our concern here. Second, ape gestures may be acquired by ontogenetic ritualization, as described in the first chapter. In this case, we would expect more individual differences and flexible use, and these would be independent of a group within a species; that is, we would not expect group-specific gestures involving cultural transmission within a specific group. Third, ape gestures may be acquired by some form of imitative learning, by the individual copying a signal either directed to it (second-person imitation) or directed to someone else (third-person imitation). In this case, we might expect some group-specific gestures, transmitted only within specific groups within the species.

Obviously, naturalistic observations cannot be definitive in deciding among these possibilities. However, there are two basic forms of evidence that are relevant. The first is looking at the patterns of individual and developmental variation. The second is looking at patterns both within and between different groups of the same species. We report here analyses using both of these kinds of evidence relevant to the question of learning. A third kind of evidence is experiments—that we do not have here, but there are several that are relevant and we review them at the end of this section.

In their analysis of chimpanzee gestures, Tomasello, George, Kruger, Farrar, and Evans (1985) found a number of striking developmental patterns relevant to the question of learning. For example, they found that juveniles used many gestures not used by adults, that adults used some gestures not used by juveniles, and that some juvenile gestures for particular functions were replaced by more adultlike forms at later developmental periods. None of these patterns is consistent with the idea that infant and juvenile chimpanzees acquire their gestural signals by imitating adults. Tomasello, Gust, and Frost (1989) also noted that many youngsters also produced signals that they had never had directed to them, for example, others never begged food, or solicited tickling or nursing from youngsters. The youngsters' signals for these functions thus could not have been a product of their imitation of signals directed to them (second-person imitation). In many cases, it was also extremely unlikely that they were imitated from other infants gesturing to conspecifics (third-person imitation or "eavesdropping") because many were only produced in close quarters between mother and child with little opportunity for others to observe (e.g., for nursing).

In the current studies, many of these same patterns hold for each of the five different ape species. First, we note that of the four species with enough individuals at the different ages to discern developmental patterns, in all cases, the number of gestures peaks during the juvenile stage (as opposed to the adult stage). Figure 8.6 displays this pattern. This is undoubtedly due in some measure to the different functions for which gestures are used at different ages; for example, play is most frequent in the juvenile period, and gestures are used quite frequently in play. But, again, these differences in function also mean that in many cases, infants and juveniles have very little opportunity to observe anyone directing certain gestures to them, and in other cases, little opportunity to observe

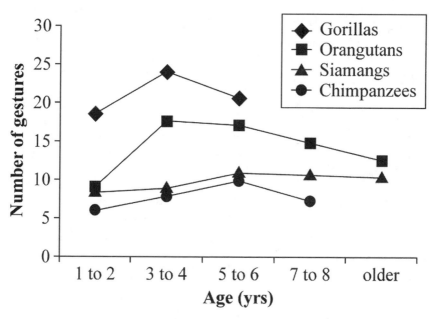

Figure 8.6.   Developmental patterns of gesture use among the five species.

others gesturing to one another. It is also important that the gestures that are shared by many youngsters—many of them for play—are gestures that are also used quite frequently by captive youngsters raised in peer groups with no opportunity to observe older conspecifics (e.g., Berdecio & Nash, 1981)—again suggesting ontogenetic ritualization, not imitation, as the major learning mechanism involved.

Also relevant is the use of idiosyncratic gestures, that is, gestures unique to particular individuals, which almost certainly are invented and learned by individuals. Tomasello et al. (1989) reported a number of idiosyncratic signals used by captive chimpanzees. Goodall (1986) also reported some idiosyncratic gestures used by individuals of the Kasakela community at Gombe in the wild. Tomasello, Call, Nagell, Olguin, and Carpenter (1994) compiled data from three longitudinal studies of captive chimpanzees and reported that 14% of the gestures were idiosyncratic. Moreover, 40% of the gestures (13 out of 30) were idiosyncratic at a given time point (i.e., only one individual used them during that particular observation period). As for the other species, Liebal (this volume) found that 10% and 20% of the gestures in orangutans and siamangs, respectively, were seemingly idiosyncratic. Similarly, Pika (this volume) found that 9% and 15% of the gestures in gorillas and bonobos, respectively, were idiosyncratic.

In terms of group-specific gestures, in the wild, there is one reasonably well-documented case of what was thought to be a group-specific gesture. Nishida (1980) observed 'leaf clipping' (an auditory attention getter) in the Mahale K group of chimpanzees, and he reported that to his knowledge, it was unique to this group. But soon after these observations, Sugiyama (1981) and Boesch (1995) observed leaf clipping in two other groups of chimpanzees across the continent in Western Africa, and Wrangham (1977) reported it in another East African group. The fact that leaf clipping has been observed in four different groups who have not had the opportunity to observe one another, speaks to the possibility that in all groups, the behavior is spontaneously invented by individuals through some kind of ritualization process. Based on all of these factors, Nishida (1994) has recently expressed his view that ontogenetic ritualization (as opposed to imitative learning) may be the mechanism responsible for the acquisition of gestures in the wild.[1]

In the current study, a few possible group-specific gestures were observed. For the chimpanzees, as reported by Call and Tomasello, there were a few between the two observation groups but they were easily attributable to differences in the materials available to these two social groups. For example, only the group with wood chips in its enclosure could throw them at others to start play. For the bonobos and gorillas, we observed here two group-specific gestures each that were not easily attributable to the different materials available in the different groups (e.g., one gorilla group often initiated play by waving straw at one another, but the other observed group had no straw in its compound). For the orangutans, we observed one group-specific gesture not attributable to environmental differences, and for the siamangs, we observed none. It is of course possible that these group-specific gestures were socially learned and culturally transmitted. But the small number of them argues that—at the very least—this is a very rare process in apes; or possibly there was some environmental factor that we did not notice, or the observation time was not long enough to see the gesture in the other groups observed.

Tomasello et al. (1997) took a more quantitative approach to the issue of variability in the gestures used by individuals within and between social groups. They observed two different groups of chimpanzees. The specific gestural repertoire of each individual was compiled. Then, a series of Cohen's Kappa statistics were used to compare each individual to each other individual to establish a degree of concordance between those two individuals—and this was done between all possible pairs both within and between groups. Mean values were then compared from individuals who lived in the same group with individuals who lived in the two different groups. Very similar values were found in the two cases, suggesting that individual variability was the main source of variance being observed, much more important than any difference between groups.

In the current study, the within-group and between-group Kappa statistics are presented in Fig. 8.7. The major finding of importance is that the Kappas within groups and between groups are very similar for each species; there is no evidence of large repertoires specific to specific groups within a species. The largest absolute and proportional difference is among chimpanzees, but in this case, the overall level of concordance is below what Fleiss (1981) considers an acceptable degree of concordance overall. In general, the overall values of these Kappa statis-

	Bonobo	Chimpanzee	Gorilla	Orangutan	Siamang
Within group kappa	0.5	0.34	0.79	0.6	0.65
Between group kappa	0.45	0.24	0.72	0.56	0.65

Figure 8.7. Within-group and between-group kappas for the five species.

tics are especially high for gorillas—what Fleiss (1981) considered an 'excellent' degree of concordance—and fairly high for orangutans and siamangs—what Fleiss (1981) considered 'fair' to 'good' degrees of concordance. This suggests that the gorillas and the two Asian apes were more similar among all individuals of the species, both between and within groups, which might suggest relatively tight evolutionary constraints, whereas the chimpanzees and the bonobos have the most individual variability, which might imply more learning.

Relevant to the question of learning is also the experimental investigation of Tomasello et al. (1997). We removed an adult female from a captive chimpanzee group and taught her two different arbitrary gestures by means of which she obtained desired food from a human (and repeated the procedure with one other adult female from another group). When she was then returned to the group and used these same gestures to obtain food from a human in full view of other group members, there was not one instance of another individual reproducing either of the new gestures (nor in the replication). The study has several limitations; for example, this is a situation in which most chimpanzees had already used other gestures successfully in the past, it was a human recipient, and only two individual demonstrators were used. But the fact is that its findings are in general agreement with those of the naturalistic observations reported here, and so it provides at least some further validity to the conclusion that imitative learning is not the major way by which apes to acquire their various gestural signals. In other experiments, chimpanzees have shown the ability to mimic human actions (Custance, Whiten, & Bard, 1995), but only after extensive training over a several month period, and never for any functional end as in gestural communication (see Call & Tomasello, 1995, for the finding that an orangutan who had been trained to mimic human actions nevertheless failed to mimic them when they were aimed at a concrete goal).

The overall conclusion about learning is thus very clear. Imitative learning processes may play some role in the case of some ape gestures; this has yet to be demonstrated conclusively, but the existence of some group-specific gestures that cannot yield easily to environmental explanations provides suggestive evidence. However, the overwhelming weight of the evidence demonstrates fairly conclusively that the main way that apes acquire their intentional gestures is through some form of social learning, presumably ontogenetic ritualization—and this is the same for all five of the ape species studied (although the chimpanzees and bonobos are more individually variable than the other species, perhaps implying more learning). How much of a role is played by unlearned behavior patterns—the degree to which individuals would gesture in these ways if they were raised outside of any social group, for instance—is at this time an open question. But flexible use would at least suggest a substantial degree of learning in how to deploy gestural signals for communicative goals, even if the behavior itself is highly constrained evolutionarily. It is therefore to the question of flexibility that we now turn.

8.3. FLEXIBILITY OF USE

The use of gestures is in many ways analogous to the use of tools as a way to solve certain problems (e.g., Gómez, 1990). Individuals are often faced with situations in which another individual controls access to a certain resource and they have to use social strategies to gain access themselves. For instance, an infant may attempt to get its mother to allow nursing or to transport it to a certain location. One may say that using a gesture to manipulate an individual is very much like using a tool to manipulate the world. To do either of these "intelligently" one must use the signal or tool flexibly depending on the particular circumstances at hand.

A key situation is when a recipient of a gestural signal does not do what the signaler wants it to do. Can signalers deploy other gestures or combinations of gestures to obtain their goal? Traditionally, much of animal communication has been based on assigning one signal to one function, which makes it quite inflexible, and primate communication has been no exception (however, see Owren & Rendall, 2001). Although primates can learn to recognize a variety of calls, including the calls of other species, and to respond appropriately, for the most part they are unable to modify their vocal production. The production of gestures, at least in apes, stands in stark contrast to the use of vocalizations in terms of its flexibility. There are three important points. First, there is a means—ends dissociation between gestures and the contexts (and functions) in which these gestures are applied. This flexibility is at odds with the traditionally assumed one-to-one correspondence between signals and functions. Second, the production of gestures is quite variable both in terms of its topography (see also Tomasello et al., 1997 for gestural variations) and also in the combinations of multiple gestures. Third, apes adjust their gestural productions for the attentional state of the recipient. (Also relevant is the fact that they can learn from humans novel gestures that are not part of their natural repertoire; see next chapter). We examine each of these three aspects in turn, the first two here and the third in the next section.

Apes and monkeys use gestures in a variety of contexts. The current studies have demonstrated that there is not a one-to-one correspondence between gestures and contexts. Many gestures are used in more than one functional context. Figure 8.8 presents the proportion of gestures that were used in more than one context for the species included in this volume. It is around half (or more) for each species. In addition, each context is served by multiple gestures. Figure 8.9 presents the percent of gestures per context in each of the ape species in the current studies. One possible caveat is that although there is not a one-to-one correspondence between signals and contexts, perhaps if one were to focus on functions more narrowly defined, rather than contexts, we might find such a correspondence. For instance, subjects may always use hand beg to request food. Although this may be true for some gestures such as rub chin in chimpanzees to request food from others, other gestures cannot be so easily classified. For example, infant chimpanzees use gentle touch to request a change of posture from the mother, a change of location, or a food transfer. Ground slap is used for calling attention (in a variety of contexts) but on other occasions, it is used once subjects are already watching and may have an intimidation or emphasis function. When apes have a goal in a certain context, they flexibly use whatever gesture they think will most likely lead the recipient to do what they want her to. Many, perhaps most, gestures can be used flexibly in this way in a variety of different communicative contexts.

It is also important that individuals sequence gestures together in single contexts. In most such cases, there is a single context and function, and the ape persists when the initial gesture does not produce the desired outcome (mainly because of an unresponsive recipient; Liebal, Call, & Tomasello, 2004a). This suggests strongly that two different ges-

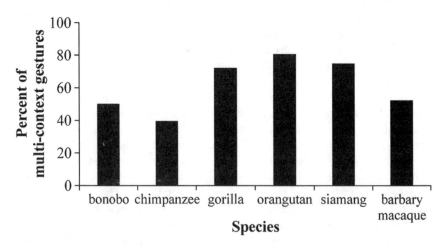

Figure 8.8. Proportion of gestures used in more than one context for each species.

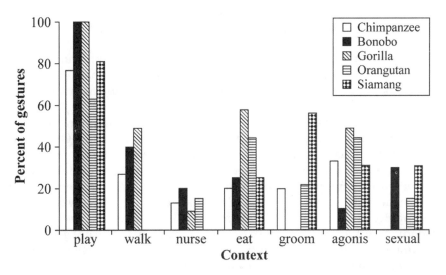

Figure 8.9. Proportion of gestures used in each context for each species.

tures are being used for the same function in the same context. The current studies have documented that approximately 20% to 30% of the total gestures produced by chimpanzees, orangutans, and siamangs appear in combinations (combinations were not quantified in the other species). There is agreement across the studies of these species that two-gesture combinations are by far the most frequent, accounting for about 70% of all the combinations. It should be noted that our definition of combination does not include cases in which attention-getting gestures are used to draw attention to involuntary facial expressions and postures—because these latter are not intentional gestures themselves. If these cases were to be included, then even a higher percentage of ape gestures could be considered as part of some kind of combination.

The majority of gesture combinations are repetitions of the same gesture, but a substantial minority involve stringing together two or more different gestures. Tomasello et al. (1994) found that 61% of the combinations of chimpanzees were formed by repetitions of the same gesture, whereas the remaining 39% were combinations of two or more different gestures. Liebal et al. (2004a) found that repetitions accounted for 45% of the combinations observed in some other chimpanzees, whereas 55% of combinations consisted of two or more distinct gestures. In most cases, even when different gestures were used in combination, they were gestures that were mostly used for the same function when they were used singly—that is, the typical pattern was something like two play gestures strung together for an unresponsive partner in a play context.

One negative finding about chimpanzee gesture combinations is also important. Liebal et al. (2004a) looked closely at chimpanzee gesture combinations with respect to the status of each gesture as an attention getter versus intention movement. Recall that attention getters are aimed at attracting attention to the self whereas intention movements are aimed at initiating a particular kind of social interaction. One possibility is thus that chimpanzees might use attention getters to attract the attention of recipients, and once their attention had been captured, they would use intention movements to request things from recipients. If this were the case, we would expect to see that attention getters would preferentially precede intention movements when the recipient was not attending. But this was not the case. When recipients were not attending, chimpanzee signalers did not use attention getters followed by intention movements, but rather they quite often walked around a potential recipient until they were facing her and then used the intention movement gesture. It thus seems that even though chimpanzees know that attention getters attract the attention of potential recipients to the self, and that visual gestures must have the attention of the recipient to be effective, they find means other than gesture combinations to make sure that they have the attention of the recipient before they make intention movement gestures. We return to this finding in the next section on adjustments for audience.

Overall, then, the current findings are very clear that all five of the ape species studied use their gestures flexibly in different communicative contexts, sometimes in combination with one another, in strategic attempts to manipulate their social partners.

8.4. ADJUSTMENTS FOR AUDIENCE

An especially important aspect of apes' flexible use of gestures is the sender's adjustments for the attentional state of the recipient. In the linguistic communication of humans, this would constitute one important component in the pragmatic aspect of the communicative interaction.

In the study of primate vocalizations, researchers speak of audience effects when the call is produced in the presence of others but not when alone. The vocalizations of many species, including nonprimates, are sensitive to social context in this very general way (Owings & Morton, 1998). But vocalizations are broadcast so that every individual in the vicinity cannot help but hear it. The sender, therefore, does not need to be attentive to other aspects of the recipients' readiness to perceive the signal and react to it—and the recipients do not really need to attend to the signals either. In contrast, many gestures take place in the visual modality, and visually based communication is not broadcast indiscriminately but, to be effective, must be directed toward an attentionally ready recipient (and the recipient must attend to the signaler to discern if the signal is directed to him as well). Many gestures thus demand, in a way that vocalizations do not, that the signaler understand something about the process by which the recipient perceives and registers the signal. In addition, it seems to be the case empirically that even auditory gestures (e.g., ground slap) are often used by signalers to gain the visual attention of the recipient—often, as argued earlier, to draw attention to some involuntary facial expression or body posture, which also indicates a sensitivity to the attentional state of the recipients. We believe that this link between gestural communication and attention to the attention of the recipient may have played a role in the evolution of complex skills of social cognition ("theory of mind") in communication, a point to which we return in the final chapter concerning the evolution of human language.

Tomasello et al. (1994) included in their observations of chimpanzee gestures the attentional state of the recipient at the moment the signaler made the gesture. Distinguishing between visual, tactile, and auditory gestures, they found that chimpanzees preferentially used visual gestures when the recipient was oriented toward them bodily (so that she could see them). In contrast, chimpanzees did not take into account the recipient's attentional state when they used tactile gestures. Auditory gestures fell in between visual and tactile gestures, being used less specifically than visual gestures but more than tactile gestures. (A possible explanation is that many auditory gestures also have an important visual component, and may be used for emphasis rather than to capture visual attention only.) These results have since been replicated in two additional studies with chimpanzees in a different group (Liebal et al., 2004a; Tomasello et al., 1997). It is also interesting in this connection that both chimpanzees and gorillas have been observed, on occasion, to use their hands to hide a facial expression that they did not want a recipient to see (de Waal, 1982; Tanner & Byrne, 1993).

In the current study, the major finding concerning adjustments for audience is that signalers in all five ape species adjust for recipients—in the sense that they use visual gestures only when the recipient is already oriented toward them. Figure 8.10 presents the data. One interesting finding is that bonobos and chimpanzees—both from the genus *Pan*, humans' closest primate relatives—showed somewhat greater specificity than the other apes in their choice of gesture modality as a function of the attentional state of the recipient. Specifically, they used visual gestures when others were looking and tactile gestures regardless of whether others were looking at them, whereas orangutans and gorillas (and siamangs to a lesser extent) used gestures (regardless of the modality) mostly when others were looking and with less specific tailoring for recipient visual fact attention.

Experimental studies have also demonstrated that apes in general are sensitive to the attentional state of the recipient when communicating gesturally. Call and Tomasello (1994) found that orangutans gestured more to a human who was facing them than to one who had his back turned (in which case they gestured just as infrequently as when he was out of the room). One human-raised orangutan was even sensitive to the state of the humans' eyes, gesturing more when they were open as opposed to closed. Povinelli and Eddy (1996) tested chimpanzees in a similar but different paradigm in which the subject had to choose which of two humans with which to communicate; for example, the subject could beg food either from a human who was looking at them or one who had his back turned. They replicated the back-turned result reported by Call and Tomasello, but they found negative results in a number of conditions in which they manipulated the visibility of the face (and the eyes). For instance, chimpanzees failed to spontaneously discriminate between a human with her face visible and one with a bucket over her head, or with her back turned but looking over her shoulder.[2]

More recently, Kaminski, Call, and Tomasello (2004) tested chimpanzees, orangutans, and bonobos in the original Call and Tomasello paradigm with only one experimenter present (see also Hostetter, Cantero, &

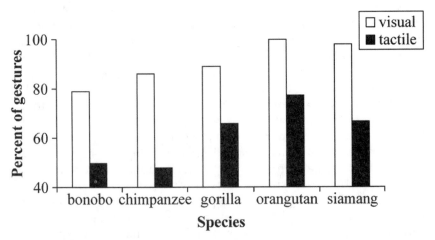

Figure 8.10. Proportion of visual and tactile gestures used when the recipients were oriented to the signaler for each species.

Hopkins, 2001). They replicated the front–back differentiation yet again, but then, contrary to Povinelli and Eddy (1996), found at least some sensitivity to the face and eyes. The novelty of this study was the systematic manipulation of face and body orientation. Thus, in different conditions subjects saw a human experimenter with (a) body and face oriented to them, (b) just the body but not the face oriented to them, (c) just the face but not the body oriented to them, (d) or neither the body nor the face oriented to them. Results indicated that apes were sensitive to the face orientation when the body was oriented toward them, but not when the body was oriented away. This was because apes extracted two types of information from the human experimenter in this situation; visual access and disposition to transfer food. The face orientation was relevant to whether the human could see their gesture, whereas the body orientation was relevant to whether the observer had a disposition to give them food (because a human with the back turned is unlikely to give food as compared with one who is oriented toward the signaler). These results thus show experimentally that apes are indeed sensitive to the attentional state of the recipient in gestural communication. Gómez (1996) found even more sensitivity to the eyes and face of the recipient in gesturing chimpanzees who had been raised by humans.

Despite the fact that all apes tested show some sensitivity to the attentional state of the recipient in communicative situations, there are some experimental data suggesting—in-line with the findings of the current studies—that chimpanzees and bonobos may be especially sensitive. First, Bräuer, Call, and Tomasello (2005) found that bonobos and chimpanzees showed greater specificity in following the gaze of a human to a location above themselves (i.e., they looked most in the experimental condition and least in the control condition) compared to gorillas and orangutans. Second, Okamoto-Barth, Call, and Tomasello (in press) found similar results with looking through barriers with and without windows. Third, Liebal, Pika, Call, and Tomasello (2004b) found greater sensitivity in bonobos and chimpanzees, as compared with gorillas and orangutans, in a situation in which subjects had to locomote some distance in order to deliver their gesture in the line of sight of a human recipient, who was sometimes faced away from them. Specifically, subjects were presented either with an attentive human or with an inattentive human (with her back turned), and with a bowl of food either in front of or behind her. The experimental set up was such that the subject had the opportunity to either use an attention getter to call the human's attention or else to walk around to face the human from the other side of the cage. All apes used more visual gestures when the experimenter was facing them than when she was not, thus replicating the results of previous studies. When the experimenter had her back turned, all species tended to move around to face the experimenter when she took the food with her. However, when she left the food in front of the subject and turned her back to her, chimpanzees and bonobos walked around in order to gesture to the human even though this meant leaving the food behind; gorillas and orangutans did not.

To summarize, all apes take into account the attentional state of the recipient when using gestures. They use visual gestures preferentially when potential recipients are oriented toward them, and therefore can see them, whereas they use tactile gestures independent of the attentional state of the recipient. Faced with an individual who is not oriented toward them, they either walk to a position where the recipient can see them and then use a visual gesture, or they use a tactile gesture directly; they do not combine an attention-getting gesture (produced first) with an intention movement to achieve this same end. There is evidence both from the current study and from experiments that chimpanzees and bonobos show special sensitivity to the attentional state of the recipient in communicative situations. This finding, in combination with the finding reported earlier that only African apes use auditory gestures designed to capture the visual attention of recipients, suggests that there may be some differences among apes in their motivations and skills for attending to and manipulating the visual attention of social partners.

8.5. CONCLUSION

All four great ape species—chimpanzees, bonobos, gorillas, and orangutans—and one species of small ape—siamangs—use gestural signals as an important part of their communication with conspecifics. An important subset of these are ones that originate mainly by means of learning and that are used flexibly in different communicative contexts. All five of these ape species have substantial repertoires of 20 to 40 intentional gestures of this type, with individuals commanding for themselves about half this number. The gestures used by chimpanzees and bonobos seem especially variable individually.

In general, previous findings with chimpanzees—concerning both how gestures are learned and how they are used—generalize to these other ape species reasonably well. The major learning process involved for ape gestures is clearly ontogenetic ritualization, in which individuals essentially shape one another's behavior by learning to predict and control what the other will do in recurrent social interactions; there is very little evidence for the imitative learning of gestures (although there are some group-specific gestures in need of explanation). These onto-genetically ritualized gestures are then used flexibly in different communicative circumstances, sometimes in combination with one another as a means of persistence to the communicative goal. All ape species use both intention movements, intended to instigate a particular kind of social interaction, and attention getters, intended to capture the attention of another onto the self (sometimes because the self is currently displaying an involuntary posture or facial expression that, to work, needs the other to attend to it). In all ape species, the signaler chooses its gestural signal—especially with regard to modality (visual, tactile, auditory)—depending on the attentional state of the recipient.

Two possible differences among species were observed. The first concerns the types of gestures used in the functions for which they are used. On several different measures, we found African apes showing different patterns from Asian apes. For example, the use of gestures to initiate travel and in exchange of food seems to be more important in the African than in the Asian apes, who use their gestures more often in a variety of other affiliative and agonistic social interactions, although some food begging gestures have been described for orangutans (Bard, 1992). Also, and perhaps of special importance, auditory attention getters are very important in the gestural communication of African apes (e.g., slapping the ground or drumming on objects to gain the visual attention of the recipient), but they are seemingly absent in Asian apes. This may suggest a greater concern among these species for the attentional state of the recipient (see also later). In some cases, the clustering of the African and Asian apes might be due to the different role of arboreality in the two taxa, although in other cases this seems unlikely, and cognitive explanations, based on genetic relatedness seem more plausible.

The second potential species difference concerns adjustments for the attentional state of the listener. In this case, the current results as well as those from some other studies, suggest the possibility that chimpanzees and bonobos are a bit more sensitive than the other ape species to the visual experience of their recipients. This finding also fits nicely with the finding that only African apes attempt to attract the visual attention of others with auditory gestures. (Also, so far there are only reports of two African apes intentionally hiding, with their hands, an involuntary display from others.) If indeed it is the case that chimpanzees and bonobos (and perhaps gorillas) are especially sensitive to the visual experience of others, and have special ways of attracting the visual attention of others with auditory gestures, this might suggest that these species communicate in ways that are especially close—although still very far from—the way human beings communicate with one another. One of the distinguishing characteristics of human symbolic communication is indeed the role played by the understanding of other "minds"—which is necessary for understanding linguistic and other kinds of symbols, as well as the pragmatic dimensions of linguistic communication.

With these considerations in mind, we turn now to an argument that in the evolution of human skills of linguistic communication, gestures may have played an especially important role, especially at the very outset. This is because our closest primate relatives, the apes (1) learn and use their gestural signals in much more flexible ways than their vocal signals; and (2) pay much more attention in the gestural than in the vocal modality—due to the inherent demands of communication in the visual channel—to the attentional state of recipients. Communicative gestures used flexibly and with attention to the attentional state of the recipient are much closer to human linguistic symbols and communication than are relatively inflexible vocalizations broadcast indiscriminately.

NOTES

1. A second possible example is the 'grooming hand clasp' reported by McGrew and Tutin (1978). This is not really an instrumental gesture, but simply involves one individual raising the arm of another to access the underarm for grooming. The behavior was also thought at the time to be unique to the Mahale K group, and it does seem to be absent from the nearby Kasakela community in Gombe. But, as with 'leaf clipping,' other researchers have since observed the behavior elsewhere; in this case in one wild and one captive community (de Waal & Seres, 1997; Ghiglieri, 1984).
2. Nonhuman primates, including some monkeys species, also show sensitivity to the visual experience of others in competitive situations (e.g., Flombaum & Santos, 2005; Hare, Call, Agnetta, & Tomasello, 2000; Hare, Call, & Tomasello, 2001; Hare, Call, & Tomasello, in press) in which case they are mostly trying to avoid the gaze of others. Communication represents a special cooperative situation in which the signaler desires the gaze of the other on the self, and it is this situation on which we focus here.

REFERENCES

Bard, K. A. (1992). Intentional behavior and intentional communication in young free-ranging orangutans. *Child Development, 63*, 1186–1197.

Berdecio, S., & Nash, L. T. (1981). Chimpanzee visual communication. *Anthropological Research Papers No. 2: Arizona State University*, 1–159.

Boesch, C. (1995). Innovation in wild chimpanzees. *International Journal of Primatology, 16*, 1–16.

Bräuer, J., Call, J., & Tomasello, M. (2005). All great ape species follow gaze to distant locations and around barriers. *Journal of Comparative Psychology, 119,* 145–154.

Call, J., & Tomasello, M. (1994). Production and comprehension of referential pointing by orangutans (*Pongo pygmaeus*). *Journal of Comparative Psychology, 108,* 307–317.

Call, J., & Tomasello, M. (1995). The use of social information in the problem-solving of orangutans (*Pongo pygmaeus*) and human children (*Homo sapiens*). *Journal of Comparative Psychology, 109,* 308–320.

Custance, D. M., Whiten, A., & Bard, K. A. (1995). Can young chimpanzees (*Pan troglodytes*) imitate arbitrary actions? Hayes & Hayes (1952) revisited. *Behaviour, 132*(11–12), 837–859.

de Waal, F. B. M. (1982). *Chimpanzee politics.* London: Jonathan Cape.

Fleiss, J. L. (1981). *Statistical methods for rates and proportions.* New York: Wiley.

Flombaum, J. I., & Santos, L. R. (2005). Rhesus monkeys attribute perceptions to others. *Current Biology, 15,* 447–452.

Ghiglieri, M. P. (1984). *The chimpanzees of Kibale forest: A field study of ecology and social structure.* New York: Columbia University Press.

Gómez, J. C. (1990). The emergence of intentional communication as a problem-solving strategy in the gorilla. In S. T. Parker & K. R. Gibson (Eds.), *"Language" and intelligence in monkeys and apes. Comparative developmental perspectives* (pp. 333–355). New York: Cambridge University Press.

Gómez, J. C. (1996). Non-human primate theories of (non-human primate) minds: Some issues concerning the origins of mind-reading. In P. Carruthers & P. K. Smith (Eds.), *Theories of theories of mind* (pp. 330–343). Cambridge, England: Cambridge University Press.

Goodall, J. (1986). *The chimpanzees of Gombe: Patterns of behavior.* Cambridge, MA: Harvard University Press.

Hare, B., Call, J., Agnetta, B., & Tomasello, M. (2000). Chimpanzees know what conspecifics do and do not see. *Animal Behaviour, 59,* 771–785.

Hare, B., Call, J., & Tomasello, M. (2001). Do chimpanzees know what conspecifics know and do not know? *Animal Behaviour, 61,* 139–151.

Hare, B., Call, J., & Tomasello, M. (in press). Chimpanzees deceive a human competitor by hiding. *Cognition.*

Hostetter, A. B., Cantero, M., & Hopkins, W. D. (2001). Differential use of vocal and gestural communication by chimpanzees (*Pan troglodytes*) in response to the attentional status of a human (*Homo sapiens*). *Journal of Comparative Psychology, 115*(4), 337–343.

Kaminski, J., Call, J., & Tomasello, M. (2004). Body orientation and face orientation: Two factors controlling apes' begging behavior from humans. *Animal Cognition, 7,* 216–223.

Liebal, K., Call, J., & Tomasello, M. (2004a). The use of gesture sequences in chimpanzees. *American Journal of Primatology, 64,* 377–396.

Liebal, K., Pika, S., Call, J., & Tomasello, M. (2004b). To move or not to move: How apes alter the attentional states of humans when begging for food. *Interaction Studies, 5,* 199–219.

Maestripieri, D. (2005). Gestural communication in three species of macaques (*Macaca mulatta, M. nemestrina, M. arctoides*): Use of signals in relation to dominance and social context. *Gesture, 5,* 55–71.

McGrew, W. C. (1992). *Chimpanzee material culture: Implications for human evolution.* Cambridge, England: Cambridge University Press.

McGrew, W. C., & Tutin, C. E. G. (1978). Evidence for a social custom in wild chimpanzees? *Man, 13,* 234–251.

Nishida, T (1980). The leaf-clipping display: A newly-discovered expressive gesture in wild chimpanzees. *Journal of Human Evolution, 9,* 117–128.

Nishida, T (1994). Review of recent findings on Mahale chimpanzees: Implications and future research directions. In R. W. Wrangham, W. C. McGrew, & F. B. M. de Waal et al. (Eds.), *Chimpanzee cultures* (pp. 373–396). Cambridge, MA: Harvard University Press.

Okamoto-Barth, S., Call, J., & Tomasello, M. (in press). *Great apes' understanding of occlusion of others' line of sight.* Unpublished manuscript.

Owings, D. H., & Morton, E. S. (1998). *Animal vocal communication: A new approach.* Cambridge, MA: Cambridge University Press.

Owren, M. J., & Rendall, D. (2001). Sound on the rebound: Returning form and function to the forefront in understanding nonhuman primate vocal signaling. *Evolutionary Anthropology, 10*(2), 58–71.

Povinelli, D. J., & Eddy, T. J. (1996). What young chimpanzees know about seeing. *Monographs of the Society for Research in Child Development, 61*(3), 1–191.

Seres, M., & de Waal, F. B. M. (1997). Propagation of handclasp grooming among captive chimpanzees. *American Journal of Primatology, 43,* 339–346.

Sugiyama, Y. (1981). Observations on the population dynamics and behavior of wild chimpanzees at Bossou, Guinea, 1979–1980. *Primates, 22,* 432–444.

Tanner, J. E., & Byrne, W. B. (1993). Concealing facial evidence of mood: Perspective-taking in a captive Gorilla. *Primates, 34*(4), 451–457.

Tomasello, M., & Call, J. (1997). *Primate cognition.* New York: Oxford University Press.

Tomasello, M., Call, J., Nagell, K., Olguin, R., & Carpenter, M. (1994). The learning and the use of gestural signals by young chimpanzees: A trans-generational study. *Primates, 35,* 137–154.

Tomasello, M., Call, J., Warren, J., Frost, T., Carpenter, M., & Nagell, K. (1997). The ontogeny of chimpanzee gestural signals: A comparison across groups and generations. *Evolution of Communication, 1,* 223–253.

Tomasello, M., George, B. L., Kruger, A. C., Farrar, M. J., & Evans, A. (1985). The development of gestural communication in young chimpanzees. *Journal of Human Evolution, 14,* 175–186.

Tomasello, M., Gust, D., & Frost, G. T. (1989). A longitudinal investigation of gestural communication in young chimpanzees. *Primates, 30*(1), 35–50.

van Schaik, C. P, Fox, E. A., & Fechtman, L. T. (2003). Individual variation in the rate of use of tree-hole tools among wild orangutans: Implications for hominin evolution. *Journal of Human Evolution, 44,* 11–23.

Wrangham, R. W. (1977). Feeding behaviour of chimpanzees in Gombe National Park, Tanzania. In T. H. Clutton-Brock (Ed.), *Primate ecology: Studies of feeding and ranging behaviour in lemurs, monkeys and apes* (pp. 504–538). New York: Academic Press.

CHAPTER 9

Ape Gestures and the Origins of Language

Michael Tomasello
Josep Call
Max Planck Institute for Evolutionary Anthropology

F or as long as there have been people speculating about the origins of human language, there have been advocates of some kind of gestural origins hypothesis (see Hewes, 1973, for the classic review). But until recently, this has been done in the absence of any detailed information about the ways in which nonhuman primate individuals communicate with one another. We believe that a comparison of the vocalizations and gestures of our nearest great ape relatives does indeed provide support for some kind of gestural origins hypothesis, but for somewhat different reasons than those traditionally invoked.

Many advocates of gestural origins for language have posited some kind of mechanical advantage for gestures, like the importance of the visual modality for humans and/or the dexterity of the hands—with modern theories emphasizing the role of mirror neurons in connecting these advantages to motor imitation (e.g., Arbib, 2004; Corballis, 2002). Others have posited that the hands are useful for conveying indexical (spatial) information in terms of directing others' attention to locations, or in conveying iconic information, as the hands can mime visual scenes in ways that the voice cannot (e.g., Armstrong, Stokoe, & Wilcox, 1995).

Important though these may be, we believe the key lies elsewhere. In fact, we believe there are two keys. The first lies in the fact that for great apes, and so perhaps for early humans, many vocalizations are used for evolutionarily urgent functions, such as signaling danger or food or separation from the group, and so they are closely tied to high emotions such as fear and excitement. Because of these urgent, emotionally charged functions, vocalizations are typically hard wired and used with very little flexibility, broadcast loudly to much of the social group at once—who are then infected with the emotion. Goodall (1986, p. 125) says that "The production of a sound in the *absence* of the appropriate emotional state seems to be an almost impossible task for a chimpanzee." Even those vocalizations such as grunts and coos that are not used for urgent functions and display more flexibility of use, are stil lvery stereotyped in terms of their production. In contrast, many (although not all) ape gestures described in this book are typically used for less urgent functions such as play and grooming, involving relatively quiet interactions between two individuals only, and seldom involving high emotions. Because gestural signals are mostly used for less urgent and emotionally charged functions, Mother Nature can relax her grip, and so ape gestures are often learned in social interaction with others and used very flexibly in different communicative circumstances— more in the manner of human linguistic symbols.

The second key is that intentional communication in the visual, as opposed to the auditory, modality requires closer attention of the communicating partners to one another and to their attentional states. The recipient has to know whether the gesture is or is not directed to her, and, even more importantly, the signaler needs to determine whether the recipient is in an attentional state conducive to successful communication—which, as we have demonstrated, apes do as a matter of course. Neither of these considerations is of great importance in vocal communication, which is typically broadcast somewhat indiscriminately, and indeed there is no evidence in primate vocal communication for audience effects other than simply the presence or absence of conspecifics (or kin). The hypothesis is that attending to others' attentional states is more important in gestural than in vocal communication, and this puts ape gestural communication closer to human language in this way as well.

Of course, ape gestural communication is still a very long way from human linguistic communication, and even from human gestural communication: The way apes learn and use their gestures differ markedly from the way humans learn and use their gestures and language. In this final chapter, therefore, we do two things. First we make the argument that ape gestural signals work in ways more similar to human communication than do ape vocal signals, particularly in terms of flexible production and attention to the attentional states of the partner. Then we attempt to identify some of the key differences between ape and human communication from the point of view of the cognitive and learning processes involved, focusing especially on those aspects dealing with the understanding and sharing of communicative intentions. We conclude with some speculations about the special role of the pointing gesture in the evolution of language.

9.1. VOCALIZATIONS VERSUS GESTURES IN NONHUMAN PRIMATES

Beginning with Dawkins and Krebs (1978), and continuing with more modern treatments such as those of Owings and Morton (1998) and Seyfarth and Cheney (2003), theorists of animal communication have stressed the importance of separating the signaler from the recipient. Recipients are individuals trying to figure out what is going on so that they can make adaptive behavioral decisions using whatever information is available. Signalers take advantage of this by evolving signals that affect the recipient's assessment of the situation and so the behavior. For example, in many species, individuals have evolved physical characteristics that make them appear larger than they really are, with the result that others are less likely to attack them. In such cases, the recipient is definitely extracting information from the signal. But it is a totally different question whether the signal is in any way 'intended'—either by Mother Nature or by the signaling individual—to manipulate the information available to others; the signal evolves (or is learned) because it affects the behavior of the other, full stop.

For example, let us take the famous example of vervet monkey alarm calls. Playback experiments and habituation experiments have demonstrated conclusively that recipients are extracting information from the different vocal signals indicating different predators. Indeed, recipients very likely form a mental representation of the predator on the basis of hearing the vocalization, and then react accordingly (Seyfarth & Cheney, 2003; Zuberbühler, 2000). In some monkey species, individuals learn to do something similar on hearing the alarm calls of various bird species, and we know that they learn to do this because individuals of the same monkey species who live outside the range of the same bird species do not react to their alarm calls in this same way (Zuberbühler, 2000). Recipients of vocal communication thus extract information from the vocal signal and use it to make adaptive behavioral decisions.

But what about the vervets making the alarm calls? Are they intending to transmit information to others? Do they have any ability to choose calls flexibly at all? It is first of all relevant to note that squirrel monkeys raised in isolation still produce their species-typical vocalizations soon after birth (see Hammerschmidt & Fischer, in press; Snowdon, Elowson, & Roush, 1997, for reviews), and when monkeys of one species are raised in groups of other species in cross-fostering experiments, only very small changes in species-typical vocalizations occur (Owren, Dieter, Seyfarth, & Cheney, 1992). So it would seem that there is very little flexibility in the actual morphology of monkeys' vocal calls. Call usage seems to have greater flexibility especially for certain calls (see Owren & Rendall, 2001; Snowdon, in press) although learning still plays a highly constrained role. Thus, in most cases, monkey vocal calls are used in adultlike contexts from early in ontogeny (with perhaps a small amount of fine tuning in identifying appropriate situations; Seyfarth & Cheney 1997, but see Snowdon, in press). In terms of audience effects, although vervet monkey alarm calls are typically not given when the signaler is alone, this could easily be an integral part of the wired-in system; and it is also the case that callers typically keep calling even after the entire group is safely aware of and away from the predator. There is no evidence that these monkeys adjust the way they call differentially for recipients in different attentional states (e.g., call louder for those farther away). Because of considerations such as these, many researchers now believe that although vervet monkey recipients extract information flexibly from all kinds of sources, including vervet monkey alarm calls, the signals themselves have evolved because they serve to change the behavior of the predator and/or the signaler's kin (Owren & Rendall, 2001). In the opinion of Seyfarth and Cheney (1994, p. 168), "Listeners acquire information from signalers who do not, in the human sense, intend to provide it."

In general, there is no evidence that the vocal communication of apes is any way more sophisticated than that of vervet monkeys (or any other monkey species). Indeed, because apes do not have referentially specific alarm calls at all, one could argue the opposite: The vocal communication of apes is in many ways less sophisticated than that of monkeys. There is very little evidence of individual differences in ape vocalizations (and there are no isolation or cross-fostering experiments—other than apes raised by humans; see following), and no systematic evidence of vocal learning. The evidence for adjustments to audience in the vocalizations of great apes—even in the sense of presence–absence of potential recipients—is very thin. There is some evidence that apes will refrain from vocalizing as they normally would when "on patrol" near neighboring groups, and when copulating with someone they are not supposed to be copulating with (see Boesch & Boesch-Ackermann, 2000, for a review)—although it is unclear whether they are monitoring the presence of potential combatants in either case when refraining. They also call more often when traveling if potential allies are nearby (Mitani

& Nishida, 1993). When chimpanzees find a large source of food, their calling is not affected by which group members are present and which are not (even if all are present—suggesting that they are not adjusting their signals to fit the communicative situation in terms of potential recipients (Clark & Wrangham, 1994; Mitani, 1996). Chimpanzees do not food call when they find small amounts of food (Hauser & Wrangham, 1987) or food that is not easily divisible (Hauser, Teixidor, Field, & Flaherty, 1993), but this is very likely tied directly to their level of excitement. And again, as in the case of monkeys, there is basically no evidence that apes adjust the way they call differentially for recipients in different attentional states (e.g., those farther away or distracted).

The case of great ape gestural communication is importantly different, especially with regard to the way things work with the signaler. Although many bodily postures and facial expressions seem to be hard wired and tied to emotional states in ways not unlike vocal calls (e.g., piloerection of the hair of chimpanzees when they are afraid or excited), others are clearly learned and used more or less voluntarily, perhaps especially those involving in some way the hands (perhaps because primate hands are used so flexibly in so many different kinds of intentional actions for pursuing so many different kinds of goals). Voluntary use enables individuals to deploy the gesture flexibly to pursue various communicative goals depending on the current circumstances, and, as we have demonstrated throughout the current studies, this is characteristic of many of apes' most important gestural signals. Our proposal is that the fundamental reality of a communicative signal—what characterizes its nature most directly—is the social, cognitive, and learning processes that underlie it, and so ape gestures are fundamentally very different from ape vocalizations. Two aspects of the process are crucial.

First, ape gestures involve learning and flexible use. As we have seen throughout this book, there are large individual differences in which individuals use which gestures, suggesting a strong role for learning. Indeed, in the current data as well as in other studies, there are a number of different reports of idiosyncratic ape gestures, used by only a single individual, which suggests that at least some ape gestures are wholly invented by individuals (or ritualized by pairs) in the face of particular communicative situations. The process of ontogenetic ritualization would seem to be the major learning process for many ape gestures, and it relies on each individual learning to anticipate what the other will do in a particular situation and react accordingly—and indeed some apes raised by humans even learn some atypical gestural signals for use exclusively with humans (see later). Nothing like this has ever been reported for vocalizations of any kind for any nonhuman primate species. In general, there are no reliable reports of major feats of primate vocal learning or invention, or highly flexible vocal use, anywhere in the literature, and indeed early attempts to teach apes aspects of human vocal language were abject failures (Kellog & Kellog, 1933). The main point in the current context is this. Because they are learned, ape gestures are used in a very flexible manner: They can be used in novel contexts, inhibited as needed, combined with other gestures, and sometimes even invented. The data in this book demonstrate repeatedly that the apes are learning or inventing many of their gestures, and they are choosing particular gestures for particular contexts, following up with other gestures if the first one does not work. Apes have social/communicative goals, and in their gestural communication much more than in their vocal communication, they are pursuing them flexibly.

Second, ape gestures work via attention to recipient attention. The current data, as well as other studies and experiments, demonstrate quite clearly that all apes adjust their gestures to the attentional state of the recipient on a routine basis. And this does not depend just on whether others are present or not, but rather, on whether the other is in a position to perceive the gesture as displayed. Although they do not use their attention-getting gestures systematically before their intention movements for nonattending recipients, apes do choose a visual gesture only when the other is attending, and even more impressively, they actively move themselves to a place where others can see their gestures when need be. Vocal communication simply does not demand this kind of attention to the attentional state of others to be effective. It is noteworthy in this context that in the current studies, we found that using auditory gestures to capture the visual attention of others (e.g., slapping the ground) is only used by African apes (chimpanzees, bonobos, and gorillas), and that there are several lines of evidence that chimpanzees and bonobos are especially attuned to the visual experience of others in communicative situations. Because these are the two closest relatives of humans, the suggestion would be that the common ancestor of chimpanzees, bonobos, and humans some 6 million years ago had begun to develop special attention to the attentional states of others—which, we would argue, is an important precursor for humanlike linguistic communication.

The main point in the current context is this. Human languages involve socially learned communicative signals (linguistic symbols), which are used flexibly in adapting to novel communicative contexts—always based on the attentional and knowledge states of the listener. The signaler (speaker) chooses from her repertoire of linguistic symbols, those that are appropriate in the current context. From the point of view of the cognitive and learning processes involved, ape gestural communication—based on learned and flexibly used signals attuned to the attentional needs of the recipient—is much more similar to human linguistic communication than is ape vocal communication and its unlearned and relatively inflexibly used signals broadcast indiscriminately. There are other dimensions to the process, but our proposal is that the gestures of early humans were closer to symbolic communication in terms of the social, cognitive, and learning processes involved, and so they were a very likely starting point on the human road to symbols and language.

9.2. HUMAN GESTURAL COMMUNICATION

Despite the fact that apes use their gestures to flexibly, intentionally, affect the behavior of others—and with attention to the attentional states of the audience—they still do not work like human gestures. In a word, humans do not just gesture intentionally to get others to do what they want, they gesture and speak in order to affect the intentional or mental states of others—and they do this for various cooperative purposes not readily apparent in either the vocal or gestural communication of non-human primates.

Let us take as the prototypical example human pointing. Pointing would seem to be a very simple gesture: The signaler simply directs the attention of the receiver to something in their common environment for some reason. Apes are perfectly capable of stretching out their arms and fingers, they know that others see things (Tomasello & Call, 2006), and there would seem to be many situations in which directing someone's attention to something external would be useful for them. But apes do not point distally to things for other apes. Possible candidates in their natural behavior are two. First, Menzel (1974) argued that apes do not point with an extended arm and finger because they point with their whole body orientation. But there is no evidence that when they are orienting their bodies—which others may very well follow in some way—that they are intentionally directing the attention of others (e.g., they do not become upset and try something different if the recipient does not orient appropriately). Second, de Waal and van Hooff (1981) argued that chimpanzees' use of 'side-directed' behavior during agonistic encounters (extended arm toward the aggressor) might be some kind of indication to allies as to who is the enemy. However, chimpanzees use an extended arm toward their potential allies as well, and so the function of this behavior is far from clear. We thus do not believe that apes produce humanlike pointing to direct the attention of conspecifics to external and distal entities (for other reasons, see later), and so the question is why not?

One reason is that communicating effectively with pointing requires a shared understanding of the current context. For example, if one human points to some object for another human, without any shared context, the response of the recipient is perplexity—why, for example, has she drawn my attention to that bucket? The pointing by itself does not display the pointer's reason for directing the recipient's attention to the bucket. But if the humans are in the shared context of searching for food, and they both know this, then the recipient sees the pointing as relevant to their shared activity, and so a reasonable inference would be that the pointing indicates that there might be some food in the bucket. There is little evidence that apes create with one another the kinds of shared contexts that would make pointing meaningful or relevant (or engage in truly collaborative acts at all; see Tomasello, Carpenter, Call, Behne, & Moll, 2005, for a review). For instance, it has been found in many studies that even when chimpanzees know that humans are hiding food from them and their job is to find it, when the human points to a bucket the chimpanzee—even if it follows the point and looks at the bucket—does not infer that there is food inside (see Call & Tomasello, 2005, for a review of these so-called object choice studies). It is as if they are saying to themselves "There's the bucket. So what? Now where's the food?" The pointing is not relevant to anything for them, because they have not created a shared understanding of the context with the human.[1]

Another reason that apes do not point for one another, or understand pointing, might be that pointing, in its human version at least, assumes a cooperative social milieu. A human baby points to an apple and its mother retrieves it and gives it to her. If a human or an ape points to an apple for another ape, the recipient would simply take it for himself. (Indeed, Savage-Rumbaugh, 1986, reports that when one of her human-raised apes pointed, the other nearby apes ignored it.) In addition, human babies also point to things—for example, a colorful bird flying past—simply to share attention and interest in things with others (so-called declarative pointing; Bates, Camaioni, & Volterra, 1975). There is no evidence that apes have this motivation to share attention or interest with others (Tomasello & Carpenter, 2005). Human babies also point altruistically to inform others of things they need to know to fulfill their goals, for example, to help them locate something they are searching for (Liszkowski, Carpenter, Striano, & Tomasello, in press)—another communicative motive so far not documented in apes or other nonhuman primates. It is also relevant that from their earliest attempts at communication, human infants engage in a kind of conversation or "negotiation of meaning" in which they adjust their communicative attempts in the light of the listener's signs of comprehension or noncomprehension (Golinkoff, 1993)—a style of communication that is essentially collaborative. Again, to our knowledge no other primate species engages in these kinds of collaborative exchanges (there are no observations of one ape asking another for clarification or repairing a communicative formulation in anticipation of its being misunderstood).

The common factor in all of this is what philosophers of action call shared intentionality; forming shared goals and attention with others. Much more than other primates, human beings seem motivated to engage with one another in collaborative activities involving shared goals, and to share experience with one another simply for the sake of doing it. (It is noteworthy that children with autism seem not to have this motivation to the same degree; Hobson, 2002.) Pointing as a communicative gesture relies on shared attention as a communicative context, and assumes in many cases shared goals (the pointing baby convinces the mother to adopt her goal that she, the baby, have the apple) or even helping others attain their goals at no benefit to oneself. Apes do not seem to participate in these kinds of shared intentionality in the same way.

A fairly dramatic illustration of this was reported by Hare and Tomasello (2004). They created for chimpanzees a competitive version of the object choice task. That is, a human first established a competitive relationship with the ape, and then subsequently reached unsuccessfully in the direction of a baited bucket (because the hole through which he reached would not enable her arm to go far enough). In this situation, with an extended arm that resembled in many ways the same pointing gesture apes fail to understand in other studies, the apes suddenly knew where the food was. One interpretation is that in this situation, the apes understood the human's simple goal or intention to get into the bucket, and from this, inferred the presence of food there (and other research has shown their strong skills for making inferences of this type; Call, 2004). Apes can understand the goals of others, and make inferences about the world based on this understanding. But without a shared attentional context or shared goals, they cannot understand the pointing gesture in which someone is attempting to inform them of something, to ask a favor of them, or to share attention with them for basically cooperative purposes.

In addition to pointing, humans also gesture to one another in many other complex ways. Many of these resemble linguistic symbols in being conventional signs, for example, gestures that vary among cultures for such things as "OK"(touching of thumb and forefinger) or "Nice going" (thumbs up) or various kinds of obscenities (what McNeil, 1992, calls emblems). Others are iconic in one way or another. Human infants produce gestures of this general type—often called symbolic gestures (Acredolo & Goodwyn, 1988; Pizzuto & Volterra, 2000)—at around the same time they begin learning language. These include such things as waving goodbye, sniffing for a flower, panting for a dog, holding arms out for an airplane, raising arms for big things, and blowing for hot things. These kinds of gestures are conventional, and so could only be learned by some form of imitation (or possibly—although there is no evidence—by individual creation in the case of iconic signs). And of course, human beings have also invented—by force of necessity—entire sign languages based on symbolic gestures, which have basically all of the defining characteristics of spoken languages. Of most importance in the current context, linguistic signs (whether gestural or vocal) symbolize in their signs various perspectives on things, which generates another layer of pragmatic inferences on the part of the comprehender (e.g., "Why did she call it an animal, as opposed to a horse or a pony?"). Apes, to our knowledge, do not use or comprehend symbolic gestures or sign languages in their natural interactions with one another.

9.3. APES' USE OF HUMAN GESTURES

Although apes in their natural habitats do not point or use sign language, those raised by humans (or who have extensive contact with humans) sometimes do learn to point or can be trained in some aspects of human sign language. This is an important fact because apes do not normally develop novel vocalizations as a result of their interactions with humans, who are talking to them constantly. So again, the acquisition of novel gestures from humans suggests that apes' skills of gestural communication are more flexible and based to a greater degree on learning than are their vocalizations.

There are numerous examples of language-trained apes acquiring the pointing gesture for use with their human trainers (Savage-Rumbaugh, Mcdonald, Sevcik, Hopkins, & Rubert, 1986; Krause & Fouts, 1997; Miles, 1990; Patterson, 1978). Most apes use the whole hand point, but some individuals sometimes use the index finger point. For instance, Krause and Fouts (1997) systematically studied the pointing of two language-trained chimpanzees and found that they were capable of pointing very accurately to various targets. In this study, humans could reliably locate the position of rewards on the basis of the information provided by the chimpanzee gestures. Menzel (2004) reported that the language-trained chimpanzee Panzee pointed to various locations to inform a naïve human about the presence of food. On some occasions, she pointed to locations after delays of several hours and was also able to indicate the correct location on a TV monitor that humans could use to find the food (see Fig. 9.1).

Figure 9.1. After touching the lexigram on her keyboard (visible in background) corresponding to the type of object hidden, Panzee points toward the location of the object. Photo courtesy of Charles R. Menzel, Georgia State University.

Recently, Leavens and Hopkins (1998, see also Leavens, Hopkins, & Bard, 1996) have shown that nonlanguage-trained chimpanzees in some circumstances can also develop pointing gestures to direct humans to locations. They found that 40% of the chimpanzees they studied pointed with the whole hand (with 5% using an index finger extension) to indicate the location of food to humans. These pointing gestures were accompanied with gaze alternation between the human and the food, and they persisted in using this gesture until they received the food (Leavens, Hopkins, & Bard, 2005). These features suggest that the pointing gestures were both intentional and referential. These gestures were only observed when chimpanzees interacted with humans, not with other chimpanzees. Because captive chimpanzees typically interact with humans extensively, and humans are especially attuned to the pointing gesture, it is perhaps not surprising that chimpanzees quickly capitalize on this and develop pointing gestures. So the current evidence indicates that chimpanzees can develop the pointing gesture to direct humans to locations or objects they desire—if they have had some history with humans. There are also some reports of pointing in monkeys: Hess, Novak, & Povinelli, 1993 and Mitchell and Anderson (1997) observed rhesus monkeys and capuchin monkeys, respectively, indicating the location of food for humans by extending their arms in the direction of hidden food; and there are numerous studies showing that monkeys will extend an arm to choose an item from an array in testing situations.

Apes can even point to direct humans to tools that are needed so that the human can get them food. Thus, Call and Tomasello (1994) found that two orangutans pointed to a hidden tool that a human needed to rake in a reward that the orangutan desired, and Russell et al. (2005) have recently confirmed these results with chimpanzees. Gómez (1996) found that an orangutan would point to the location of a key that a human needed to open a box to get some food for the orangutan, and Whiten (1996) obtained analogous results with a language-trained chimpanzee. In each case, the orangutans and chimpanzees pointed for humans to objects that were a means to get the goals that they desired. But impressive though this use of pointing is, even the apes raised by humans use their pointing only as an imperative gesture to request objects or actions they want from humans, or they want humans to use toward some further goal. Unlike human children, apes do not use pointing declaratively to draw someone's attention to something in which they wish to share interest, or informatively to inform a human about the location of an object she may be seeking. The use of pointing exclusively for imperative purposes suggests that apes do not communicate cooperatively with others, as human infants do from before language acquisition even begins.

Turning now to symbolic gestures, it is clear that even though apes do not develop these spontaneously in their interactions with humans, as they do pointing gestures, nevertheless they can be trained to use some aspects of a human sign language (e.g., Fouts, 1975; Gardner, Gardner, & van Cantfort, 1989; Miles, 1990; Patterson, 1978). Most studies have used ASL (American Sign Language) or some version of it. The average size of the sign repertoire varies between 100 to 200 signs (Miles & Harper, 1994) although some investigators have reported repertoire sizes beyond these figures (Patterson, 1978). Apes use the signs to communicate with humans (although there are some reports of them using signs with one another or to themselves; Jensvold & Gardner, 2000). In some cases, these signs are iconic (i.e., their topography is reminiscent of the referent they represent) whereas in other cases they are arbitrary. But importantly, no matter the type of sign or sign combination, language-trained apes use their signs almost exclusively to request things from humans, not to point out things to them declaratively or informatively (about 95% of all intelligible speech acts were imperatives in the only two systematic studies: Greenfield & Savage-Rumbaugh, 1990; Rivas, 2005). It is also important that signing apes do not initially or readily learn signs by imitating humans—as human infants acquiring a sign language do naturally and from the very beginning. Early researchers noted that apes had some difficulty learning signs by observing and reproducing the hand configuration of another speaker, and so they physically shaped the hands of the apes to produce the desired configuration (Fouts, 1972; Miles, 1983; Patterson, 1978; although Fouts, 1972 and Miles, Mitchell, & Harper, 1996 reported that with greater experience, their apes began to acquire their gestures via imitation).

Having argued that apes do not naturally point or use other kinds of human gestures or sign language with one another—and that when they learn to do these things for humans, they still lack important features—we would nevertheless emphasize that apes' in interaction with humans do learn important new ways of gesturing that are communicatively adaptive in their human environments. Basically nothing of the kind happens with vocalizations. (Although there are some reports of the bonobo Kanzi mimicking some human vocal patterns, as reported earlier, these vocal modifications do not seem to be used communicatively.) Thus, when we consider the influence of humans on apes' communication, there is no question that the modality most easily influenced, shaped, or trained is the gestural modality, although apes do not thereby begin to gesture in all of the ways that humans do.

8.4. THE EVOLUTION OF LANGUAGE

The conclusions from these considerations are thus two. First, from a functional point of view, ape gestural communication is much more similar to human communication than is ape vocal communication, especially with regard to the social, cognitive, and learning processes involved. More specifically, in contrast to ape vocal signals, which are mainly unlearned and inflexibly used, ape gestures are mostly learned, and they are used flexibly for multiple communicative ends, in combination with one another, and adjusted for the attentional state of the recipient. There are certainly very good evolutionary reasons for this difference between modalities, one possibility being the strong connection between vocalizations and evolutionarily urgent situations and emotions, in which broadcast communication has certain advantages, and another being the strong connection between gestural communication and attention to the attention of the other. For these reasons—and perhaps other more 'mechanical' reasons as outlined by Corballis (2002), Arbib (2004), and Armstrong et al. (1999)—it would seem likely that early humans might very well have found it easier to move from communicative signals to communicative symbols in the gestural, rather than in the vocal, modality.

Second, to make this move, humans had to begin interacting with one another in some new ways. In the current hypothesis, they needed to begin interacting with one another collaboratively, forming shared goals and intentions, and to begin to enjoy sharing experience with one another for its own sake (see Dunbar, 1996, on the hypothesis that human language arose not to help humans work together, but simply to gossip, leading to social cohesion). Human linguistic communication is itself a collaborative activity (Clark, 1996) in which signaler and recipient share the goal that the recipient receive the message accurately, and so they work together toward this end. The communicative goals for human communicators depend in virtually all instances on the assumption of cooperative partners, who will help, or at least not interfere with, the signaler once the message is received. It is not clear when in human evolution these skills and motivations of shared intentionality might have evolved, but given the artifactual record on the emergence of differentiated and coherent cultural groups, the most likely candidate is modern humans—with these new skills and motivations representing the major adaptive advantage that led them to outcompete other hominids.

Our specific hypothesis—based on all of these facts about the way apes and humans communicate—is that in the evolutionary transition from activities based more on individual intentionality to those based more on shared intentionality, a key role was played by the pointing gesture. Specifically, in the domain of communication, in the transition from apelike to humanlike communication, the key transitional stage was some form of deictic pointing. Thus, when individual apes are raised in a humanlike, helpful, cooperative environment, they often develop the pointing gesture in one of its functions, namely, the imperative. This suggests that imperative pointing might have arisen in human evolution simply as a result of individuals becoming more tolerant and helpful toward one another, without any additional cognitive machinery. Helpful responses to imperative pointing from recipients might then have set the stage for signalers to anticipate the needs of others and point for them informatively, to help them by providing them with needed or desired information. The more cooperative forms of pointing require more in the way of co-constructed shared contexts, and so skills and motivations for other aspects of shared intentionality might then have been favored in human evolution. Once we get to full-blown co-operative human pointing—involving shared context, shared reference, cooperative motives—we are more than halfway to linguistic symbols. It is possible that iconic gestures—which are basically not used by apes and not used by human children until after pointing—might have emerged as still another step before linguistic symbols, and might have paved the way taking different perspective on the same thing, the key innovation in linguistic symbols (Tomasello, 1999, 2003).

As with all gestural theories of language origins, one must also tell some story about how and why humans eventually settled on the vocal modality for language. We do not have such a story—there are plenty around—but in general we would stress that to explain something as complex and multifaceted as language, we will need many evolutionary stories. Language is not one thing, but rather it is a complex mosaic of skills. Some of these component skills evolved before humans had even appeared on the scene, and they are shared by many species. Other component skills are very recent and perhaps uniquely human, at least among primates; for instance, speech production occurs with much voluntary control (although dolphins, parrots, and songbirds may also have open, independently evolved vocal production programs). Thus, although there may also be some unique ingredients to human language, such as the motivation to share with others as we have argued here, many other components are not unique. It is the novel combination of many components that makes human language such a special form of primate communication.

We have devoted this book to what we believe is one of the fundamental building blocks for language; primate gestural communication and the cognitive and social processes that support it. The comparative study of the gestural communication of our closest living relatives has enabled us to provide new support for the gestural origins of language hypothesis by focusing on the functional aspects of communication; learning, flexible use, adjustments for audience, and so forth. Our analysis has revealed three important milestones in the evolution of language; the flexible production of communicative signals in the manual modality, increased sensitivity to the attentional states of others due to the demands of the visual (as opposed to the auditory) modality, and the development of an intrinsic interest in understanding and sharing and intentional states with others.

NOTE

1. The species that do best on the object choice task are either animals that have been domesticated by humans (i.e., dogs) or ones that have interacted extensively with humans (marine mammals and enculturated apes). Enculturated apes or trained apes and monkeys can learn to use a pointing cue in these studies, but only after many dozens of trials of training with explicit feedback (e.g., Itakura & Tanaka, 1998; Itakura & Anderson, 1996).

REFERENCES

Acredelo, L. P., & Goodwyn, S. W. (1988). Symbolic gesturing in normal infants. *Child Development, 59,* 450–466.

Arbib, M. A. (2004). How far is language beyond our grasp? A response to Hurford. In K. Oller & U. Griebel (Eds), *Evolution of communication systems: A comparative approach* (pp. 315–322). Cambridge, MA: MIT Press.

Armstrong, D., Stokoe, W., & Wilcox, S. (1995). *Gesture and the nature of language.* Cambridge, England: Cambridge University Press.

Bates, E., Camaioni, L., & Volterra, V. (1975). The acquisition of performatives prior to speech. *Merrill-Palmer Quarterly, 21,* 205–224.

Boesch C., & Boesch-Achermann, H. (2000). *The chimpanzees of the Taï Forest: Behavioural ecology and evolution.* Oxford, England: Oxford University Press.

Call, J. (2004). Inferences about the location of food in the great apes (*Pan paniscus, Pan troglodytes, Gorilla gorilla,* and *Pongo pygmaeus*). *Journal of Comparative Psychology, 118,* 232–241.

Call, J., & Tomasello, M. (1994). Production and comprehension of referential pointing by orangutans (*Pongo pygmaeus*). *Journal of Comparative Psychology, 108,* 307–317.

Call, J., & Tomasello, M. (2005). What do chimpanzees know about seeing revisited: An explanation of the third kind. In N. Eilan, C. Hoerl, T. McCormack, & J. Roessler (Eds.), *Issues in joint attention* (pp. 45–64). Oxford, England: Oxford University Press.

Clark, A. P., & Wrangham, R. W. (1994). Chimpanzee arrival pant-hoots: Do they signify food or status? *International Journal of Primatology, 15,* 185–205.

Clark, H. (1996). *Uses of language.* Cambridge, England: Cambridge University Press.

Corballis, M. C. (2002). *From hand to mouth: The origins of language.* Princeton, NJ: Princeton University Press.

Dawkins, R., & Krebs, J. (1978). Animal signals: Information or manipulation. In J. Krebs & N. Davies (Eds.), *Behavioral ecology: An evolutionary approach* (pp. 282–309). Oxford, England: Blackwell.

de Waal, F., & van Hooff, J. (1981). Side-directed communication and agonistic interactions in chimpanzees. *Behaviour, 77,* 164–198.

Dunbar, R. (1996). *Grooming, gossip and the evolution of language.* London: Faber Faber and Harvard University Press.

Fouts, R. S. (1972). Use of guidance in teaching sign language to a chimpanzee (*Pan troglodytes*). *Journal of Comparative Psychology, 80*(3), 515–522.

Fouts, R. S. (1975). Chimpanzees and sign language: A research report. In L. S. Wrightman & F. H. Sanford (Eds.), *Psychology: A scientific study or human behavior* (p. 371). Monterey, CA: Brooks Cole.

Gardner, R. A., Gardner, B. T., & Van Cantfort, T. E. (Eds.). (1989). *Teaching sign language to chimpanzees.* Albany: State University of New York Press.

Golinkoff, R. (1993). When is communication a meeting of the minds? *Journal of Child Language, 20,* 199–208.

Gómez, J. C. (1996). Nonhuman primate theories of (nonhuman primate) minds: Some issues concerning the origins of mindreading. In P. Carruthers & P. K. Smith

(Eds.), *Theories of theories of mind* (pp. 330–343). Cambridge, England: Cambridge University Press.

Goodall, J. (1986). *The chimpanzees of Gombe: Patterns of behavior.* Cambridge, MA: Harvard University Press.

Greenfield, P. M., & Savage-Rumbaugh, E. S. (1990). Grammatical combination in *Pan paniscus*: Processes of learning and invention in the evolution and development of language. In S. T. Parker & K. R. Gibson (Eds.), *"Language" and intelligence in monkeys and apes* (pp. 540–578). Cambridge, England: Cambridge University Press.

Hammerschmidt, K., & Fischer, J. (in press). Constraints in primate vocal production. In U. Griebel & K. Oller (Eds.), *The evolution of communicative creativity: From fixed signals to contextual flexibility.* Cambridge, MA: The MIT Press.

Hare, B., & Tomasello, M. (2004). Chimpanzees are more skillful in competitive than in cooperative cognitive tasks. *Animal Behaviour, 68,* 571–581.

Hauser, M. D., Teixidor, P., Field, L., & Flaherty, R. (1993). Food-elicited calls in chimpanzees: Effects of food quantity & divisibility. *Animal Behaviour, 45,* 817–819.

Hauser, M. D., & Wrangham, R. W. (1987). Manipulation of food calls in captive chimpanzees. A preliminary report. *Folia Primatologica, 48,* 207–210.

Hess, J., Novak, M. A., & Povinelli, D. J. (1993). 'Natural pointing' in a rhesus monkey, but no evidence of empathy. *Animal Behaviour, 46*(5), 1023–1025.

Hewes, G. W. (1973). Primate communication and the gestural origins of language. *Current Anthropology, 14,* 9–10.

Hobson, P. R. (2002). *The cradle of thought.* London: Macmillan.

Itakura, S., & Anderson, J. (1996). Learning to use experimenter-given cues during an object-choice task by a capuchin monkeys. *Current Psychology of Cognition, 15,* 103–112.

Itakura, S., & Tanaka, M. (1998). Use of experimenter-given cues during object choice tasks by chimpanzees (*Pan troglodytes*), an orangutan (*Pongo pygmaeus*), and human infants (*Homo sapiens*). *Journal of Comparative Psychology, 120,* 119–126.

Jensvold, M. L. A., & Gardner, R. A. (2000). Interactive use of sign language by cross-fostered chimpanzees (Pan troglodytes). *Journal of Comparative Psychology, 114*(4), 335–346.

Kellogg, W. N., & Kellogg, L. A. (1933). *The ape and the child.* New York: McGraw-Hill.

Krause, M. A., & Fouts, R. S. (1997). Chimpanzee (*Pan troglodytes*) pointing: Hand shapes, accuracy, and the role of eye gaze. *Journal of Comparative Psychology, 111,* 330–336.

Leavens, D. A., & Hopkins, W. D. (1998). Intentional communication by chimpanzees: A cross-sectional study of the use of referential gestures. *Developmental Psychology, 34,* 813–822.

Leavens, D. A., Hopkins, W. D., & Bard, K. A. (1996). Indexical and referential pointing in chimpanzees (*Pan troglodytes*). *Journal of Comparative Psychology, 110,* 346–353.

Leavens, D. A., Hopkins, W. D., & Bard, K. A. (2005). Understanding the point of chimpanzee pointing: Epigenesis and ecological validity. *Current Directions in Psychological Science, 14,* 185–189.

Lizskowski, U., Carpenter, M., Striano, T., & Tomasello, M. (in press). 12- and 18-month-olds point to provide information for others. *Journal of Cognition and Development.*

McNeill, D. (1992). *Hand and mind: What gestures reveal about thought.* Chicago, IL: University of Chicago Press.

Menzel, C. R. (2004). Unprompted recall and reporting of hidden objects by a chimpanzee (*Pan troglodytes*) after extended delays. *Journal of Comparative Psychology, 113,* 426–434.

Menzel, E. W., Jr. (1974). A group of young chimpanzees in a one-acre field: Leadership and communication. In A. M. Schrier & F. Stollnitz (Eds.), *Behavior of nonhuman primates* (pp. 83–153). New York: Academic Press.

Miles, H. L. (1983). Apes and language: The search for communicative competence. In J. de Luce & H. T. Wilde (Eds.), *Language in primates: Perspectives and implications* (pp. 43–61). New York: Springer-Verlag.

Miles, H. L. W. (1990). The cognitive foundations for reference in a signing orangutan. In S. T. Parker & K. R. Gibson (Eds.), *"Language" and intelligence in monkeys and apes.* (pp. 511–539). Cambridge, England: Cambridge University Press.

Miles, H. L., & Harper, S. E. (1994). "Ape language" studies and the study of human language origins. In D. Quiatt & J. Itani (Eds.), *Hominid culture in primate perspective* (pp. 253–278). Denver, CO: University Press of Colorado.

Miles, H. L., Mitchell, R. W., & Harper, S. E. (1996). Simon says: The development of imitation in a signing orangutan. In A. Russon, K. Bard, & S. Parker (Eds.), *Reaching into thought: The minds of the great apes* (pp. 521–562). Cambridge, England: Cambridge University Press.

Mitani, J. C. (1996). Comparative field studies of African ape vocal behavior. In W. McGrew, L. Marchant, & T. Nishida (Eds.), *Great ape societies* (pp. 241–254). Cambridge, England: Cambridge University Press.

Mitani, J. C., & Nishida, T. (1993). Contexts and social correlates of long-distance calling by male chimpanzees. *Animal Behaviour, 45,* 735–746.

Mitchell, R. W., & Anderson, J. R. (1997). Pointing, withholding information, and deception in capuchin monkeys (*Cebus apella*). *Journal of Comparative Psychology, 111*(4), 351–361.

Owings, D. H., & Morton, E. S. (1998). *Animal vocal communication: A new approach.* Cambridge, MA: Cambridge University Press.

Owren, M. J., & Rendall, D. (2001). Sound on the rebound: Returning form and function to the forefront in understanding nonhuman primate vocal signaling. *Evolutionary Anthropology, 10*(2), 58–71.

Owren, M. J., Dieter, J. A., Seyfarth, R. M., & Cheney, D. L. (1992). Evidence of limited modification in the vocalizations of cross-fostered rhesus (*Macaca mulatta*) and Japanese (*M. fuscata*) macaques. In T. Nishida, W. C. McGrew, P. Marler, M. Pickford, & F. B. M. de Waal (Eds.), *Topics in primatology: Human origins* (pp. 257–270). Tokyo: University of Tokyo Press.

Patterson, F. (1978). Linguistic capabilities of a lowland gorilla. In F. C. C. Peng (Ed.), *Sign language and language acquisition in man and ape* (pp. 161–201). Boulder, CO: Westview Press.

Pizzuto, E., & Volterra, V. (2000). Iconicity and transparency in sign languages: A cross-linguistic cross-cultural view. In K. Emmorey & H. Lane (Eds.), *The signs of language revisited* (pp. 45–71). Mahwah, NJ: Lawrence Erlbaum Associates.

Rivas, E. (2005). Recent use of signs by chimpanzees in interactions with humans. *Journal of Comparative Psychology, 119,* 404–417.

Russell, J. L., Braccini, S., Buehler, N., Kachin, M. J., Schapiro, S. J., & Hopkins, W. D. (2005). Chimpanzee (*Pan troglodytes*) intentional communication is not contingent upon food. *Animal Cognition, 8*(4), 263–272.

Savage-Rumbaugh, S. (1986). *Ape language: From conditioned response to symbol.* New York: Columbia University Press.

Savage-Rumbaugh, S., McDonald, K., Sevcik, R., Hopkins, W., & Rupert, E. (1986). Spontaneous symbol acquisition and communicative use by pygmy chimpanzee (*Pan paniscus*). *Journal of Experimental Psychology: General, 115,* 211–235.

Seyfarth, R. M., & Cheney, D. L. (1994). The evolution of social cognition in primates. In L. Real (Ed.), *Behavioral mechanisms in evolution and ecology* (pp. 371–389). Chicago: University of Chicago Press.

Seyfarth, R. M., & Cheney, D. L. (1997). Behavioral mechanisms underlying vocal communication in nonhuman primates. *Animal Learning and Behavior, 25,* 249–267.

Seyfarth, R. M., & Cheney, D. L. (2003). Signalers and receivers in animal communication. *Annual Review of Psychology, 54,* 145–173.

Snowdon, C. T. (in press). Contextually flexible communication in nonhuman primates. In U. Griebel & K. Oller (Eds.), *The evolution of communicative creativity: From fixed signals to contextual flexibility.* Cambridge, MA: MIT Press.

Snowdon, C. T., Elowson, A. M., & Roush, R. S. (1997). Social influences on vocal development in New World primates. In C. T. Snowdon & M. Hausberger (Eds.), *Social influences on vocal development* (pp. 234–248). Cambridge, England: Cambridge University Press.

Tomasello, M. (1999). *The cultural origins of human cognition.* Princeton, NJ: Harvard University Press.

Tomasello, M. (2003). *Constructing a language: A usage-based theory of language acquisition.* Princeton, NJ: Harvard University Press.

Tomasello, M., & Call, J. (2006). Do chimpanzees know what others see—Or only what they are looking at? In M. Nudds & S. Huley (Eds.), *Rational animals?* (pp. 371–384). Oxford, England: University Press.

Tomasello, M., & Carpenter, M. (2005). The emergence of social cognition in three young chimpanzees. *Monographs of the Society for Research in Child Development* (279), 70.

Tomasello, M., Carpenter, M., Call, J., Behne, T., & Moll, H. (2005). Understanding and sharing intentions: The origins of cultural cognition. *Behavioral and Brain Sciences, 28,* 675–735.

Whiten, A. (1996). When does smart behaviour reading become mindreading? In P. Carruthers & P. K. Smith (Eds.), *Theories of theories of mind* (pp. 277–292). Cambridge University Press.

Zuberbühler, K. (2000). Interspecific semantic communication in two forest monkeys. *Proceedings of the Royal Society of London B., 267*(1444), 713–718.

Author Index

Note: *t* indicates table.

Subject Index

Note: *f* indicates figures; *n* indicates endnote; *t* indicates table.

Author Index

Note: *t* indicates table.